FRAMING A
NATIONAL NARRATIVE

FRAMING A NATIONAL NARRATIVE

The Legend Collections of
Peter Christen Asbjørnsen

Marte Hvam Hult

Wayne State University Press
Detroit

Copyright © 2003 by Wayne State University Press,
Detroit, Michigan 48201. All rights are reserved.
No part of this book may be reproduced without formal permission.
Manufactured in the United States of America.
06 05 04 03 02   5 4 3 2 1

Library of Congress Cataloging-in-Publication Data
Hult, Marte H.
Framing a national narrative : the legend collections
of Peter Christen Asbjørnsen / Marte Hvam Hult.
p. cm.
Includes bibliographical references and index.
ISBN 0-8143-3006-1 (cloth : alk. paper)
1. Asbjørnsen, Peter Christen, 1812–1885. Norske huldreeventyr og
folkesagn.   2. Romanticism—Norway.   3. Nationalism—Norway.   I. Title.
PT8802 .N67 2003
398.2'09481—dc21   2002029640

ISBN 0-8143-3006-1

♾ The paper used in this publication meets the minimum requirements of the
American National Standard for Information Sciences—Permanence
of Paper for Printed Library Materials, ANSI Z39.48-1984.
This volume was done with the assistance of a fund established by
Thelma Gray James of Wayne State University for the
publication of folklore and English studies.

For my Mother
GERD NORA HVAM
and the memory of my Father
OLE HVAM

Contents

Acknowledgments 9

1. THREADS IN A TAPESTRY:
Norwegian Nation-Building

11

2. ASBJØRNSEN AND MOE:
The Genesis of *Norske folkeeventyr* and Its Relationship to *Norske huldreeventyr og folkesagn*

33

3. THE SPACE AND PLACE OF *NORSKE HULDREEVENTYR OG FOLKESAGN*:
Appropriation of the Norwegian Countryside

57

4. ORAL NARRATIVE IN ITS PERFORMANCE CONTEXT:
The Created Informants and Contexts of *Norske huldreeventyr og folkesagn*

87

5. From the Supernatural to the Human Other:
The Marginalized Storytellers of
Norske huldreeventyr og folkesagn
119

6. Spirits of the Woods, Fields, and Mountains:
The Tradition Content of
Norske huldreeventyr og folkesagn
141

7. From Danish to Dialect:
The Myriad Voices of
Norske huldreeventyr og folkesagn
167

8. The Tapestry Woven:
A Gobelin of Nature, Folklore, and Language
193

Notes   197
Works Cited and Consulted   233
Index   247

Acknowledgments

I left Norway as a young child, not of my own volition, and my deepest gratitude goes first to my parents, who worked hard, even as we were becoming Americans, to prevent our Norwegian language and traditions from withering and dying on the hot prairies of western South Dakota. I am always saddened when students tell me that their grandparents or other relatives spoke Norwegian "when they didn't want us to understand what they said." That is a tremendous loss.

This book is a revised and expanded version of my doctoral dissertation at the University of Minnesota, and I would like to acknowledge the contributions of the thesis committee: My adviser, William Mishler, who made valuable suggestions for reading and writing throughout the thesis process; Kaaren Grimstad for meticulous reading and sensitive insights; Monika Zagar; John Rice; and most particularly Jack Zipes, without whose enthusiasm and assistance this book would not be a reality. The Department of German, Scandinavian and Dutch at the University of Minnesota generously provided financial support through a dissertation grant in 1998.

I would like to acknowledge Ellen Stekert, whose folklore classes were influential. Mariann Tiblin and Charles Spetland at Wilson library were always willing and eager to help me navigate through the tremendous Scandinavian collection, and Eddy Wighus at the University Library in Oslo was most helpful in locating rare sources. My thanks to my cousin Dr. Martin Hvam for help with zoological translations, and Nina Witoszek for supplying her original English quotations. My friends and colleagues Micheline van Riemsdijk and Torild Homstad were always willing to listen and offer thoughtful suggestions. I am grateful to my sister Anne Hvam, who drew the illustration that appears on the jacket and title page of this book.

My thanks to the following who granted copyright permissions: Steven P. Sondrup at *Scandinavian Studies* for permission to quote John Lindow's article; Lars Alldén at Aschehoug for permission to cite extensively from the 1949 edition of *Norske huldreeventyr og folkesagn* and from the Universitetsforlaget publication of Anne Cohen Kiel's article; Arnhild Fjose and Eirin Hagen at Cappelen for permission to quote Julian Kramer's article; Perry Cartwright at The University of Chicago Press for permission to cite from Christiansen's *Folktales of Norway;* and to Gudleiv Bø for permission to quote his lecture at the University of Minnesota. I am deeply obliged to Arthur Evans, director of the Wayne State University Press, for his support of the project and wish also to thank editors Jennifer Gariepy and Tom Ligotti, and all those involved in the design, production and marketing of the book for their fine work, as well as the anonymous reviewers whose suggestions were most helpful. Finally I want to thank my son Erik for the continual reminder that I have a life outside of books and the nineteenth century, and my dear husband Michael, whose unwavering support and encouragement have helped to make that life, if not a fairy tale, at least so very happy.

CHAPTER 1

THREADS IN A TAPESTRY:
Norwegian Nation-Building

I am no Frenchman!
I am a Norwegian, by God!
—HENRIK WERGELAND, *Hasselnøtter*

INTRODUCTION: THE QUEST FOR A NORWEGIAN NATIONAL IDENTITY

The current revival of interest in nationalism and nation building, reflected in a spate of recent publications, is not limited to emerging new countries of Eastern Europe or liberated colonies of the third world; Norwegians have been debating national identity in one form or another for at least two hundred years, and this preoccupation with *Norskhet* [Norwegian-ness] shows no signs of abatement in the first years of the twenty-first century.[1] There is, in fact, ample evidence that "the development of Norwegian national identity has not yet been completed" (Sørensen 1994, 33).

This development of Norwegian national identity has been a long and involved process which began in earnest with the Treaty of Kiel in 1814, when Norway was ceded as a spoil of war from Denmark to Sweden, and continues with modifications in our own time. And while this ongoing historical process is too complex and multifaceted to be more than briefly summarized here, it must nevertheless be stated that, although this is primarily a literary study, the concept of nation building and the rise of Norwegian national romanticism in the nineteenth century are the warp on which the various threads of the story will be woven, much as the silken threads on Norwegian poet Olaf Bull's *Gobelin* pillow, which, while they may detour around a path in the forest, and stop at the herbal garden, or disappear around a bend, always in the end come together to create a whole picture. In this poem, from 1913, Bull's little daughter Merete is mesmerized by a pastoral scene on a gobelin pillow, and Bull takes her by the hand and embarks on an imaginary stroll along the path in the tapestry, into a world where dream and reality intertwine. At the end of the poem, the walk ends when they realize that the lovely imaginary journey was "just pitiful silk embroidery" (Bull [1913] 1999, 50).[2] The juxtaposition of reality and fairy-tale as reflected in Bull's poem of a woven tapestry pillow is perhaps an apt metaphor for the "imagined community," in Benedict Anderson's words, that is Norway, and is most certainly an appropriate one for Peter Christen Asbjørnsen's *Norske huldreeventyr og folkesagn* [Norwegian Hulder Fairy Tales and Folk Legends], which appeared in its first collections in 1845 and 1848, and which is as fine an example of the synthesis of the real and the imagined as one is likely to find in nineteenth-century Norwegian literature.

This collection of stories of Norwegian folklore, which Asbjørnsen encapsulated within separate frame narratives, is a classic of the Norwegian national romantic period, but if it is true, as Jørgen Haugan says, that "Norway has never dusted off its classics" (Haugan 1991, 50), then *Norske huldreeventyr og folkesagn* is long overdue for a thorough literary analysis and a reevaluation of its position in a period of Norwegian history when the search for a unique Norwegian identity was in full flower.

Peter Christen Asbjørnsen was born on 15 January, 1812 in Christiania, as Oslo was then called. He was the son of Andreas Asbjørnsen, a Christiania glazier, and Thurine Elisabeth Bruun who, because of a mental illness, *saw* supernatural creatures and was inordinately superstitious. Asbjørnsen's childhood in the glazier's shop would have been filled with the stories of apprentices, travelers, and customers, as well as those of a rather drunken grandmother who lived with the family for some time. Here he spent his childhood, playing with the neighborhood children in the churchyard and throughout the nooks and crannies of the large, old *nabogaard*, a tumbled-down old building with attics, lofts, and dark and mysterious hallways. Only a few minutes walk would have brought him and his friends into the countryside, where they picked berries and played in the woods.

Asbjørnsen was not a good student, and it has been suggested that he was not much interested in school. A friend from his school days, Carl Andersen, later wrote that Asbjørnsen did not advance in school because, "Folk books and fairy tales, and later namely his dear Walter Scott, had a much too irresistible power of attraction for him" (cited in Hansen 1932, 32–33). While not much is known about his early education, he was enrolled in the Cathedral School in Christiania in 1825. But the studies did not go well and the next year his father sent him for special university entrance examination preparation in the countryside in Ringerike. It did not go much better there however, since Asbjørnsen was, according to one account, a "lazy rascal, who would much rather roam around in the woods and fields than sit inside and cram Latin expressions" (Krogvig, intro to Moe 1915, 17).[3] His father was not satisfied with his progress and brought him back to the Cathedral School in Christiania the next year. But Asbjørnsen's time in Ringerike was decisive. It was here that he met Jørgen Moe, who was to become his collaborator on the famous Norwegian folk tale collections *Norske folkeeventyr* [Fairy Tales of the Norwegian Folk]. Jørgen Moe's letters to Asbjørnsen after he returned to Christiania indicate that Asbjørnsen was not altogether well at this time of his life and indicate also that Asbjørnsen was already engaged with writing. But Asbjørnsen was also occupied with helping his father build meteorological instruments and had not relinquished his favorite pastimes of hunting and fishing. He did not take the university entrance examination until 1833 and, because of poor results, did not matriculate at the university but became instead a live-in tutor in Romerike. Asbjørnsen could not afford to continue his studies in Greek, arithmetic, and geometry, the subjects he had failed, and did not finally finish his examinations until 1835.

Asbjørnsen himself never spoke much about his life during the three years he worked as a tutor, and there is some disagreement about where he taught. His biographer Knut Liestøl believes it was at Børke in Sørum. After two years here, he moved to Fjeldstad in Gjerdrum. It was during his time in Romerike that Asbjørnsen began writing in earnest, and it was here that he collected many of the stories and observations of the landscapes which were to form many of the frames for *Norske huldreeventyr og folkesagn*. During his stay at Fjeldstad, Asbjørnsen had become secretly engaged to Caroline Marianne Grinder, and the plan was that she was to wait for him while he studied medicine. Her parents, however, preferred a richer and better connected suitor, and in May of 1838 she married Nicolay Kolderup. Opinions vary as to whether or not the loss of Caroline was a tragedy which marred Asbjørnsen's life, or whether he actually recovered quite quickly. Whichever is true, he never married.[4]

The collection of Norwegian folk tales, *Norske folkeeventyr*, began to appear in 1841. This collection of folk tales sparked debate about how the Norwegian language should be represented in print. Until that time, few had made a concentrated effort to recreate the dialects of the people, but Asbjørnsen and Moe realized that the folk tales had to be read as they were spoken by the local informants who told the stories. Asbjørnsen had already begun his work, independently of Moe, on several of the stories later incorporated in the first edition of *Norske huldreeventyr og folkesagn*. In 1852, *Norske folkeeventyr* was published in a second edition, and shortly thereafter, Moe turned his collected manuscripts over to Asbjørnsen and devoted the remainder of his life to his clerical duties, eventually becoming the Bishop of Kristiansand in 1875. Asbjørnsen turned more and more to natural science after 1850. Already by that time he had published a six-volume natural history for young people. He wrote and translated widely, primarily in the field of zoology, introduced Darwin to Norway, and discovered a new starfish on one of his zoological field-trips. He became interested in forestry, and in 1856, with a stipend from the Norwegian government, he began studying forestry in Germany. From 1860 to 1864 he was the forester in Trøndelag, and from 1864 to 1876 he worked in the management of the peat industry for the state. Despite his wide-ranging interests, Asbjørnsen never lost interest in hearing and telling stories and personally edited three editions of his legend collections, the latest in 1870, as well as publishing additional editions and supplements to *Norske folkeeventyr*. When he died in 1885, he had himself become a legend as the "King of Fairy Tales."

Asbjørnsen and Moe's *Norske folkeeventyr* has rightfully received much attention and acclaim as a pivotal nation-building text of the nineteenth century in Norway, primarily because of its influence on the development of the written Norwegian language, which was enormous. But, although long recognized as a classic of national romanticism, stories from Asbjørnsen's quite different independent work, *Norske huldreeventyr og folkesagn*, are often carelessly included in anthologies, both Norwegian and English, with a quite medieval disregard for authorship. As recently as 1995, a well-respected scholar credited a quotation from Asbjørnsen's "An Old-Fashioned Christmas Eve" to "Asbjørnsen and Moe, 1963, 18–21"[5] Both *Norske folkeeventyr* and *Norske huldreeventyr og folkesagn* are classics of the Norwegian literary canon, but no full-length study of *huldreeventyr* as an independent literary work has been written, nor has it received the position within the canon that it clearly deserves as an autonomous literary text, rather than as a work of folklore. *Norske huldreeventyr og folkesagn* demonstrates a rich microcosm of mid-nineteenth century societal currents which reflects a wide range of issues, from language questions to socioeconomic concerns. If the modern Norwegian, despite endless introspective musings on *Norskhet,* and a search for an articulated national identity, feels to some extent that this identity is splintered, can this not be at least partially attributed to a literature which may have both reflected and created this dichotomy? This study will "dust off" Asbjørnsen and his legend collection and position it as a text of great importance in the establishment of the Norwegian national narrative, a critical link in the development of the modern Norwegian novel, and a work relevant in its themes to modern Norwegian society.

"Nation, nationality, nationalism—all have proved notoriously difficult to define, let alone to analyse." For Anderson the point of departure is that nationality or nation-ness and nationalism are "cultural artefacts of a particular kind," and he analyzes the processes, among them the development of vernacular languages and the rise of print capitalism, that create his definition of a nation as "an imagined political community—and imagined as both inherently limited and sovereign" (Anderson 1991, 3, 3, 6). There appear to be as many definitions of nationalism as there are scholars studying the phenomenon, but what they seem to have in common is an emphasis on abstract economic and political theories and on the historical processes of modernization. While definitions are helpful in delineating the parameters for discussion, they focus on the abstract and on the general, and do not, perhaps, take us very far in understanding a nation in particular. As Michael Herzfeld notes, "The relationship between theory and practice troubles scholars in virtually all fields of cultural analysis and criticism" (Herzfeld 1987, 2).

If all happy families are alike, so too perhaps all imagined communities are alike, at least on the dry page; but despite academic definitions, nations do, after all, exist in the real world, with real people, real political systems, and real, if fluid, borders and boundaries of various kinds. One of these borders, whose meaning must be clarified, is the distinction between "state" and "nation." These terms are often used interchangeably, but they are, of course, quite different. Walker Connor explains, "A dictionary designed for the student of global politics defines the state as 'a legal concept describing a social group that occupies a defined territory and is organized under common political institutions and an effective government.' By contrast, a nation is defined as 'a social group which shares a common ideology, common institutions and customs, and a sense of homogeneity'" (Connor 1972, 333). According to Connor, less than 10 percent of states can truly be called nation-states, a state where the population is essentially homogeneous. Until very recently Norway would have been considered such a true nation-state.

To understand any actual nation-state, the cultural artifacts of that state must themselves be the basis of study, and no cultural artifact is more important in this regard than literature and the language in which it is transmitted. "The rise of the modern nation-state in Europe in the late eighteenth and early nineteenth centuries is inseparable from the forms and subjects of imaginative literature" (Brennan 1990, 48–49). But it is critical to remember that these cultural artifacts, or what Anthony Smith, in his *Theories of Nationalism*, calls cultural markers, "derive their meaning from particular historical contexts, and their effects vary with those contexts rather than with any presumed consequences of 'modernisation'" (Smith 1983, xx). Cultural artifacts of literature do their work within specific contexts of time and place.

In *Belated Modernity and Aesthetic Culture: Inventing National Literature*, Gregory Jusdanis discusses how literature functioned in the formation of the nation-state of Greece, which became independent in 1827. In some respects, Jusdanis' model contains several striking parallels to the Norwegian situation. Belated modernity was certainly not an exclusively Greek phenomenon, as anyone familiar with the delayed industrialization and limited communications of the Norwegian state would acknowledge. In addition, Jusdanis stresses the conflict between proponents of Classical Greek and those who favored the use of the demotic. "The most important instrument for the creation of a national consciousness is the vernacular." Quoting Dimitrios Katartzis, the leader of the demotic camp, he continues, "A language should be written as it is spoken; only in a shared idiom can members of a society communicate with each other" (Jusdanis 1991, 41, 44). The Scandinavianist has no difficulty in recognizing a parallel to the Norwegian language situation, in which a written Danish language competed with a vast array of local Norwegian dialects. But when Benedict Anderson writes that "in the case of Norway, which had long shared a written language with the Danes, though with a completely different pronunciation, nationalism emerged with Ivar Aasen's new Norwegian grammar (1848) and dictionary (1850), texts which responded to and stimulated demands for a specifically Norwegian print-language" (75), it is evident that he is greatly oversimplifying the emergence of nationalism in Norway. Language is but one thread in the loom, although an important one, and it will receive a great deal of attention in this study of Asbjørnsen's classic work, but it is also necessary to consider some of the other elements that contribute to a nation's feelings of solidarity, and specifically how these factors apply to Norway.[6]

Most authors who touch at all on the topic of the development of Norwegian national identity agree that it is a process fraught with paradox. "Norway is a country which has problems with its identity" (Haugan, 14). Haugan believes that this identity problem is due to Norway's youth as a state; to him Norway finds itself in the unclear and difficult stage of puberty. This view, of course, presupposes that national identity is dependent on the modern political entity of the state, rather than on the less clearly defined but certainly viable cohesion of community based on an ethnic homogeneity, with shared language and traditions: a nation. This viewpoint, that Norwegian national identity and culture was something that had to be developed after 1814, is the prevalent one among scholars today. "Have nation—need culture!" is the title of a chapter in Brit Berggreen's 1989 text *Da kulturen kom til Norge* [When Culture came to Norway]; though dominant, this is not the sole viewpoint.

That Danes and Norwegians were considered separate "nations" already long before 1814 is clear in the works of the eighteenth century Danish theologian Erik Pontoppidan. He writes, "The Norwegian peasant, in point of politeness, exceeds the Danish Burgher; and the Norwegian Burgher, especially of the mercantile class, in this respect, equals at least the Danish Nobility" (Pontoppidan 1755, 250). Throughout this work, Pontoppidan writes of the Norwegian and his country as separate entities from Denmark. In his Danish atlas from 1763, when writing of the length and breadth of Denmark, Pontoppidan describes the perimeters of the country of Denmark much as we know it today. Norway is not mentioned at all. A more modern proponent of the notion that Norway was a distinct "nation" before 1814 is the Norwegian historian Kåre Lunden. Lunden utilizes contemporaneous materials in his book *Norsk grålysing* to show that there did exist a belief in a distinct Norwegian national character already before 1814. Lunden's work is particularly influenced by Adam Smith's *Theories of Nationalism*, in which Smith differentiates between primitive and developed nationalism, and further subdivides nationalistic movements. The case of Norway is categorized by Smith as a "pre-independence ethnic nationalistic movement."

As Jusdanis points out, "[P]olitical independence is not necessarily coterminous with the construction of a nation, an imagined realm of shared identity" (40). To Lunden, and those who share his opinion, a feeling of national identity arose in Norway before Norway was a separate sovereign nation-state. Much of Lunden's argument rests on the works of the young Norwegian writers of the late eighteenth century, many of whom studied in Copenhagen before Norway had a university of its own. There the sometimes homesick young students gathered together, wrote songs and poems, told jokes and drank wine punch. They formed a literary society, Det Norske Selskapet, which functioned in some respects in opposition to the Danish literary society. From its inception in 1774 until about 1790 a number of men from early Norwegian literary history were members of this group: Johan Herman Wessel, Claus Fasting, Johan Nordahl Brun, Peter and Claus Frimann, and Jens Zetlitz, to mention only the most well known. What many of their songs and poems had in common was an idealization of the far-off Norwegian landscape, particularly the mountains and especially Dovrefjell (Bull 1923, 70). To the young Norwegian expatriates in Denmark, Norway was not just an imagined community; it was a very real and concrete physical space which inspired love and longing. Interestingly enough, here it is not language that is the unifying force but rather concrete physical geography. As the cultural geographer Yi-Fu Tuan notes, "It is a characteristic of the symbol-making human species that its members can become passionately attached to places of enormous size" (Tuan 1977, 18). Any study of the importance of literature in nation-building in Norway cannot be undertaken without attention to how this attachment has been symbolized narratively through the utilization of physical geography to create "place" from "space."[7]

Whether one shares Haugan's or Lunden's point of view as to when the process of the development of Norwegian national identity began, and bearing in mind that both Haugan and Lunden have political agendas of their own with respect to Norway's position within or without the European Community, there is no doubt that the process intensified after 1814. Richard Dorson summarizes nicely the task at hand as it was seen in 1814:

> Norway achieved independence from Denmark in 1814, and immediately embarked on a quest for her national identity through history, folklore, and language. The task of nationalists in Norway, as in other late nations with a proud antiquity—Greece and Italy come at once to mind—was to forge links with remote glories across a dismal interregnum. Independent scholars set for themselves the tasks of reconstructing the history, gathering the ballads and tales, and studying the dialects, which together contained the soul and essence of the Norwegian people. According to the romanticist ideas of the mid-nineteenth century, the true character of the old, pure Norway, unsullied by foreign invasions, was to be discovered in the conservative peasant. (Dorson 1966, 289)

So far, so good, but in truth, discovering the true character of this conservative peasant, or *bonde* as he is called in Norwegian, became a paradoxical undertaking.[8] It must also be remembered that although Norway received more autonomy as a result of the constitution of 1814, the country did not achieve total independence until 1905, when the union with Sweden was dissolved. Norwegian national identity was formed in a period when colonial consciousness was very much a part of the contemporary circumstances, although not necessarily identified in these terms.

The role of folklore in the search for the purely Norwegian character cannot be over-estimated, based as it was on the romantic nationalistic ideas of the German scholar Johann Gottfried Herder, who believed that folk tales were the clearest revelation of the folk spirit and whose ideas motivated much of the collection of folklore throughout Europe during the early nineteenth century. Among other ideas, Herder came to believe, following Montesquieu, that the physical environment occupied by a country contributed to a "national character" or a "national soul," one which was different for each nation. Herder "reminded his readers that every nationality must develop in accord with its own innate abilities, in line with its own cultural pattern."[9] And this national character could best be discovered and renewed through the study of the people's folk poetry.

It was not the folk poetry itself that was of primary interest to Jacob and Wilhelm Grimm, the German brothers whose folk tale collections became a model for Asbjørnsen and Moe, as well as for other collectors during the remainder of the century. "In fact, from the beginning, their principal concern was to uncover the etymological and linguistic truths that bound the German people together and were expressed in their laws and customs" (Zipes 1988, 10). For the first Norwegian collectors, it became even more imperative to discover these same etymological and linguistic truths as they applied to Norway, since the Norwegian written language had virtually disappeared after the ravages of the Black Death in the fourteenth century annihilated much of the literate population of the country. The written Norwegian language never recovered, since the union with Denmark in 1380 brought Danish rule and the Danish written language into use in all official business. In the joint collections of Asbjørnsen and Moe, the intent was always to retell the folk tales in a manner that would incorporate what Asbjørnsen and Moe considered to be *særnorske* [uniquely Norwegian] characteristics, including a language that would contain some Norwegian, rather than Danish, vocabulary. The collection and dissemination of the folk poetry was to serve in the development of the young nation by uncovering the "spirit of the people" that had been kept alive throughout the years of Danish colonialism in the stories of the countryside. But, at least in Norway, the search for the spirit of the folk, the *edel bonde* [noble peasant, farmer] itself created as much folklore as it uncovered.

Much has been written about the role of Norwegian intellectuals in the process of defining a national character out of what in reality were local customs and local loyalties. A good overview is presented by Øyvind Østerud, who has identified five paradoxical features of the nation-building process from 1814 to 1905, a period he calls the "grand classical phase," in which Norway developed from an ideal and idea of the political elite to an historical reality for a community of citizens (Østerud 1986). In the first place, the new Norwegian nation state was created through the old dynastic principle, the trading really of one monarchy for another, and not at all a new form of government as such. Secondly, Norway as a national entity was not a rediscovered fact but an historical and literary idea, created first in Copenhagen, subsequently in Christiania, and formulated in Danish. Thirdly, there was no statistical common basis for Norwegian culture. "The 'Hidden Norway' did not suddenly present itself in the middle of the nineteenth century, but was localized, unveiled, distilled, and interpreted by civil servants and intellectuals" (12). In the fourth place, nationalism became important when the folkloristic tradition began to become artificial, and it became important for those who really were outside of the tradition. And finally, it was for the most part nationalism that shaped the Norwegian nation and not the opposite. The uniquely Norwegian was partly postulated and partly produced.[10]

If we accept Østerud's conclusions, which are in agreement with much dominant current thought on nationalism, that Norwegian uniqueness is an historic and literary construction, then it becomes evident that the role of literature is the crucial element which has the ability to create a national entity of imagination, to nationalize the local, because only through print language could people "come to visualize in a general way the existence of thousands and thousands like themselves" (Anderson, 77). The state

> requires a network of linked values and sentiments to hold it together. Nation building entails the invention of collective narratives, the homogenization of ethnic differences, and the induction of citizens into the ideology of the imagined community. . . . At the initial stage of nation building . . . the carriers of nationalism are eager to set up those institutions that designate and codify a national consciousness. Literature is one such institution.

But what is often forgotten is that "literary historians selected a series of indigenous texts, sanctified them into a canon, and then proclaimed them the embodiment of a people" (Jusdanis, 28, 40, 121). Certainly this is what happened with the collection of folk tales collected and published by Asbjørnsen and Moe. In May 1940, the Norwegian novelist Sigurd Hoel asked the question, "Which Norwegian literary work of the last hundred years has all-told had the greatest meaning for the entire Norwegian people?" He considers in turn the poetry of Henrik Wergeland, P.A. Munch's history of the Norwegian people, Ivar Aasen's language work, Ibsen's *Peer Gynt*, and Bjørnson's stories of the Norwegian peasantry before concluding that all of these must be secondary to the folk-tale collections, and that because in the final analysis they are "for better or for worse, the most completely Norwegian [thing] we own and have." Hoel does not distinguish between the folk tale collections of Asbjørnsen and Moe and the independent work of Asbjørnsen alone: "The first of the collections was published in booklet form from 1841 to 1844. These were followed by other collections, edited partly by Asbjørnsen and Moe together, and partially by Asbjørnsen alone. However it is fully justifiable to view all these collections as one work" (Hoel 1948, 98, 114, 98). It may be justifiable for the average Norwegian to consider this rich folkloristic heritage as one work, but it is hardly justifiable for the folklorist or the scholar.[11] The codification of "Asbjørnsen and Moe" as one entity within the Norwegian literary canon will be challenged in this book, and the widely held belief that there is essentially no difference between the joint folk tale and the independent legend collections will be contested. But before embarking on this insistence on genre differentiation, and the analysis of Asbjørnsen's independent work, it is necessary to briefly examine the wider European context in which both collections were produced.

THE EUROPEAN CONNECTION: EARLY INFLUENCES

While it is true that the Norwegian folk tale collections were inspired by the work of the brothers Grimm in Germany, and that theirs was the over-riding influence, there were, of course, other influences and factors that were important in the genesis of the work that has forever tied Asbjørnsen and Moe together in the minds of their countrymen. Many literary historians have traced the impulses that led to the fertile national romantic collecting of folklore in the 1830s and 1840s and the rise of national romanticism in art, music, and literature, and it can be enlightening to see how literary history also reflects the biases and prejudices of its own time. One of the late nineteenth-century scholars who was influential in determining future perceptions of Asbjørnsen and Moe was Moltke Moe, Jørgen Moe's son. Moltke Moe, a respected scholar in his own right, traced the literary advent of romanticism in Scandinavia in "The National Breakthrough and its Men." His explanation of the trends in Scandinavia during the first part of the nineteenth century shows how belief in a Nordic uniqueness permeated the prose of the scholar as much as it did the creative artist. But Moe's summary gives one perspective on the context in which Asbjørnsen and Moe undertook their classic work.[12]

The first ripples of romanticism in Scandinavia did not emanate from Jacob or Wilhelm Grimm. They came from MacPherson and Percy, from Klopstock's heroic poetry in the pre-romantic period, and finally from the oldest school of romanticism in Germany. The influence was palpable already with Ewald in Denmark and it continued with some of the *norske selskabs* writers and with

Baggesen. But only with Oehlenschläger's breakthrough in 1802 did the movement triumph and conquer creative literature. From the same origins and in a similar way the movement penetrated Swedish literature some years later. And not long after, Johan Storm Munch and the short story writer Maurits Hansen in Norway walked in the footsteps of German sentimental romanticism. In Norway this influence was not felt until that of the Grimms', which only little by little made its influence felt in the nordic countries.

In Scandinavia the movement did not often take such an inflated and excessive course as it often did in Germany. The reason is not just found in the people's more objective national character, according to Moe; there was another reason. Denmark had very early collected and published its old folk songs. Anders Sørenssøn Vedel's *It hundrede Vdvaalde Danske Viser* [One Hundred Selected Danish Ballads] had been published already in 1591, and, especially in Peder Syv's edition of 1695, became astonishingly popular, not less so in Norway than in Denmark, and was continually being reprinted in new editions. (Peder Syv added another hundred songs and the edition came out under the title *200 Viser om Konger oc Kemper oc Andre* [200 Ballads about Kings and Heroes and Others]). At the time Moltke Moe was writing it was still known and discussed around the countryside as "Kjempeboki" or "Tvohunder-viseboki." After Peder Klaussøn's translation of Snorre and along with Petter Dass' outspoken folk poetry, Peder Syv's book of ballads was the work that the Norwegian farmers drew on the most, apart from religious texts. Vedel's and Syv's collections had an extraordinary influence, and Moe claims that they permeated into the quiet folk-consciousness of the people. Although there is almost no trace of the ballads' influence in the literary development of the first half of the nineteenth century, Moe believes that they were remembered and served to dam the excesses of German literary romanticism. When the time was ripe for the recognition of the Grimms' contribution, it was easier for Scandinavians to separate the wheat from the chaff because of the native roots of the ballad tradition.

In the second decade of the nineteenth century, interest in folk poetry and folk belief really made itself evident in Scandinavia. The movement became visible at almost the same time in both Danish and Swedish literature, but the Danes Werner Abrahamson, Rasmus Nyerup, and Knud-Lyne Rahbek were a little ahead with the publication between 1812 and 1814 of a five-volume collection of Danish ballads from the Middle Ages, *Udvalgte danske Viser fra Middelalderen*. Here the emphasis was not on linguistic sources or historical data in the songs, as was the case with Vedel and Syv, but rather on poetry. The editors were familiar with Percy, Herder, "Des Knaben Wunderhorn," Walter Scott, and Jamieson's collections from Scotland. What they wanted to do was establish the Danish songs on the same level with these foreign ones. None of the Danish editors were in the romanticism camp, but they were all influenced by the new movement and made an honest effort to see with romanticist eyes. Their first models were Arnim and Brentano, along with Walter Scott, but long before the first volume appeared, they had found a new guide. In 1811 Wilhelm Grimm's German translation from Vedel and Syv, *Altdänische Heldenlieder*, was published, and it was this text after which the Danes patterned their work. Grimm's translation was a masterpiece, both scientifically and poetically. His introduction and commentary was for a long time the best material written about the Danish folk songs. Although the five-volume Danish collection was inferior in nearly all respects to Grimm's translation, it was extraordinarily influential on the literature of Denmark's "Golden Age."

In 1814, the first volume of a Swedish collection of folk songs and ballads, *Svenska folk-visor från forntiden* [Swedish Folk Songs from the Past] appeared. This three-volume work was compiled by Erik Gustaf Geijer and Arvid August Afzelius and was inspired by the Danish examples and with the same background of impulses from the German, English, and Scottish folk song collections. The Swedish collection was the only one of the Scandinavian collections which obtained most of its songs from living tradition as opposed to old hand-written variants. Geijer's essay "Om omqvädet" and the introduction to the collections were of great importance for all Scandinavians, influencing Magnus Landstad, a collector of Norwegian songs, as well as Jørgen Moe and, in Denmark, Svend Grundtvig. In 1816, Nyerup published a literary history about the Danish/Norwegian folk books called *Almindelig Morskabslæsning;* in 1817, J. M. Thiele published *Prøver af danske Folkesagn* and between 1818 and 1823 his influential *Danske folkesagn* in four small volumes. Moe cites Jacob Grimm, who in a 1818 review of Thiele's *Prøver af danske Folkesagn* expressed the wish that also Norway and Sweden would begin to collect folk material since it would be a great gain for the joint German/Scandinavian history. Moe writes,

> It would be a long time before Grimm's wish was fulfilled in Norway. Fifteen years would pass before the first freezing swallow appeared, and one swallow does not make a summer. Neither did Andreas Faye's *Norske Sagn* (1833), but it was an omen of summer. Faye's book is the point of departure for the national work, which in the 1840s and thereafter would be the most substantial element in Norwegian science, art, and literature. (Moe 1927, 49)

Faye's collection has over the years been the subject of considerable deprecation. But it is necessary to remember that he was attempting to preserve the folklore material and was not a creative artist. He simply recorded the legendary material in a somewhat dry and systematic way. It was to be Jørgen Moe and Peter Christen Asbjørnsen who would shape the Norwegian folk tales into an incomparable style that reflected the realities of the Norwegian national landscape and character. They were truly in the right place at the right time, with the preliminary work accomplished by others, they were positioned to exert enormous influence over establishment of the Norwegian national identity and the Norwegian language. To Moltke Moe, the discovery of the traditional folk material was fortuitous. He writes that it was lucky that it happened when Maurits Hansen's reputation was at its highest.[13]

"With his unhealthy foreign romanticism and his mass production he otherwise could have led our young literary world astray. As it was, Maurits Hansen is the only important Norwegian writer who was a real romanticist in the German sense" (Moe 1927, 49). But Maurits Hansen was also the writer perhaps most admired by the young Asbjørnsen and Moe.

Moe's emphasis is on a long written and oral tradition of folk material with which the Norwegian *bonde* was familiar and it was, according to Moe, because of this established tradition that Norway's romanticism movement differed considerably from the German. But if the folk songs from Vedel's and Syv's collections "permeated into the quiet folk-consciousness of the people," then they must have slipped completely into the subconscious of Henrik Wergeland, Norway's greatest lyric poet, whose oft-quoted (and sometimes misquoted) reply to a query by Frederika Bremer was that he thought there was folk poetry but that it was hard to access and was in decline, a conclusion based on the fact that hundreds of pastors had gone into the valleys without having collected or remarked about any folk songs at all. Earlier in the letter he writes that it is the spirit of the age that songs and legends are dying, and nothing is coming to replace them. Norwegians sang in the hopeful years of 1808–1814, but have since fallen silent. People even need songbooks to sing the national patriotic songs, and he writes that even "the ultra-patriot Henrik Wergeland will not take it upon himself to sing one through to the end" (Wergeland 1867, 130, 127).

Writing in 1932, Asbjørnsen's biographer Hans Hansen has a slightly different perspective on the impulses that fueled national romanticism in Norway. He writes that Norwegian romanticism is, as in other countries, not a heterogeneous and sharply defined chronological epoch. In this country it is also divided into several periods, which spring from different sources. In the first period, Henrich Steffens and the speculative German romanticist philosophy manifest themselves.[14] And through the romantic writings of Maurits Hansen, Tieck and Fouqué have a great influence on Norwegian romanticism. In the second period it is folk poetry—and Herder, and especially the Grimms' theoretical considerations over it—which seem to give life to and nearly dominate Norwegian romanticist art and literature. (Hansen 1932, 132). But Hansen goes on to say that it is Steffens more than anyone else who tunes the instruments of the romanticist movement, giving them the mysterious undertone which characterizes the entire romantic period. And although his influence was critical to Wergeland and probably also to Welhaven, it is far less evident in the romanticism of the 1840s and 1850s, when philosophy was not at all a factor. Hansen cites the importance of Danish, rather than German, aesthetics to the Norwegian romanticists and particularly the work of Johan Ludvig Heiberg, but notes the influence on Jørgen Moe of the German Jean Paul Richter's *Vorschule der Esthetik*. Hansen continues:

> One can most likely say that the influence of Richter on Jørgen Moe is the single example of German romantic philosophy's direct effect on Norwegian romanticism since Henrik Steffens. But on the other hand the importance of German romanticism on the Norwegian is overwhelming as it concerns the greatest source of all romanticism in the various countries: folk poetry. So great was the German influence on Norwegian intellectual life in this respect that one can safely say that at no other time did Germany mean so much for Norwegian art as it did in this time, in the real national romantic period. Not just for literature, but also for painting, music and other arts. For Asbjørnsen and for Moe the German influence is completely determinative. The way in which the Germans retold their folk materials had such a dominating influence on the folklore projects of the two that all other influences were minor in comparison. This influence comes first and foremost from the Grimm brothers' *Kinder und Hausmärchen* and their *Deutsche Mythologie*. The first book gave for Asbjørnsen, as for Moe, the direction for their

method of retelling the Norwegian folk tales. And *Deutsche Mythologie* became the big arsenal from whence they took their theories about fairy tales and legends. (137)

Most Norwegian literary historians agree that romanticism in Norway was much more about nationalism than it was about philosophy, but that the movement is difficult to define.

> It is the essence of romanticism that it resists definition; it breaks down borders, is multifaceted and full of contradictions. It rejects all norms, both in subject and form and cultivates individual and national uniqueness . . . romanticism did not come to Norway like a rush of spring weather, but seeped slowly in. Only when it was disintegrating in most other countries, did it break through forcefully with Wergeland, and then with the union of a legacy from the enlightenment with a modern liberalism, but first and foremost with a powerful personal originality which gave to everything its own form. Soon after, poetic realism manifested itself. "The National Breakthrough" in the 1840s did not only bare the stamp of a romantic basic viewpoint, but also of a growing respect for concrete reality. (Beyer and Beyer 1978, 121, 124)

These summaries and descriptions give an insight into the *zeitgeist* of the time in broad sweeping terms, but a more intimate and perhaps revealing picture emerges when we examine some of the books and periodicals that Asbjørnsen was reading from early days in 1830 until 1845, the year *Norske huldreeventyr og folkesagn* appears in its first edition. One is immediately struck by the depth and breadth of Asbjørnsen's interests and can understand Jørgen Moe's remark in a letter of 1836, in which he calls Asbjørnsen, *Du levende Lexicon over Alting!* (Moe 1915, 141) [You the living all-knowing encyclopedia!]. The books he checked out of the University library during these years are almost evenly divided between the natural and social sciences and literature. Conspicuous by their absence are any works by

Maurits Hansen or Steen Steensen Blicher, so it is reasonable to suppose that Asbjørnsen owned works by these favorites.[15] Well represented are the influential texts mentioned above; he read Baggesen and Oehlenschläger, Steffens and Herder.[16] He read Nyerup, Rahbek, Thiele, Geijer and Afzelius. He borrowed Nyerup's *Almindelig Morskabslæsning* many times. He read Cooper and Scott. He read world histories, language histories and grammars, Heiberg's mythology, and had a fondness for travel writing. He read Goethe, Schiller, Heine, Tieck, Stagnelius, Swedenborg, Paludan-Müller. He returned again and again to Byron and Tullin.[17] In the reading room, he read encyclopedias and dictionaries; newspapers, magazines, and periodicals: *Maanedsskrift for Litteratur, Svea, Zeitgenossen, Athene, Kjøbenhavns flyvende Post, Ursins Magazin, Nordisk Tidsskrift, Prometheus, Frey,* and others. Although the Norwegian national romanticism movement may have been more about nationalism than it was about philosophy, this did not prevent Asbjørnsen from reading Threschow's lectures on Kant and several other philosophical works. Of the nearly 500 books he borrowed, the classics of antiquity are well represented, especially in the early years when he was studying for his examinations; in some years, works on zoology, chemistry, or botany are prevalent. But throughout the listings of the works he borrowed, one name stands out, year after year: Grimm.

The first book Asbjørnsen checked out of the University library by either of the Grimm brothers was *Deutsche Grammatik,* vol. 1 on 6 December 1832. In May of the following year, he checked out the second volume, and on 21 November the influential *Irische Elfenmärchen,* the Grimms' brothers translation of *Fairy Legends and Traditions of the South of Ireland.* Asbjørnsen borrowed this book again on 29 April 1838 and 17 June 1842; on January 15 of 1843, 1844, and 1845, it was automatically renewed since it had not been returned before the end of the year. In the meantime, he discovered *Kinder- und Haus Märchen* and *Deutsche Sagen* in early 1835. One or another volume of either or both of these works must have been almost continually in his possession through 1845, according to the library records. In those years when most of the borrowings were in the physical sciences, 1840 through the first part of 1842, *Kinder- und Haus Märchen* seems incongruous in long listings of works on chemistry and zoology.

The legacy of the enlightenment was very much alive in the nature of P. Chr. Asbjørnsen, and the blending of national romanticism with a scientific rationalism is evident also in the collaborative work of Asbjørnsen and Moe on the famous folk tale collections, where sound common sense is usually rewarded. To understand why *Norske folkeeventyr* has been so highly regarded by the Norwegian public over the years is to understand how texts are canonized to reflect the perceptions of the "imagined community," perceptions with which that community can identify. How and why Asbjørnsen's independent work has been appropriated into that canon as part of the "Asbjørnsen and Moe" entity is a fascinating record of how a nation perceives itself and its literary icons. The story begins with *Norske folkeeventyr*, the folk fairy tale collection, and the literary fairy tale tradition in Europe, because the context in which Asbjørnsen wrote his legend collections must be understood. But this is not a story about fairy tales and happy endings; it is the story about the much more real and complex world that Asbjørnsen both created and reflected in *Norske huldreeventyr og folkesagn*.

CHAPTER 2

Asbjørnsen and Moe: The Genesis of
Norske folkeeventyr and Its Relationship to
Norske huldreeventyr og folkesagn

> *Every fairy tale is, in its own way,
> something of a dragon slayer.*
> —Max Lüthi

ASBJØRNSEN AND MOE AND THE LITERARY FOLK TALE TRADITION

There are no dragons in the Norwegian fairy tales, but there are numerous nasty trolls, and they are inevitably dispatched by the cunning and resourceful young Espen or Askeladden, or even the chubby little Butterball. There are also plenty of unscrupulous officials, greedy ministers, and the occasional haughty princess to be dealt with, and the young hero, who is just as often called simply *gutten* [the boy], or the occasional heroine, is able eventually to conquer all and reinforce the triumph of wits over brawn or power. The Norwegian folk tales are truly splendid ones, and the story of their creation is also a story of triumph over circumstances. So many things could have gone wrong, or happened differently, and the folk tale collection would have been something quite different than it finally became.

Jørgen Moe and Peter Christen Asbjørnsen first met in 1827 when Moe was fourteen and Asbjørnsen a year older, as students at the Støren brothers' prep school at Norderhov in Ringerike. The two became fast friends, a friendship that would last for life, and a friendship that would eventually lead to their collaboration on the collection and retelling of the Norwegian folk tales.[1] It is fortunate for the Norwegian literary canon that both Moe and Asbjørnsen loved nature and outdoor life, since it was likely this interest that drew them together. In personality they were really quite different, Moe given to melancholy and a sensitive and poetic idealism, Asbjørnsen much more practical and even-tempered. The combination was a fortunate one for their collaboration.

This collaboration has been the object of considerable speculation over the ensuing years. Whose idea was it initially to collect the folk tales, as the Grimms had done in Germany? Who was primarily responsible for the characteristic style of the retelling, so *Norwegian*?[2] These questions have never been, and probably cannot be, answered with complete certainty, and most scholars today are content to consider the questions moot, although the current prevailing consensus generally attributes the discovery of the importance of the folk tales to Moe, and also considers him the better stylist of the two.[3] In general, perhaps one can say that most scholars of the twentieth century tend to value Moe's contribution above Asbjørnsen's. One exception is Hallvard Bakken, who, speaking of the folk tale collection, writes, "It has been customary to claim for Jørgen Moe the primary share of this work, and particularly Anders Krogvig, who one must say tends to overestimate Moe in all respects, has tried to reduce Asbjørnsen's contribution" (Bakken 1935, 470).[4] Earlier scholars were more apt to give Asbjørnsen the credit for first collecting the tales, based on a small notebook containing three stories dated from 1833. Moltke Moe claims that Asbjørnsen must have made an error in dating the small notebook, since he did not visit the places where the tales came from until 1835. Or, Moe explains, he could have added the date later and simply made a mistake in the year (Moe 1927, 81).[5] Moltke Moe dates Jørgen Moe's first efforts in collecting from 1834. In a letter to his sister in the fall of this year Jørgen Moe asks her if she knows the fairy tale about the seven foals. He asks her to refresh her memory of it, because he has a need for it.

Perhaps the most objective point of view regarding the genesis and style of the famous collaboration is given by Hans Hansen in his 1932 biography of Asbjørnsen. Hansen summarizes the points of view on these questions taken by scholars up to that time and concludes that it may perhaps never be possible to ascertain the genesis or the origin of the style of the folk tales for certain because of lack of documentation, although he is perhaps more likely to believe that Asbjørnsen could have been collecting as early as 1833. Hansen writes, "All things considered, one must be cautious in attaching too much significance to these two questions. The work on the folk tales ought for all time without reservation be tied to the names of both men, and the honor be equally divided between them" (Hansen 1932, 162). The important fact is that the two agreed that the method of retelling the tales had to be in the "voice of the people." And regardless of which of the two first starting collecting folk tales, there is no doubt that the first written evidence of the value of the folk tales comes in a letter to Asbjørnsen from Jørgen Moe in 1836:

> If I ever become really healthy again, I am going to start telling fairy tales. I have read those that Adam [Oehlenschläger] published; My God! Now that's something! But of course they are not Norwegian, and a Norwegian fairy tale would have about the same relationship to the southern countries' tales as Bergen's nature has to Sjølundes. There is a theme from "when I was little" which awakened to full power when I read Tieks (sic) "Blond Eckbert." He is almost Norwegian; in his temperament, his heart, he is so entirely; the dark, dim, deep feeling (the sharply outlined shadows of the peaks of Bergen), which suddenly in a kind of half despairing abandonment gives vent to melancholy, as when the sun in that nature suddenly hits the glaciers on the peaks and these reflect a radiance the eye cannot tolerate without pain. But his imagination is too eastern. The Norwegian can offer Bergen's overflowing fragrant abundance of flowers, but not the radiance and refulgence which sparkles along the banks of the Ganges or the Euphrates. Nor does he in his fairy tales have enough sense to be Norwegian; even in fantasy's most capricious creations the Norwegian will have common sense, which Tieck unrightfully despises. If I ever become

really vigorously healthy again, you will hear one about the seven foals that will be Norwegian! This isn't bragging since the conditions for the fulfillment of this promise aren't likely. (Moe 1915, 144)

Ill though he was at the time, it seems evident that Moe was thinking of using the folkloristic material as a basis for the creation of an art fairy tale. Moltke Moe, who was closest to both of the great collectors, says of the letter just cited, "Here Moe still sees the fairy tales primarily through the eyes of Tieck and Oehlenschläger; the folk tale's meaning as historical and nationalist documents still isn't clear to him, even if he realizes the uniquely Norwegian, characterized by our Norwegian folk tales, clearly enough. But right after this came the breakthrough. In the late fall of 1836 the Grimms' *Kinder- und Haus-Märchen* fell into his hands. Studying them opened his eyes to a new important side of folk tales: their scientific worth, and here too was the pattern for the correct retelling" (Moe 1927, 85).[6]

The two friends met in Oslo and in Moss in 1837 and agreed to collect and publish the Norwegian folk tales and the first small effort came out already at the end of that year, in *Nor*. Here, under Asbjørnsen's name, were published five fairy tales and three legends, including early versions of several which would eventually appear in the first edition of *Norske huldreeventyr og folkesagn*. Jørgen Moe had gone through the work and "deloused" it, to use Asbjørnsen's expression, and had also written an introductory poem. And if Asbjørnsen did learn from Moe to write with more Norwegianisms, "With Asbjørnsen's contribution to *Nor*, his apprenticeship ends," according to Moltke Moe, who continues,

> In the rendering of the big collaborative folk tale collection both writers have a full grasp of the tone of the folk diction and both have equal ability to strike it. And even if it was Jørgen Moe who, through the memories of his upbringing, first comprehended the folk poetry with interest and understood its meaning for our young literature, and who

first mastered the style of the people, then this is offset by Asbjørnsen's prolonged work on the common project. And in the fundamental work, the first collection of *Norske folkeeventyr*, both writers are fully and completely equal, both have the same part. (Moe 1927, 86)[7]

But *Norske folkeeventyr* did not come into existence easily. Both Asbjørnsen and Moe, after all, wrote Danish and they had to collect not only the folk tales, but also many of the Norwegian expressions used by the people, and they did not find it easy to write as the people spoke. Although the manuscript for the first collection is lost, it is evident from other sources that the two friends and collaborators wrote and rewrote until they were satisfied that they had hit the mark. Moe was often plagued with illness, to the point where he sent Asbjørnsen some of his work to be published after his death with the proceeds to be used for publication of the folk tales. In addition, neither of the two had much money; Asbjørnsen sometimes could not even afford postage, and finding a publisher willing to publish the project was daunting. Asbjørnsen was at this time writing articles for *Skillings* magazine, and in 1838, its publisher, Carl August Guldberg, agreed to publish the tales, but only if the young authors could guarantee a certain number of sales by signing up subscribers ahead of time. In December of 1838, Moe wrote to Asbjørnsen that they must delay publication of the subscription until after his spring examination. Moe believes that they must have more material and explains to Asbjørnsen the advantages of publishing the collections as *books* rather than pamphlets. He writes, "Let us wait, dear Peter! Our future literary reputations will undoubtedly to a great extent depend on how we appear with this really important work" (Moe 1915, 167–168).

The subscription offer was published in 1840 and was written by Moe. Hans Hansen calls it "a little masterpiece," but it did not have the desired effect, unfortunately, and in a charming letter-poem of 4 February 1840, Moe queries Asbjørnsen about subscribers in his part of the country, along with other questions about the project. Moe's words also give a glimpse of the personality of his friend, whom Moe sometimes berates for being less than attentive to their project, or for not writing to him:

> Men dernæst har jeg Et og Andet,
> hvorom jeg vilde tale med dig,
> Ifald Du har en Time ledig
> Fra Punschen og fra Fiskevandet . . .
> Saavidt jeg veed, har vores ene
> Landsmandske Hersteds-Abonnent
> Lagt til Abonnementets Kjæde
> Nok een, og *det* jeg skulde mene
> Er, hvad vi vente kan omtrent.
>
> (MOE 1915, 180–181)[8]

Both Asbjørnsen and Moe were determined that the collection would be published, even if they were to lose money on the undertaking. With few subscribers, Guldberg withdrew as publisher, but with the help of P. A. Munch, the Danish-born publisher Johan Dahl agreed to the project and towards the end of 1841, the first small collection of *Norske folkeeventyr, collected by Asbjørnsen and Jørgen Moe* appeared. It was an unprepossessing little volume, ninety-six pages, with a bluish-gray cover without a title, without authors' names or the name of the publisher. But it immediately caused quite a stir. Most critics did not know what to make of the little book. Hans Hansen explains,

> It was not surprising that the critics felt disoriented when the fairy tales were published. It was the first time a book was printed in the Norwegian people's own language. But in educated circles, it was looked at as something "coarse." The fairy tales were, from the view of language history, revolutionary and were also felt as revolutionary. But it helped that Welhaven expressed himself favorably. Jørgen Moe, who had come to Oslo by now, could shortly after the publication write to his friend Peter Broch: "The fairy tales, incidentally,

are extraordinarily successful here, almost creating a furor, since Jahn with his aesthetic absolute power has decided that it is 'a splendid book,' and they will soon be reviewed in Nella by a capable hand. . . ." P. A. Munch, who had understood the historic importance of Asbjørnsen and Moe's work long before the folk tales were published, almost gave them the stamp of European approval when he reviewed the tales in *Leipziger allegemeine Zeitung* (1843), in which he called them "the most successful of anything our young literature can show." And when Jacob Grimm himself declared that the Norwegian folk tales almost unconditionally were superior to all other folk tale collections, people started to realize what a great national work Asbjørnsen and Moe had given us (Hansen 1932, 148–149).[9]

And the Norwegian folk tale collection grew with additional publications in 1842, 1843, and 1844. A new edition was published in 1852, and in 1865 Moe sent Asbjørnsen his remaining collections, in five notebooks, asking him to share with Sophus Bugge. After this, subsequent editions were published by Asbjørnsen alone.

The Norwegian folk tales have been translated into many languages and are well known around the world.[10] Those qualities that made them typically *norsk* to their contemporaries included a use of many Norwegian, as opposed to Danish, words; idiomatic expressions, and the short, concise retort. Jørgen Moe wrote in his famous introduction to the 1852 edition that the Norwegian tales are characterized by a form of humor that can only be developed in a country where people live in a hard natural environment. Moe also sees the Norwegian folk tale in some respects as a continuation of the saga poetics, in the sense that the folk tales contain the same directness and a mode of expression that arises from simplicity. Moe sees the same splendid intrepid humor throughout the folk tales that one also finds in the sagas. Moe's introduction to this edition was tremendously influential, as one might expect. How better to forge a link across the intervening centuries and appropriate a claim to a glorious past than by finding in the people's folk tale characters a connection with the great Old Norse medieval literature of Norway/Iceland?

But when Asbjørnsen and Moe published their first collection of tales in 1841, a collection comprised mostly of fairy tales, the fairy tale as a genre already had a long history. This evolution of the fairy tale, from its oral roots in a dim past to the literary fairy tale as it has been reformulated to serve particular segments of various societies, is a long and complex story. This evolution has been traced by Jack Zipes in his introduction to *Spells of Enchantment: The Wondrous Fairy Tales of Western Culture*. Zipes writes that

> during its inception, the fairy tale distinguished itself as a genre both by appropriating the oral folk tale and by expanding it, for it became gradually necessary in the modern world to adapt the oral tale to the standards of literacy and make it acceptable for diffusion in the public sphere. The fairy tale is only one type of appropriation of a particular oral storytelling tradition: the wonder folk tale, often called the *Zaubermärchen* or the *conte merveilleux*. (Zipes 1991c, xii)

The fairy tale derives from the oral wonder tale, which Zipes further defines and refines by reference to Vladimir Propp's famous thirty-one basic functions, which Zipes condenses into eight steps, and which give an archetypal story form, one which facilitates recall, and which invariably requires a wonder or miracle to bring about the desired effect. Zipes observes that

> rarely do wonder tales end unhappily. They triumph over death. The tale begins with "Once upon a time" or "Once there was" and never really ends when it ends. The ending is actually the beginning. The once upon a time is not a past designation but futuristic: the timelessness of the tale and its lack of geographical specificity endow it with utopian connotations—utopia in its original meaning designated "no place," a place that no one had ever envisaged. (xiii)

By the time the brothers Grimm and somewhat later Asbjørnsen and Moe began appropriating oral wonder tales in order to preserve them for the study of the "folk spirit," there was already established a long literary tradition of the literary fairy tale in Europe. Zipes discusses the evolution of this tradition from the appearance of the first major literary fairy tale, Apuleius' "Cupid and Psyche" in the second century, through the Italian and French texts of the sixteenth and seventeenth centuries, the introduction of the oriental tale into the French tradition, and the publication of inexpensive editions of tales in the eighteenth century, which were sold to the lower classes in France and central Europe. "The fairy tales were often abridged; the language was simplified; and there were multiple versions, which were read to children and nonliterates. Many tales were appropriated by oral storytellers, so that the literary tradition became a source for an oral tradition." It is important to remember that all transcribers of folk tales in eighteenth-century Europe were carrying on a dialogue with an already established written tradition, even those who claimed to be merely recording the stories of the peasants without modification. This is, of course, true of *Norske folkeeventyr* as well. The Norwegian joint folk tale collection is a collection of wonder, or fairy, tales, fables, and jocular tales which contain the motifs and tale types familiar in other national collections, set in a Norwegian context.[11] Asbjørnsen's *huldreeventyr*, on the other hand, are migratory local legends set in literary frames.

It may be likely that Peter Asbjørnsen learned a great deal from Jørgen Moe during their collaboration on the fairy tale collections; but Asbjørnsen's own work with the legends has been appropriated by Norwegian literary historians and scholars as part of the "Asbjørnsen and Moe" codification, as has been shown in several citations: "It is fully justifiable to view all these collections as one work" or "The work on the fairy tales ought for all time without reservation be tied to the names of both men." Of course no one would dispute that this is true with respect to the joint folk tale collection, but in fact, Asbjørnsen's own independent contribution to Norwegian nation building through the legends of *Norske huldreeventyr og folkesagn* has not been properly recognized nor has the text been given the autonomy it deserves. The cavalier dismissal of Asbjørnsen's independent work by including it as a part of an "Asbjørnsen and Moe" joint literary oeuvre does an injustice not only to Asbjørnsen's literary reputation, but also overlooks the considerable differences between the fairy tale and the legend.

Already the Grimm brothers discussed the difference; in *Deutsche Sagen*, Jacob Grimm writes that the fairy tale is more poetic and the legend is more historical. Citing Grimm, Bengt Holbek notes that the comparative form is apt since "there are all kinds of overlapping and hybrid forms" but "fairy tales create a make-believe universe . . . [T]hey are visits to a better world, the world as-it-should-be" (Holbek 1987, 198, 201). It is the literary fairy tale based on the oral wonder tale that comprises the majority of the stories in Asbjørnsen and Moe's famous *Norske folkeeventyr*.[12] The stories selected for inclusion were those that conformed, or could be made to conform, to Moe and Asbjørnsen's ideas about what constituted the uniquely Norwegian, within the boundaries of the wonder tale. No one, except perhaps small children, seriously believe that fairy tales are true, and that is not in itself of any great importance to its audience, whose concern is with the wonder of the story.[13] Fairy tales take place in the atemporal world of never-never land, in a fantasy realm of magic and talking animals, where flat characters, either good or evil, perform a series of actions for which they are rewarded or punished. On the other hand, veracity is of primary interest in the type of oral material utilized by Asbjørnsen in his *huldreeventyr*, the legend. Legends "are considered narratives which focus on a single episode, an episode which is presented as miraculous, uncanny, bizarre, or sometimes embarrassing. The narration of a legend is, in a sense, the negotiation of the truth in these episodes. That is not to say that legends are always held to be true, as some scholars have claimed, but that at the core of the legend is an evaluation of its truth status" (Oring 1986, 125). Despite the emphasis which scholars have placed on *Norske folkeeventyr* as a nation-building text, it is my contention that fairy tales are in many respects too formulaic to have much intrinsic nation-building value; they appear to me much more suited to polarization of groups and classes than to the unification of these elements.[14]

THE LEGEND COLLECTION: NORSKE HULDREEVENTYR OG FOLKESAGN

Norske huldreeventyr og folkesagn is a collection of twenty-seven separate stories which appeared in three editions edited by P. Chr. Asbjørnsen himself, from the first collection of 1845 to the third edition in 1870. As early as 1835 Asbjørnsen was collecting legends for Andreas Faye, but soon thereafter he must have thought about a collection of legends of his own. He published the first stories which would later appear in *Norske huldreeventyr og folkesagn* in 1837 in *Nor*. Included were the stories "The King of Ekeberg" and "Matthias the Hunter's Stories." Several of the stories which were later to appear in the first collection of *Norske huldreeventyr og folkesagn* were first published in the newspaper *Den Constitutionelle* in 1843 and 44. Among these were "Berthe Tuppenhaug's Stories," which appeared as "A Wise Woman's Stories" in two issues of *Den Constitutionelle* in 1843; "The Hulder Clan," which originally was entitled "Birdsong and the Hulder Clan" when it appeared in 1843; "An Old-fashioned Christmas Eve," which was published right before Christmas in 1843; and "The Giant and Johannes Blessom" which appeared in 1844.

By the time *Norske huldreeventyr og folkesagn* reached its third edition, in 1870, it was already considered a classic of Norwegian national romanticism. In fact, as a reviewer noted with reference to minor changes in orthography or word selection in a review of the third edition, "These improvements naturally had to be undertaken with a certain amount of caution, since it was a question of preserving the character through which these descriptions of Norwegian nature, folk life, and folk belief have, after all, won so many friends through the years" (Halvorsen 1870, 810).

The folklore presented in *huldreeventyr* is composed largely, but not exclusively, of recognizable migratory legends which are localized by the use of fictionalized and, for the most part, rural, storytellers, set within a frame story recounted by an educated urban first-person narrator. The dialectic between the narrator of the frame story and the created folk storytellers and their tales is the dialectic between the urban and rural, the refined and unrefined. Asbjørnsen himself considered the stories he was relating in the *huldreeventyr* to be representative of the current folk beliefs of the people, and his motivation in the publication of *Norske huldreeventyr og folkesagn* was in some respects different from the motivation he and Moe shared in publishing the folk tales. In a reply to P.J. Collett's review of the first collection of *huldreeventyr*, printed in the newspaper *Den Constitutionelle*, Jørgen Moe expresses the difference between the traditional material in the two collections:

> The difference in the nature of the material is mainly because: fairy tales of the sort in the collection [*Folkeeventyrene*] are no longer created by the people. . . . They are not created any longer, they are only told. . . . But with the legend, or the "huldre" fairy tale, which daily is being created . . . it is quite different; just because they are still being created, their structure is not nearly as firm and completed as the fairy tales', which is also why the writer can treat the legend in versatile interpretive ways. (Moe 1845)[15]

In some respects it is perhaps unfortunate for the literary reputation of *Norske huldreeventyr og folkesagn* that the public was already aware of Asbjørnsen as a collector of folklore and as a collaborator on *Norske folkeeventyr*. It is likely that the scanty critical attention to *Norske huldreeventyr og folkesagn* as an autonomous literary work is due, at least in part, to this fact and to the inherent dichotomy in the work itself. Considered folklore by literary scholars and literature by folklorists, the text does not fit easily into any preconceived body of texts against which, and through which, it could be studied, unlike the established literary fairy tale tradition. In the preface to their comprehensive study of Scandinavian folk belief and legend, Reimund Kvideland and Henning K. Sehmsdorf explain that "in selecting our texts, we have emphasized faithfulness to belief tradition rather than to literary quality. Some of the better-known texts, for example, those published by Peter Chr. Asbjørnsen during the nineteenth century, have not been included here because they were edited to conform to the literary standards of the time" (Kvideland and Sehmsdorf 1988, xxi).

One is tempted to ask Kvideland and Sehmsdorf which texts are *not* so edited.[16] But of course, the problem is clear: the text is a literary one, not a faithful transcription from an informant, however much Asbjørnsen may have claimed otherwise. Asbjørn Aarseth agrees, speaking of both Asbjørnsen and Moe, he writes: "The fact that the two collectors have such high prestige rests not least on their ability for literary formation of the oral material they were confronted with. They are both in their own way exceptional stylists. But precisely this condition renders them less suitable for finding genuine folkloristic texts as objects for analysis" (Aarseth 1976, 108).

If the folklorists are suspicious that the folklore is corrupted by literary treatment, surely then one would expect the literary critics to eagerly engage a work of such classic proportions? And, in the beginning, it looked as though the work might be considered an imaginative, creative collection of novellas or short stories containing folkloristic elements and a personification of Norwegian nature. Jørgen Moe, in the newspaper article cited earlier, writes that each of the stories in *huldreeventyr* can claim "to be something quite apart, to be an independent little short story" (Moe, 1845).[17] And an anonymous reviewer in *Morgenbladet* goes even further, dispelling the traditional canonical view that the frame narrator in *Norske huldreeventyr og folkesagn* is no one other than a thinly disguised Asbjørnsen himself: "The narrator shows up as a city-dwelling man of letters, as a student and tutor in the country, even as a lieutenant. We must not be under the illusion that we are dealing with Mr. Asbjørnsen's own person; the 'I' that appears in the book is neither him nor Per nor Pål, but rather a whole class. It is us, his readers, whether we are lieutenants or students or whatever."[18] But despite this early realization that *Norske huldreeventyr og folkesagn* was in fact more than an autobiographical travel journal, only nine years later Camilla Collett could write to Johan Ludvig Heiberg in June of 1854, with respect to the lack of Norwegian literary talent, "We have not had a short story writer since Maurits Hansen" (cited in Steen 1947, 242). This is perhaps all the more puzzling since Camilla Collett herself wrote portions of the frame narrative in several of the *huldreeventyr*. It is clear that she at least did not consider *huldreeventyr* to be part of that genre. What happened to the early literary aspirations of *Norske huldreeventyr og folkesagn*?

One explanation may be that the literary historians, scholars, and others of the elite who were constructing the Norwegian national identity may have realized intuitively or consciously that the text could subvert efforts to idealize the Norwegian *bonde*. Far from the hero of the folk fairy tale, with his saga ancestors, the Norwegian *bonde* as he appears in the legend collection is a much less admirable character. Asbjørnsen's process of cultural creation, with its critical view of the faults and failings of the *bonde* is a far different construction than what was done in Germany by the Grimms, or for that matter, in Bjørnson's idealized *Bondefortellinger* [Stories of the Farmers]. Asbjørnsen, in fact, distances the implied reader from the Norwegian peasant by a variety of methods which creates a two-tiered view of the Norwegian. And as Jusdanis notes, "The literary and philosophical canons . . . cannot tolerate pluralism . . . the canon serves as a utopian site of continuous textuality in which a nation, a class, or an individual may find an undifferentiated identity" (Jusdanis 1991, 58–59). And as Georg Johannesen writes, with customary irony, "Any thought that could not have been thought by Bjørnstjerne Bjørnson is forbidden in Norway" (Johannesen 1994, 88).

A recurring argument against considering the text as an imaginative literary work is Asbjørnsen's lack of depth in characterization. Virtually all critics view his characterizations as stereotypical, his sketches of people as one-dimensional recreations of persons he had actually met, lacking complexity. But the text was immensely popular, and who can argue that popular literature is less influential than that which is canonized as great literature by academics or literary critics? Popular literature has always been at least as influential as the literature canonized by an intellectual standard-setting elite. Jane Tompkins, in her influential *Sensational Designs*, shows how texts which are not part of the current American literary canon because of perceived deficiencies in characterization or plotting were vastly more popular and influential at the time of their reception, because they were read with different preconceived assumptions than those of today. Tompkins sees that "the presence of stereotyped characters, rather than constituting a defect in these novels, was what allowed them to operate as instruments of cultural self definition. Stereotypes are the instantly recognizable representatives of overlapping racial, national, ethnic, economic, social, political, and religious categories; they convey enormous amounts of cultural information in an extremely condensed form" (Tompkins 1985, xvi).

Conceding that characterization in *Norske huldreeventyr og folkesagn* is stereotypical does not negate its literary value. The characterizations must be the way they are in order to function as a performance context for the traditional material. It is nevertheless true that Asbjørnsen himself contributed to the non-literary view of his work, stating in the preface to the first edition, for example that "there is not much to add regarding the narrative method of these huldre tales and folk legends. They are told as they still live in the mouths of the common people; nothing is added or removed. Only in a few places are a couple of accounts combined, where some less sharply delineated local traditions are supplemented with those that are more complete and prevalent" (Asbjørnsen 1845, v).

Although this may be true so far as the internal legends are concerned, it does not address the frame narration. Asbjørnsen states that he "wished to transmit them [the legends] in their original scent and color" (iv) and, in so doing, he in effect created a performance context for folklore long before the importance of such a context was realized. But it was a *created* context, a literary construct, not a carefully annotated actual description; in fact, it will be shown that Asbjørnsen showed no compunction in improvising his created folk narrators, combining variants and otherwise freely constructing the storytelling milieux. And although there is no clear indication that Asbjørnsen *himself* felt that in *Norske huldreeventyr og folkesagn* he was writing imaginative literature, that he was nonetheless doing so is one of the premises of this book, and it is in this light that the text will be considered. It is of interest to note in passing that the Intentional Fallacy has been, and still is, a dominate characteristic of much Norwegian literary criticism, bound as that criticism still is in the historical/geographical method.

"THERE HAVE BEEN TOO FEW POINTS OF VIEW."

In the case of *Norske huldreeventyr og folkesagn*, scholarly criticism is, with a few exceptions, confined mainly to short evaluations in the various literary histories, since the text has never attained the stature of creative literature to the extent that it has seemed to require much interpretation, and has often simply been integrated into anthologies as part of the enshrined "Asbjørnsen and Moe" canon entity.[19] There are nevertheless several early commentaries that indicate that before the time of the third edition of *Norske huldreeventyr og folkesagn* in 1870, Asbjørnsen's text was considered more than simply a faithful rendition of Norwegian folklore.

In what is considered by many to be Norway's first literary history, Hans Olaf Hansen's *Den Norske Literatur fra 1814 indtil vore Dage*, [Norwegian Literary History from 1814 to the Present] which was published in 1862, when its author was only nineteen years old, Hansen says of Asbjørnsen, "No other Norwegian writer has delivered so many poetic nature descriptions as he has; neither has anyone else produced so many characteristic features of the common man's life and nature as he. Therefore his *Huldreeventyr og folkesagn* does not just possess great value as a collection of tales, but has also—perhaps an even greater—value as a literary work" (Hansen 1862, 106).[20] Edvard Brandes, in comparing Asbjørnsen's *huldreeventyr* with Svend Grundtvig's collection of Danish folk tales writes that

> Asbjørnsen's collection has a different character than Grundtvig's, for the Norwegian author, who mixes different accounts together as a matter of course in order to get good stories from them, and who has a quite singularly fresh and entertaining narrative style, is much more the poet than the scientist in his treatment of the material. He can actually be considered the Norwegian H. C. Andersen, and his collection will be read with a great deal more interest than the Danish one by all those who aren't attracted to this literature for reasons of scientific inquiry. (Brandes 1877, 326)[21]

In 1883 Henrik Jæger published a little volume entitled *Norske Forfattere* [Norwegian Writers] which includes what could be considered the first attempt to examine *Norske huldreeventyr og folkesagn* from a literary critical perspective, within the context of Norwegian national romanticism. It is this work that has had "fundamental influence over that which was later written about Asbjørnsen the collector of folklore, the teller of fairy tales, and the man" (Aarseth 1981, 44). Speaking of the *huldreeventyr* in opposition to the joint folk tale collections, Jæger notes that "their popularity has been more local, and because of this the critical elucidation has been limited by our domestic literary conditions. While there has not been a lack of recognition, there has undoubtedly not been enough incisive analysis. There have been too few points of view, and those points of view have been too similar. It is necessary to find new points of view" (Jæger 1883, 1–2). Jæger places the text within the larger framework of *huldreromantik*, a historical survey of which occupies over half of his article. Jæger situates Asbjørnsen within the circle of literary figures of the 1840s like Welhaven and Andreas Munch who, as Jæger says, made all mythology into nature symbolism.[22] At first, Asbjørnsen too saw the legends of the people in the light of national romanticism; as he wrote in the preface to the first edition, "these legends are nothing other than nature itself," but, according to Jæger, Asbjørnsen soon outgrew this romantic phase and came to understand the legends anthropomorphically. The people's ideas of the supernatural were shaped after themselves.

After a summary of the milieu in which the *huldreeventyr* were created, Jæger gives the obligatory biographical background of his author and, finally, fifty-two pages into his article, turns his attention to the text for the remaining thirty pages, beginning with a discussion of possible models for the format of *Norske huldreeventyr og folkesagn*. Andreas Faye's early collection of legends from 1833 would only have shown Asbjørnsen the difficulties in re-telling the legends, since Faye's work is generally considered dry and prosaic. It seems clear that the likely model was Crofton Croker's *Fairy Legends and Traditions of the South of Ireland* from 1825, a work which was influenced by Walter Scott and which Asbjørnsen knew in the Grimms' translation as we have seen. The remainder of Jæger's analysis consists of an attempt to show how Asbjørnsen in his stories gradually shifts the emphasis from the tales in the first collection of 1845 to their tellers in the second collection from 1848. Jæger writes that

> in the first collection, the legends themselves furnish most of the names. The sketches are partly named directly for the legends ("The King of Ekeberg," "The Huldre Clan," "Legends of the Mill," etc.), partly for whomsoever tells the stories ("Mathias the Hunter's Stories," "Berthe Tuppenhaug's Stories," "The Gravedigger's Stories"), and partly they are named after the time of the day or year when the legends are told and the circumstances in which they are told ("An Old-fashioned Christmas Eve," "A Night in Nordmarken," "An Evening by the And River," etc.). In the second collection, on the contrary, it is what the author himself describes, and

not the legends, which give the title: "Mountain Images," "A Grouse Hunt in Holleia," "The Lumber Haulers," "A Wise Woman," "The Gypsies." The reason for this difference is that what had originally been the main concern for the author has become secondary, and what originally was an unimportant side issue has become the main concern. Originally Asbjørnsen's main purpose was to tell legends, now his main concern has become to describe curious types and situations. To begin with, the original part of Asbjørnsen's sketches [the frame] was just a pretext to give the opportunity of telling the folk traditions; now these traditions have almost become a pretext in order to have the opportunity of describing the people. (69–70)[23]

For Jæger, as for Hansen, Asbjørnsen was responsible for bringing a new realism to Norwegian literature with his descriptions of nature and of the people. This type of realistic writing has often been termed "poetic realism" by later literary historians. However, in his overview of how the concept of realism had shifted from the 1830s to the 1980s, Asbjørn Aarseth takes exception to that prevailing view of Asbjørnsen as a realistic writer, placing him in fact squarely back in the flowering of national romanticism, and, in what can be considered one of the few modern critiques of a story from *Norske huldreeventyr og folkesagn*, also takes exception to Henrik Jæger's contention that Asbjørnsen progressed from romanticism to realism in the years between the writing of "The Hulder Clan" in 1843 and "The Lumber Haulers" in 1848.

In "The Hulder Clan," a young live-in tutor, traditionally considered to be Asbjørnsen himself in his role of frame narrator, tries to become more intimately acquainted with the daughter of the household during a sojourn in an old look-out cabin during a summer rain shower. His advances are repulsed as the girl warns him that she has a *hulder* for an ancestor. This frame construction introduces a series of stories about the *hulder*. Aarseth claims that Jæger's analysis of "The Hulder Clan" is an example of a naturalistic reading of a romantic text, because Jæger stresses the distinction between the more primitive folk beliefs of the rural people and the young storyteller, who is educated and does not take the stories the girl tells seriously. Aarseth criticizes Jæger's concern to spare Asbjørnsen's feelings, since Asbjørnsen was still living at the time of Jæger's critique, and would presumably find remarks about his unfortunate engagement distressing.[24]

More critical still is Aarseth of Jæger's reading of "The Lumber Haulers" as a naturalistic text, an assessment which is still prevalent today. In this story, told without a frame narration, Asbjørnsen describes a typical wayside pub frequented by the workmen who haul lumber to market. The rowdy, quarrelsome crowd play cards and tell stories about the devil until the festivities are broken up by a general mêlée. Jæger asserts that this story is a fine naturalistic and scientific description of the actual lumber haulers. Aarseth, on the contrary, insists that the milieu is carefully crafted by means of utilization of animal metaphors and language to create a context for stories about the devil.

> In this text, as in the others, Asbjørnsen is first and foremost a creative writer. . . . We have in "The Lumber Haulers" as in "The Hulder Clan" a typical example of the author's creative method, his stress on creating a uniform text, that is to say, to match the people and surroundings of the frame with the tone of the actual legend material. And of course it is not just a question of an appropriate wrapping; it is more precise to call it a complete integration of the frame environment and the propagation of the traditional material. (Aarseth 1981, 50, 52)

For Asbjørn Aarseth, Asbjørnsen's work is not an example of realism or naturalism at all, but rather romanticism of a kind not recognized by Jæger from his perspective of the 1890s. For us, Aarseth continues, romanticism has a wider definition than it had for Jæger. We include qualities such as an interest in the darker side of life, a tendency to demonize, and a sense for the grotesque and morbid in descriptions of environment in our modern definition of romanticism (51).

Although brief, Aarseth's defense of "The Lumber Haulers" as a carefully integrated literary work is a step in the right direction, although his concern is primarily with the shifting concept of what realism means in literature, and his choice of Asbjørnsen's text only one of several he discusses. A more ideologically focused point of view of one of the *huldreeventyr* is undertaken by Walter Baumgartner in a 1993 article. Baumgartner summarizes Aarseth's work and recognizes Aarseth as the first scholar to consider the *huldreeventyr* as an integrated literary text. But while Aarseth chose "The Hulder Clan" and "The Lumber Haulers" to illustrate his conclusions, Baumgartner selects the most political of the stories, "An Evening in the Squire's Kitchen" for his purposes. Baumgartner claims that "*An Evening* is a fictional attempt at mediation between folk culture and high culture. This story implies a declaration of a program, a justification and a reception-linked launching for Asbjørnsen and Moe's folkloristic project, a project that in many respects was politically and ideologically highly explosive and disputed" (Baumgartner 1993, 312).[25] According to Baumgartner, Asbjørnsen sets up an opposition between the world of the salon, where the squire carries on a tirade on a litany of political matters, and the kitchen, where the servants, the blacksmith, and even the squire's wife are engaged in storytelling. Since the squire is portrayed in a very unfavorable manner, the contemporaneous reader, who most probably would have shared the squire's opinion of the kitchen stories as "stuff and nonsense, and lying rigmarole!" (A 1: 64, Trans. Brækstad) becomes more inclined to react favorably to the proceedings in the kitchen. The stark opposition between the two spheres is also reflected in the use of light/dark metaphors.

Baumgartner is not primarily interested in the content of the folkloristic stories told in the kitchen, but rather in the difference between the monopolistic discourse and lack of response in the salon and the egalitarian give-and-take of the dialogues in the kitchen. Baumgartner is reminded of Bakhtin's opposition between "the monologue of high culture and the dialogical culture of laughter of the people" (316). The squire tries to invade the sphere of the kitchen, but fails in his attempt to send the small boys off to bed, and loses his authority to the blacksmith. "The little boys, over whom grandfatherly authority no longer held any sway when the blacksmith promised to tell fairy tales." (A 1: 78–79). For Baumgartner, the power struggle between the squire and the tale-telling blacksmith, a power struggle which the blacksmith wins, is reflected in the contrasting lighting metaphor between the dark salon and the bright and cheerful kitchen. Tying the light metaphor to the Norwegian word *opplysning*, which means enlightenment, particularly in this context the enlightenment of the people through education, Baumgartner finds a daring contradiction between the prevailing idea in the 1840s, espoused by Welhaven and others, that "the light must come from above" (318) and the actual conditions found within "An Evening," in which the "light" must find its way from the common people into the world of the squire and the higher classes.

Baumgartner's attempt to find in Asbjørnsen a radical sympathizer with the lot of the rural peasant marks an important step in the literary criticism of *Norske huldreeventyr og folkesagn* because of his critical endeavor to situate the literary work within its historical context, something to which this text has seldom been subjected. Important also is his emphasis on the reception of the story; the idea that the text could bring home its emancipatory ideas to the common people, and his realization that the stories of *Norske huldreeventyr og folkesagn* contain the dialogic discourse that Bakhtin has shown to be characteristic of the language of the novel.

Nevertheless, the narrator distances himself from the blacksmith as much as the reader distances himself from the squire, and Baumgartner concludes that "my story about Asbjørnsen's *huldreeventyr* and a possible rural peasant proletarian counterculture can unfortunately in spite of everything not have a clear happy ending" (320). Perhaps Baumgartner would have done well to remember Anders Krogvig's words in his introduction to Jørgen Moe's letters: "As we can see from 'An Evening in the Squire's

Kitchen,' Soelvold and his manner were really almost a comical phenomenon for Asbjørnsen—moral indignation was simply not his cause" (Krogvig, intro to Moe 1915, 20).[26]

But if Asbjørnsen lacked moral indignation, he did not lack a sense of irony and the ability to see the incongruities in the folk life of mid-nineteenth-century Norway. His *Norske huldreeventyr og folkesagn* is animated by a dialectic between the urban narrator and the polyphonic voices of a still nearly tribal folk population. If the text can be read as both a classic of poetic realism and an example of national romanticism *par excellence*, then there is no doubt that the text transcends the romanticism out of which it grew. And while these period labels are certainly useful for literary historians and as an aid to classification, caution is called for. In 1926 Jørgen Bukdahl, in speaking of the rift between the Danish-Norwegian ruling culture and the culture of the countryside wrote that "damage has also been done by the artificial borders of literary history. As if a people's cultural life has anything to do with romanticism and realism. What really happened in the 1840s was simply that the Dano-Norwegian literary circle discovered a hidden Norway, and that cultural struggle, which Norway is in the middle of, began in earnest: the attempt to weld together the two forms of culture" (Bukdahl 1926, 24).

What is ultimately important about *Norske huldreeventyr og folkesagn* is not its classification as a romantic or realistic text in the literary histories, labels which predetermine a reader's orientation before opening the book, however useful such terms may be for literary historians. What is important is how the text works, how it impacts the reader, what effect the stories have had, both at their initial reception in the mid-nineteenth century and later, as the Norwegian literary canon was being formed. Jane Tompkins articulates the critical point of view that will form the basis for this study of Asbjørnsen's text. Although she is writing about American novels, her words are applicable for any society in a nation building phase. She writes that

> I see them as doing a certain kind of cultural work within a specific historical situation, and value them for that reason.

> I see their plots and characters as providing society with a
> means of thinking about itself, defining certain aspects of a
> social reality which the authors and their readers shared. . . .
> It is the notion of literary texts as doing work, expressing and
> shaping the social context that produced them, that I wish
> to substitute finally for the critical perspective that sees them
> as attempts to achieve a timeless, universal ideal of truth and
> formal coherence. (Tompkins 1985, 200)

How Asbjørnsen's classic text both reflected its society and helped to shape it through its representations of nature, folklore, and language as part of an ongoing process of development of a Norwegian national narrative will be the focus of the following chapters. Perhaps by looking behind the unexamined surface reality of this text as it has stood for over 150 years, the threads of nature and geography, ethnology, folklore, and language can be woven into a new and richer picture of an old classic, a more complex *gobelin* of interrelated strands that may even cast a light on contemporary Norwegian society, just as it illuminated a segment of an earlier society for the original readers of *Norske huldreeventyr og folkesagn*.

CHAPTER 3

The Space and Place of *Norske Huldreeventyr og Folkesagn*: Appropriation of the Norwegian Countryside

> *The placing of a story in a certain setting, like the building of a house, a wall, or a road, makes that place habitable.*
> —J. Hillis Miller

A NATIONAL IDENTITY BUILT ON NATURE

Most scholars who write of Norwegian national identity stress the Norwegian's close affinity to nature, to an almost totem-like relationship of the Norwegian to his physical space.[1] Situated on the margins of Europe, with huge tracts of uninhabitable land, the creators of a Norwegian national identity had to deal early and forcefully with a difficult natural environment.[2] Groups of inhabitants which were widely divergent, and separated by this natural environment into almost tribal entities, somehow had to be inspired to feel a loyalty to the larger state; and anecumenical mountain ranges and often barely arable land had to be redefined as positive symbols rather than as the often bleak and inhospitable tracts that they actually were. The fiercely independent Norwegian *bonde* was, in some respects, a part of this natural topography as well. Particularly during the nation-building phase after 1814, the Norwegian cultural philosopher Gunnar Skirbekk notes that

> The close relationship between people and nature has been secured through a long history. One can say that of all people, especially those who have lived for a long time in a region of distinctive natural living conditions. But for Norway, there was something else in addition: a modern state which more

> or less builds its national identity on nature.... There was
> no national nobility who could personify the nation. But
> the *bonde* was there.... There was little in the way of outer
> splendor to be seen—houses and huts but no castles, but there
> were mountains and fjords, forests and the sea. Norwegian
> nature is like the Creator's own cathedral.... So nature
> became, along with the sagas and the *bonde*, the main feature
> in the national consciousness. (Skirbekk 1984, 16–17)

But how does a nation build its national identity on nature? Writing about the role of mountain photography in the constitution of a Slovenian national identity, Aleš Erjavec explains that to a large extent, the topography of a country has to be symbolically appropriated:

> In most cases the "place" where a nation is located is
> primarily a cultural community which can exist even in
> Diaspora. In the second case, the "place" is a very real
> and relatively well defined *territory*. It can, of course, be
> designated on the basis of "historical" borders, but it can
> also be based on geographical divisions such as mountains or
> rivers. In this sense it has to be protected or appropriated.
> It need not be populated, but it must be symbolically
> appropriated, otherwise it does not really belong to us.
> (Erjavec 1994, 212. Erjavec's italics)

And if the territory is not populated, this symbolic appropriation will take place mainly through the dissemination of literary and artistic texts—texts *doing work*. "Literature was conscripted into the service of nationalism because of the capacity of stories both to promote popular identification with territory and history and to instill national symbols into daily practice" (Jusdanis, 162). That *Norske huldreeventyr og folkesagn* played a role in the appropriation and the subsequent intensification of nature as a defining feature of Norwegian national identity can be demonstrated in the study of its reception and continued influence throughout the rest of the nineteenth century. "The historical essence of the work of art lies not only in its representational or expressive function but also in its influence" (Jauss 1989, 15. Trans. Bahti). Asbjørnsen was able to claim the topography of southeastern rural Norway and the mountain tracts of central Norway for the urban educated residents of the city of Christiania, establishing the countryside as a "middle ground" between city and wilderness, and he was able to do so in such a way that he also integrated the Norwegian *bonde* as a natural part of the scenery. He created a symbolic representation of space through a repository of meanings which were then utilized by subsequent writers and artists to symbolically appropriate the Norwegian natural world.[3]

TOPOGRAPHIC NORWAY: EARLY DESCRIPTIONS

A brief review of attitudes towards nature and early travel writing is necessary in order to understand the historical context into which Asbjørnsen's work was received, and the "work" that his text effected in helping to create a more or less unified Norwegian national attitude towards a nature that presented great physical challenges to such a unification.

The modern attitude towards landscape and scenery, and especially mountains, was not shared by the early inhabitants of northern Europe. A shift in perception occurred during the eighteenth century. Before that time, lively debates over the origins of mountains occurred. The problem was simply that God had created a perfect world, a perfect world of symmetry and roundness. Mountains did not fit into this mold, so where and when did they arise? Many people believed that the world at the time of creation was smooth and round. The mountains must have come later, probably as a result of the flood, and hence they were a punishment from God. Mountains were symbols of human sin, "monstrous excrescences on the original smooth face of Nature" (Nicolson 1959, 83).

This aversion to the unsymmetrical, abhorrence of mountain peaks, and a total disregard for what today is called "scenery" is evident in very early travel writing describing Norway. Who cannot empathize with the terror evident in the following passage written in 1685, describing the infamous *Vaarstigen*, a path that had to be traversed during certain times of the year over Dovrefjell:

> Then there follows a terrible and very high and steep mountain, on which one rides up the side, having on one side this terrible rock and on the other side absolutely nothing but to look down from this precipice as though out into an abyss, and this path, which is cut out along the edge of the mountain, is so narrow that a horse cannot without danger pass another, so that if one were to fall with one's horse from this narrow path, which easily could happen with carelessness, there would be no possible human rescue, since there is absolutely nothing to grasp to stop oneself, but one would fall down into the river. (Backer 1952, 34)

Appreciation of nature has no place in the harsh reality of early travel.

In his book *Norsk naturfølelse i det nittende aarhundrede* [Norwegian Feelings towards Nature in the Nineteenth Century], Theodor Caspari laments the lack of any feeling for nature in Norway in the early years of the nineteenth century and partially attributes this lack to ignorance of any areas not in close proximity to the towns. This ignorance, Caspari shows, could be related to the difficulty of travel in the Norway of the eighteenth and early nineteenth centuries. To demonstrate how rarely Norwegians traveled for pleasure in the early years of the nineteenth century, Caspari cites from Nils Hertzberg's notes about travelers in Hardanger: "During the whole long period between 1804 and 1836 he could only document twenty-three *Norwegian* travelers—three university professors and twenty students and graduate students" (Caspari 1917, 15). The italics above are Caspari's, and they underscore the reality of early travel explorations in Norway. When travelers did brave the treacherous roads and difficult conditions, they were as likely as not to be wealthy Englishmen, who early discovered the fishing rivers and opportunities for hunting in Norway. As Mary Louise Pratt notes in her highly acclaimed study of travel writing on the imperial frontier, *Imperial Eyes*, these early English accounts of travel within Europe are not far different from accounts which describe meetings with indigenous peoples in South America or Africa.

> Readers of European travel books about Europe have pointed out that many of the conventions and writing strategies I associate here with imperial expansionism characterize travel writing about Europe as well. . . . The discourses that legitimate bourgeois authority and delegitimate peasant and subsistence lifeways, for example, can be expected to do this ideological work within Europe as well as in southern Africa or Argentina. (Pratt 1992, 10)

That this was certainly the case with early English travelers to Scandinavia is clear from even a cursory exploration of that early literature, since most of these early travel accounts offer evidence that not only was travel difficult, but that dealings with the indigenous people were often difficult also, and that these encounters are described in a fashion that does most certainly delegitimate peasant lifeways.

During her travels in Denmark, Sweden, and Norway at the end of the eighteenth century, Mary Wollstonecraft was one of the first to reflect on the beauties of Norwegian nature, while abhorring the ignorance of the inhabitants. With the typical English arrogance evident in much early travel literature, she writes on her inability to speak to many of the guests at a dinner party: "As their minds were totally uncultivated I did not lose much, perhaps gained, by not being able to understand them." And again, "Nothing, indeed, can equal the stupid obstinacy of some of these half alive beings" (Wollenstonecraft [1796] 1889, 81, 137). In the summer of 1820, a certain A. Brooke found the scenery on Dovrefjeld to be "of the sublimest and most imposing nature," although a "melancholy wildness" prevailed at the summit. His first contact with the "natives," however, was less imposing: "The rapaciousness of the inhabitants was extreme, and it was only by keeping a watchful eye, that their attempts at pillaging my baggage were frustrated" (Brooke 1823, 137, 79). Writing of her trip to Norway in 1827, the Marchioness of Westminster devotes most of her description to the whirl of social activities with which she was inundated, but she too found time to comment upon the general wretchedness of the common people. "The women, among the peasants, are hideous and dirty beyond description" (Westminster 1879, 59). As the Swedish ethnologist Jonas Frykman explains, "Individuals who for one reason or another are on the fringes of our existence are classified as dirty" (Frykman and Löfgren 1979, 139). And the Norwegian peasant was certainly on the fringes of existence, not only to the British tourists, but also to the Danish educated *embets*-class of his own country.

At about the same time that Asbjørnsen was beginning his collecting trips around southern Norway, yet another Englishman, Robert Bremner, wrote a two-volume work, *Excursions in Denmark, Norway and Sweden*, which paints another unflattering picture of the Norwegian peasant:

> No change is more perceptible on entering Norway than that which takes place in the character of the people. We found our new acquaintances rude and contentious to a high degree . . . the Norwegian is naturally ingenious, and might be made much of were he more industrious . . . considering the general state of civilization, it is still a question with many, whether the Norwegians are fit for so free a form of government as that which they now enjoy? . . . The Norwegians have often been described as a highly moral people; but it did not appear to us that they have any right to this distinction. . . . Among the Swedes a quarrel is the exception, among the Norwegians it is the general rule . . . the peasants, even when not drunk, seem to be naturally rude. (Bremner 1840, 20, 50, 75, 78, 187)

But Bremner does not reserve his criticism only for the rural peasants; he found Christiania to be "the dullest capital we ever set foot in" and the ladies of the town "far inferior to those of Sweden. They are emphatically large, and dress in a way that would not be tolerated in a country-town with us" (28, 32).

Finally, perhaps the best example of what Pratt calls "urban discourse about non-urban worlds, and a lettered bourgeois discourse about non-lettered peasant worlds" (35) is to be found in an 1857 text, *A Long Vacation Ramble in Norway and Sweden*, by two anonymous authors, X and Y. These authors found "the primitive habits of the people somewhat amusing," but also lamented, "One seeks in vain in the degenerate children of these times, ground down with toil, their every thought and aspiration bounded by present need, for one spark of the old Vikings' fiery valour." But at least the natives in northern Norway were sensible enough to appreciate the honor conferred upon them by the visitors: "Never was more genuine hospitality more freely accorded; the memory of our night at the North Cape will long survive, and let us hope that the visit of the three Englishmen to Skarsvaag will be called to mind, not without pleasure, by those kind and hearty folks, and serve perhaps to beguile the tediousness of some few hours of their long and dreary winter." Upon leaving Norway for Sweden, the authors conclude that the people are warm at heart, with little notion of social rank, and that he who can accept this Norwegian notion of equality will "find in them much to interest and much to study" (X and Y 1857, 16, 54, 53–54, 146–47).

But despite the general consensus that the Norwegian native was a simple and primitive sort, desperately in need of improvement, the English travelers in the first half of the nineteenth century were united in their praise of the natural topography. While the mountains were still often viewed with a combination of dread and awe, all could agree to the sublimity of the Norwegian waterfall, and the beauty of the forests; even so, it is not uncommon in these texts to find as well an aversion to a natural landscape devoid of human monuments. Bremner writes, in true nineteenth-century romantic fashion, of the environs of Drammen: "There are so many trees of richer foliage than the pine, and so many tufts of blushing lilac, with fields of such healthful green smiling through them, and scarce a rock or barren spot in sight, that the imagination wanders to another clime. There is nothing *wild* in the prospect; it is *beautiful,* and in the highest degree; were a grey ruin or two scattered on the heights, it would have no superior in Europe" (86–87).

Although the English tourists may have been the first to write about the beauties of the Norwegian countryside, it does not necessarily follow that the native inhabitants were totally without aesthetic appreciation; but the difficult struggle for sustenance left little time or inclination for aesthetic speculations. If "appreciation of landscape is an urban aesthetic . . . depending upon an urban elite," (Tuan 1993, 135) then the lack of large cites in Norway certainly delayed the development of this aesthetic appreciation among the Norwegians themselves. When Asbjørnsen started his ramblings through the countryside near the city, collecting stories and impressions, Christiania had only about twenty thousand inhabitants, hardly a large city. In addition, it is well known that it can require the creative eye of a visitor to truly see what has been accepted and ignored by the inhabitants of a region. "The visitor's evaluation of environment is essentially aesthetic" (Tuan 1974, 64). In some respects, because he was a town boy, perhaps Asbjørnsen did experience parts of the countryside with the eyes of a visitor. He certainly saw the Norwegian landscape through the eyes of a naturalist and a sportsman, and he was the first to describe it in a way which led others to want to experience it in the same way. His descriptions of nature in the frame stories are not the idealized rhapsodies of the lyric poet. Caspari says of Asbjørnsen's respect for nature that he "always serves up nature, if one dares to put it this way, naturally" (42).

"A RATHER CLUMSY GAMBIT"

Despite the small size of Norway's capital city, sometimes even twenty thousand persons were far too many inhabitants for the often impecunious and debt-ridden young Asbjørnsen. Perhaps one of the most often quoted sentence fragments in Norwegian literature is the opening line of the 1843 story "Kværnsagn" [Legends of the Mill], the first story in the first volume of *huldreeventyr*, although not the first written—"Når verden går meg imot." [When the world goes against me]. Per Arneberg writes: "These classic words open up a world. With them an alive and kicking, modern and unconventional artist grasps his contemporary by the hand and takes him along on the first journey into a closed world, a kind of Scandinavian Tibet" (Arneberg 1958, 292). And because it was a hitherto closed world, full of folk belief and folk stories which had not before been considered worthy of print, a world that was in many ways uncharted, Asbjørnsen had a similar problem to the one which Walter Ong describes for Chaucer:

> We should think more about the problems that the need to fictionalize audiences creates for writers. Chaucer, for example, had a problem with the conjectural readers of the *Canterbury Tales*. There was no established tradition in English for many of the stories, and certainly none at all for a collection of such stories. What does Chaucer do? He sets the stories in what, from a literary-structural point of view, is styled a frame. A group of pilgrims going to Canterbury tell stories to one another: the pilgrimage frames the individual narratives. In terms of signals to his readers, we could put it another way: Chaucer simply tells his readers how they are to fictionalize themselves. He starts by telling them that there is a group of pilgrims doing what real people do, going to a real place, Canterbury. The reader is to imagine himself in their company and join the fun. (Ong 1975, 16)

Of course, this is exactly the problem that faced Asbjørnsen in *Norske huldreeventyr og folkesagn:* There was no established tradition in Norwegian for the retelling of the oral migratory legends. Asbjørnsen utilizes a technique with which he would have been familiar to tell his readers how they are to become part of what

Peter Rabinowitz would term the "authorial audience," that is, the hypothetical audience for whom the author writes (Rabinowitz 1987, 21).[4] In almost all of the *huldreeventyr*, the actual legends are recounted by created rural narrators, but before the reader can hear these stories, the frame narrator, the civilized urban voice, sets the stage by describing not only the physical location, but the folk narrator. There may be a new world to explore, but the experience must be mediated for the reader by the frame narrator, who will tell him/her not only where (s)he is going and how (s)he will get there, but also how (s)he is to interpret what (s)he experiences along the way, and what the response should be to both people and landscape.[5] An examination of several contemporaneous reviews of the first edition of *huldreeventyr* indicates how truly remarkable Asbjørnsen's landscape descriptions were seen to be at the time of their appearance, and also in subsequent literary histories. It is not an exaggeration to state that the modern Norwegian's love-affair with *friluftsliv* [outdoor life] is first articulated in a realistic literature in *Norske huldreeventyr og folkesagn*.

In the newspaper *Den Constitutionelle* for 3 August 1845, P. J. Collett acknowledges the favorable reception of Asbjørnsen's text by noting that the book is "in everyone's hands." The reviewer sees the book as one of the more interesting publishing phenomena of recent years, bringing as it does, "a greeting from our wild, fresh, always youthful nature. . . . It is as if we perceive the smell of pine needles and forest anemones as we read" (Collett 1845). Collett may have been the first but was certainly not the last to notice the appeal to the senses other than sight in Asbjørnsen's nature descriptions. In another newspaper article, Jørgen Moe writes that however good Asbjørnsen's descriptions of the life of the people may be, "they could not by a long shot be compared to his nature pictures. The latter are truly brilliant; they portray, with a few definite features and a very simple language, a physiognomy of landscape with remarkable clarity and certainty" (Moe 1845).

To the writer Andreas Munch, the stories are more than their titles imply, "It is not just 'Norwegian hulder fairy tales and folktales' but scenes of Norwegian folk life and life of nature, in which the legends lie like pearls in a worthy setting" (Munch 1848). The first reviews were not limited to Norway; a review by C. F. B. appeared in the Swedish journal *Frey*. The author finds: "No one can better paint a summer morning in the forest and let the sun's rays mirror themselves in the clear dewdrops than Mr. Asbjørnsen."[6]

If it is true that the frame story, as a narrative tool, is a "rather clumsy gambit but one that a good narrator can bring off pretty well when he has to" (Ong 1975, 16), then Asbjørnsen had several models from which to choose when he selected the device that was to include some of the best loved nature descriptions in Norwegian literature. Most scholars agree that the pivotal text to influence Asbjørnsen's story structure was Crofton Croker's *Fairy Legends and Traditions of the South of Ireland*, published in English in 1825, which Asbjørnsen knew in the Grimm translation and which he so often borrowed from the university library. Knut Liestøl makes it quite clear in his Asbjørnsen biography that Croker was the source:

> While Asbjørnsen was still living, Henrik Jæger asserted in an article about Asbjørnsen and the *huldreeventyr* that this [Croker's] was the model. Moltke Moe unreservedly agreed, and there is reason to believe that both of these men, who were so close to Asbjørnsen, had heard this from him. Croker tells many legends about Irish supernatural creatures: elves, pixies, changelings and so forth. In a long and remarkable introduction [to the German translation] William Grimm points out the relationship between these creatures and those of other countries—especially the Germanic ones. This introduction must have led Asbjørnsen to think of the Norwegian tradition. Croker does not tell the legends in the same method used by the Grimms in *Deutsche Sagen*, Thiele in *Danske Folkesagn* or Faye in *Norske sagn*. His style is lively and expressive and sometimes he places the story in the voice of a folk storyteller. Then he gives a description of the storyteller and tells how he came to tell the tale. (Liestøl 1947, 136)

Although Asbjørnsen used Croker as a model, all critics agree that *Norske huldreeventyr og folkesagn* far surpasses its predecessor both in form and content. Other influences on the style of *huldreeventyr* was the Norwegian short story writer Maurits Hansen, whom, as we know, both Asbjørnsen and Moe idolized while still students, and the Danish novelist and short story writer Steen Steensen Blicher. The beginning of Blicher's story *Hosekræmmeren* is echoed in the opening lines of Asbjørnsen's *Kvernsagn*. It is unfortunate that Asbjørnsen's first effort at a novella is lost, because his debt to Hansen and Blicher was clearly evident in the early work. After reading this lost story, Jørgen Moe gave his friend his detailed critique in a letter of July 1834. Moe found that the story was too similar in construction to Blicher's *Himmelbjerget*, but along with other criticisms he also found that "with more practice and a more thorough study of character, you most certainly can become a little Maurits." Although Hansen was important, it was Blicher who most influenced Asbjørnsen's style. Especially important to Asbjørnsen would have been Blicher's example of the departure from omniscient narration and early use of the unreliable narrator (Ingwersen 1996, 68). Liestøl explains that "Asbjørnsen must in several respects have felt an affinity with Blicher. They both found consolation in nature when times were difficult; they were both ardent hikers and hunters" (Liestøl 1947, 138). It is telling that what Moe found best in Asbjørnsen's early effort was his "fluid talent at painting landscape" (Moe 1915, 130, 129). It is interesting that Moe uses the verb "paint" in his assessment because it is this ability to infuse the landscape descriptions with color and form that makes Asbjørnsen's *huldreeventyr* so adept at evoking a sense of place.

Theodor Caspari wrote in 1917: "One never tires of his nature descriptions. Hamsun, Thomas Krag, Jacob Bull can in the long run seem monotonous, Asbjørnsen never" (Caspari 1917, 42). To a very large extent that statement is as true today as it was nearly a century ago when Caspari was writing, and certainly this narrative ability to engage the reader diachronically helps to explain the text's attraction. An example from a literary history of 1924 illustrates this ability:

When he in "A Night in Nordmarken" describes his
wandering along Skjærsjøen, there is an atmosphere of the
forest and summer, despite the distance in time and changing
conditions, it is the Nordmarken as it exists in every Olso
boy's mind. And how superb the expression of the night
feeling in "Legends of the Mill," the humming of the mill,
the rushing of the river, and the unsettled lighting through
which characters pop up and disappear. . . . And absolutely
first rate is the atmosphere of nature in "A Summer Night
in the Krok Forest"—the description of the warm day up
by Lyse in Sørkedal; of the evening at the lonely deserted
cabin, of the night wandering through the forest and the fear
which gripped him; and finally the splendid painting of the
loggers by the bonfire. Every image succeeds here, so that
anyone who ever walks the same way to the Krok forest has
Asbjørnsen's story in mind—the atmosphere of the story
blends with the rustling of the forest and the roar of the river.
(Elster d.y. 1924, 261–62)

In the introduction to his 1949 edition of *Norske huldreeventyr og folkesagn*, Knut Liestøl discusses how some localities become so identified with literary texts that one is unable to experience them without thinking of the fictional overlay; he points to the Wessex of Thomas Hardy, Walter Scott's Border Country, or the Iceland of the Sagas. "And who can come to Sel in Gudbrandsdalen and see the Jørund farmyard without having a multitude of impressions well up from Sigrid Undset's *Kristin Lavransdatter.*" *Norske huldreeventyr og folkesagn* is this kind of text. Liestøl quotes Sigrid Undset: "If you only knew how we Oslo kids, who tramped in all directions through Nordmarka and the Krog forest, loved Asbjørnsen's stories and how we felt that these paths were still *his*" (Liestøl, intro to A 1: v, vii. Undset's italics). In his biography of Asbjørnsen, Liestøl remembers his first encounter with an Asbjørnsen story:

Huldreeventyr seems to have something for everyone: the
folklorist, the hunter, the sports-fisherman, the hiker in

Nordmarka or Rondane, etc. The book has a remarkable power over the mind whether one is young or old. When I read "A Night in Nordmarken" for the first time in elementary school, I thought it was an extremely splendid piece; to find time to appreciate it properly, I set myself the task of writing out the beginning letter by letter in the next penmanship class. And when I was going to Ringerike for the first time, it was a matter of course that I would follow Asbjørnsen's trail in "A Summer Night in the Krog forest." . . . In descriptions of walking trips, one sometimes reads that here and there one is following one of Asbjørnsen's trails. With its many nature pictures and its richness of folk characterization, *huldreeventyr* has been a source of inspiration for a number of our foremost artists, and their pictures have done their part to make the book so popular. (Liestøl 1947, 142–43)

CREATING "PLACE" FROM "SPACE"

How does one account for the "remarkable power" this text has had to create "place" from "space"? It is possible to isolate three distinct elements in Asbjørnsen's style which help to explain the power of attraction of *Norske huldreeventyr og folkesagn*. First, the manner in which the reader is asked to fictionalize himself; second, the realistic physical descriptions which localize the stories, a result of Asbjørnsen's personal interests and abilities; and finally the use of actual place names in both the frame narrative and informant stories.

What sets the frame narration of the text apart from the short story tradition of Maurits Hansen and Steen Blicher is the manner in which Asbjørnsen engages the reader through the use of a narrative technique which does not become dated, because each new reader is asked to fictionalize him/herself as a more or less boon companion of the frame narrator. An examination of descriptions from the text will illustrate this technique of engaging the reader in the story, this appropriation of the country landscape for the reader.

In the early story "Legends of the Mill," the frame narrator, after a short fishing trip which includes listening to tales told by the workers at a mill, is on his way back to Christiania in the early evening, accompanied by a young boy who is afraid of the dark:

> We followed the path under the Grefsen ridge down along the hills towards Grefsen. White mists swirled over the river basin and the marshes down in the valley. Akershus rose up over the smoky haze of town, and its towers were mirrored in the fjord, into which Nesodden threw itself out as a huge sharp shadow. The sky wasn't completely clear, and there was some motion in the clouds and in the air; the moonlight mingled with the dawn of the summer night and lessened the contours in the foreground of the landscape that was spread before our feet. But over the fjord the moonlight lay clear and shining, while the Asker and Bærum hills, visible dimly in bluish-black shadows, rose above each other high up in the air and formed a distant frame for the scene. (A 1: 29–30)[7]

"Asbjørnsen takes his reader by the hand," says Arneberg, but he does not delve deeper into *how* Asbjørnsen is able to draw the reader *into* the narrative. The task is accomplished through the manner in which Asbjørnsen fictionalizes his reading audience. "We followed the path under the Grefsen ridge down along the hills towards Grefsen." The reader is pulled into an intimacy with the narrator because it is assumed that the reader *knows* that there *is* such a path. "*Akershus* rose up over the smoky haze of town, and its towers were mirrored in the fjord, into which *Nesodden* threw itself out as a huge sharp shadow" (italics mine). There is no need to tell the reader what Akershus and Nesodden are, the reader *knows*. There is a similarity to the narrative technique which Hemingway utilizes by his use of the definite article or the demonstrative pronoun *that*, as Walter Ong explains in his discussion of the opening sentences of *A Farewell to Arms*:

"The late summer of that year," the reader begins. What year? The reader gathers that there is no need to say. "Across the river." What river? The reader apparently is supposed to know. "And the plain." What plain? "*The* plain"—remember? "To the mountains." What mountains? Do I have to tell you? Of course not. *The* mountains—*those* mountains we know. We have somehow been there together. Who? You, my reader, and I. (Ong 1975, 13. Ong's italics)

Asbjørnsen often uses the definite article to invoke this same type of familiarity in the frame narratives of *Norske huldreeventyr og folkesagn*. The reader is expected to know not only familiar landmarks, but also various cultural information shared by the authorial audience. In the first paragraph of "A Grouse Hunt in Holleia," we read, "On one of the first days of May—this was long before the hunting law was hatched—we went up the hillside from Tyristranden to watch the mating dance of the wood grouse the next morning at Skjærsjøhaugen, which had the reputation of being the best place in the area to see this" (A 2: 99).[8] Asbjørnsen finds it necessary to explain that the early May hunt was undertaken before the enactment of the hunting law of 1845, which limited hunting of wood grouse between 1 April and 15 August. The authorial audience would have been aware of this law, and the narrator feels the need to clarify that he is not poaching. Again and again in the frame narrative of *Norske huldreeventyr og folkesagn*, the reader is treated as a familiar and trusted companion; for this reason the reader soon trusts the narrator as a reliable narrator, and one who is "controlling, interpreting and judging the other discourses" (Lodge 1990, 47), characteristic of the classic realist text. This will become particularly important when the narrator describes his informant, that unknown creature, almost a part of the natural landscape, the Norwegian *bonde*, to whom we shall return in a later chapter.

This ability to engage the reader in the physical topography enabled Asbjørnsen's work to serve as a guide for the appropriation of the Norwegian natural world for his contemporary readers, the urban elite whose task it was to build a Norwegian national identity.[9] As Olaf Bull leads his little daughter into the fantasy world of imagination by following the path on his *Gobelin* pillow, so too does Asbjørnsen lead the reader into his created picture of Norwegian nature, articulating a collective narrative, essentially explaining to the reader of his time, and readers since, how that reader is to relate to the natural environment, framing a national narrative grounded in the belief of a pristine and idyllic natural world, a natural world of refuge from day-to-day struggles, but also a natural world to be used and enjoyed.

> So, in the 1830s, little by little, quietly and unobtrusively, but also with unerring certainty, the young tutor started conquering the natural scenery of Østlandet. . . . One township after another: Eidsvold, Ullensaker, Hurdalen, Hadeland, Toten, Biri, Hallingdal, Valdres,—all the way up to the summer dairy cabins. . . . If one wants a truly vivid impression of how remarkably far the Norwegian feeling for nature changed in the thirteen short years from 1835, one has only to read "A Sunday Evening at the Mountain Dairy" and "A Reindeer Hunt in the Rondane Mountains." (Caspari 1917, 40, 41)

Of more than semantic interest is Caspari's use of the expression "to conquer." Some scholars who interest themselves in the phenomenon see a similarity between the colonization of primitive third world societies and the situation in Norway, which, after all, was a virtual colony of Denmark for four hundred years, and was jointly ruled with Sweden at the time of Asbjørnsen's work.[10] How did this young tutor "conquer the natural scenery," open up a "kind of Scandinavian Tibet" for his countrymen, and help to symbolically appropriate Norwegian nature as an element for a truly *Norwegian* national identity?

Asbjørnsen had always been intensely interested in the natural world, he loved to fish and hunt, sometimes to the detriment of other obligations. An irritated Jørgen Moe writes his friend in December of 1843,

> During the fall I have written to you three times, partly about things that interested me, partly about corrections to the fairy tales and the summer trip. The first subject I will drop so as not to bother you too much, but for the last two, which are, after all, joint concerns, I must once again request a few words. I approached Dahl [A and M's publisher] about the publication on the presumption that the delay came from there, but received the answer that they were waiting for the manuscript, and this presumably because *you* were so often out hunting and so forth. I would think that you could find the time to send my manuscript down to the printers, for God's sake. (Moe 1915, 246. Moe's italics)[11]

But because of Asbjørnsen's keen and unwavering interest in the natural world, in the animals and plants that inhabited the Norwegian fields and forests, the descriptions of that world in *Norske huldreeventyr og folkesagn* gave his contemporary readers the first realistic portrayal of how eastern Norway and the mountains actually appeared. He saw the Norwegian landscape that he described through eyes unclouded by the romanticism that was so prevalent in the lyric poetry of his time:

> Towards the west and north the unending mountain plateau spread out before our feet, gray-green, brownish, sorrow-awakening distances. . . . Through this partially transparent air the sun poured its ocean of light over the West mountains' glaciers of snow and ice. Wine-colored clouds with gilded edges drifted over them, and the reddish glittering gold radiance the mountains rested in reflected high up into the air and flashed through the whole northwestern sky. (A 2: 56–57)[12]

Caspari declares that from these few lines, "Asbjørnsen has already painted the first Norwegian mountain picture—in words" (47). As is evident in this example, it is clear that Asbjørnsen paints a visual image with words; not for nothing was he a good friend of many of the most famous contemporaneous landscape artists! And, of course, this influence traveled both ways: When Adolph Tidemand painted "Signekjærring" in 1848, it was because he was familiar with this personage through Asbjørnsen's story.[13]

Because of his interest in natural science, Asbjørnsen's descriptions often include much more specific information than simply the lay of the land; he knew the species of trees and flowers, he knew the birds by their song. In the story "The Hulder Clan," the narrator, in this case a young tutor, describes the surroundings as he, his young charges, and the lovely young lady in whom he is interested begin their walk from the farm Bjerke back to their home on a fine summer morning:

> We wandered up through the leafy groves of Bjerke's orchard, where the redstart thrushes and chaffinches were celebrating the day at the top of the alders with quick, harmonious warbling; flycatchers were fluttering around between the branches adding their say, while the cheerful song of the garden warbler, shyly hidden in the leaves, streamed out from the thick, dark crown of the trees. The morning was so still and warm; the leaves of the birch trees hardly moved, and when we came up from the path through the meadows, we saw in a sunbeam pearls of dew glistening on the clover and on the folded leaves of the blades of grass. The swallows swooped low for the dragonflies; the swallow thrush sat rocking on a thistle and chirped in the field. We heard the song of larks from the blue sky, which was encircled on all sides by light summer clouds, which shielded us against the hot sun. (A 1: 83)[14]

Later in the same story, after a rain shower during which the tutor and the girl take shelter in a tumbled down look-out cabin, the description continues: "The rich foliage of mosses and lichen that covered the damp log walls sparkled in the brilliant sunlight, refreshed by the rain. Outside, in the forest, there was a delight in all the plants and birds. Pyrols and twinflowers sent out streams of fragrance, and the spruce trees showered us with their perfume" (92).[15] While some critics have found this detailed descriptive quality to be somewhat superfluous, it is precisely this wealth of detail, encompassing visual, aural, and olfactory elements, which creates for the reader a totality of experience, and which creates the necessary "repository of meanings," to use Tuan's phrase, which leads to space becoming place. In his notes to this story, Knut Liestøl gives a two page, small-print explanation of where the story "really" took place. It is possible, he says, to trace the route taken by the description given. This, of course, would be of no importance whatsoever if the work had not become, in a sense, a collective narrative of a people, a type of written road map of "nature as culture" to be re-possessed by subsequent generations. One indication of how well Asbjørnsen succeeded in helping to build a collective national consciousness based on nature, and that this success was appreciated as such even during his lifetime, is evidenced, in part, by his selection in 1870 as the only honorary life-time member of the Norwegian Tourist Association in recognition of his "superior services rendered to the development of tourist life in this country" (Norske Turistforening Årbok 1870, 119).

In addition to the fictionalization of the reader as a boon companion to the frame narrator, and the realistic physical descriptions which help create place from space, *Norske huldreeventyr og folkesagn* contains a multitude of actual place names—farms, rivers, mountains, valleys, and a variety of given names—which contribute to an overriding sense of the place in the text. It is not only the frame narrator who utilizes the specifics of who and where; the created informants who tell their stories pepper their accounts with names of localities and add a local color that is totally missing from the "once upon a time" generic world of the fairy-tale. In "Legends of the Mill," for example, the narrator, with a fishing pole in his hand, walks "up through the meadows on the east side of the Aker river past Torshaug and Sandaker, through Lillohagen to the outlet by Maridal Lake" (A 1: 19).[16] When he gets to Brekkesagen, the sun is sinking; he talks to an old worker by the mill who came from Gudbrandsdalen thirty years before. And so it continues in the stories and in the frames: Gamlebyen, Brekke, Beierbroen, Grefsenåsen, Grefsen, Akershus, Nesodden, and Asker and Bærumsåsene. In "Matthias the Hunter's Stories," the action is set a bit further afield. The narrator arrives one lovely Saturday in November 1836 at his friend's house in Nittedalen. Here he is entertained so royally that he nearly forgets his hunting plans for the next day: "The sun was already at the rim of the ridge, and if I wanted to get there while people were still up, it was out of the question to walk the long way past Dals church up to the Middle Woods and from there go through most of Gjerdrum on the poor trail over the Myr [swampy] clearing, which by now would be doubly nasty and uneven after the November cold we had had." So he finds himself a local fellow at Nybråten to guide him on the shortcut across the hills, past the old *seter* at Askvangen, where old Matthias begins to tell stories about the *hulder* that he encountered on the big road between Bjerke and Mo, and continues with other stories until, "We came out on the Kulsrud ridge, from where one can see out over the big plain of Upper Romerike . . . right below me were Heni and Gjerdrum churches" (A 1: 40, 50).[17] Of course Asbjørnsen did not create the place names, but by their use in the frames and legends he created a rich topography of symbolically appropriated "place" throughout the *huldreeventyr*: farms, rivers, hills, mountains, whole districts, all charted as though on a map, charted as a collective narrative for the imagined community of Norway.

"HAVE YOU EVER SEEN THE RIDGE OF GJENDIN?"

If *Norske huldreeventyr og folkesagn* in its time opened up a "closed world, a kind of Scandinavian Tibet," by its descriptions of the Norwegian natural world and its inhabitants, it fell upon others to build upon that description, to further people the landscape that had been symbolically claimed. The work accomplished by *huldreeventyr* in this respect served as an inspiration to myriad other Norwegian writers and artists. "His nature descriptions and descriptions of the life of the people have meant much to later writers. When the students greeted him on the occasion of the twenty-fifth anniversary of the first edition of *huldreeventyr*, Bjørnson thanked him in these words: 'God knows I would not have amounted to much if you had not lived.'" (Beyer and Beyer, 1978, 162).[18]

Other contemporaries found Asbjørnsen's style infectious. Camilla Collett was thought by some to be the author of Asbjørnsen's "Bird Song and Hulder Clan" when it appeared in *Den Constitutionelle* in March of 1843. Only two months later Collett's work, "Badeliv og Fjeldliv" appeared. Ellisiv Steen notes:

> Without in any sense being an imitation, this piece is completely in Asbjørnsen's spirit and style, and the thought is irresistible that Camilla, after having been suspected of writing one of Asbjørnsen's works, wanted to show what she could do in his special genre. Nothing was more foreign, not to say impossible, for Mrs. Collett's inflexible nature than literary imitation; that she could write in Asbjørnsen's manner was because this manner in reality was natural to her as well. (Steen 1947, 187)

It is evident that Asbjørnsen's work served not only as a catalyst for other artists of his time, but also was a response to an ongoing formulation of Norwegian nature as culture. Of course Camilla Collett later worked with Asbjørnsen in writing portions of several frame stories for the *huldreeventyr*.

Probably the most well known and remarkable example of an appropriation of Asbjørnsen's themes for a later literary work, and one which because of its wide-reaching cultural influence must be considered in depth, is Henrik Ibsen's use of the legendary character Peer Gynt; this is not to prove influence, since no literary work is created without influence, but as an illustration of the process by which national narratives are constructed.

> In the triangle of author, work, and public, the last is no passive part, no chain of mere reactions, but rather itself an energy formative of history. The historical life of a literary work is unthinkable without the active participation of its addressees. For it is only through the process of its mediation that the work enters into the changing horizon-of-experience of a continuity in which the perpetual inversion occurs from simple reception to critical understanding, from passive to active reception, from recognized aesthetic norms to a new production that surpasses them. (Jauss 1982, 19. Trans. Bahti)

And one of the "addressees" of *Norske huldreeventyr og folkesagn* was Henrik Ibsen and a "new work that surpasses" was *Peer Gynt*.[19]

As Ibsen scholars are aware, Ibsen was notorious for denying that he had ever been literarily influenced by anyone, but in a letter to his publisher on 8 August 1867, he writes:

> If it is of interest to you, Peer Gynt was an actual person who lived in Gudbrandsdal, either at the end of the last century or the beginning of this one. His name is still well known amongst the common people up there, but not much more is known about his exploits than what is found in Asbjørnsen's *Norske huldreeventyr* (in the piece "Mountain Images"). So there wasn't much for me to build the poem from, but then again that has also left me greater freedom. (Ibsen 1904, 151–52)

Many people are vaguely aware that Ibsen borrowed the name and several motifs for his famous play from Asbjørnsen's retelling of a legend that had been orally transmitted for years, but a close reading and comparison of Asbjørnsen's two stories, "A Reindeer Hunt in the Rondane Mountains" and "A Sunday Evening at the Mountain Dairy," which were published together as "Mountain Images" with Ibsen's play *Peer Gynt*, will reveal that virtually the whole two first acts of *Peer Gynt*, despite Ibsen's efforts to minimize his reliance on the source material, elaborate motifs from Asbjørnsen's stories, and that Ibsen set the first acts of his play in the landscape made symbolically habitable by Asbjørnsen's figuratively groundbreaking work.[20]

In the story "A Reindeer Hunt in the Rondane Mountains," the folk narrator Per Fugleskjelle tells a series of stories about the legendary Per Gynt, a hunter in Kvam in the old days. In the first of these vignettes Per encounters a strange creature indeed:

> When he came up to Høvringen, where he was going to stay in a cabin overnight, it was so dark that he couldn't see his hand in front of his face, and the dogs started to really bark, so it was actually spooky. Suddenly he came close up against something, and when he touched it, it was cold and slimy and large, and he didn't think he had gone off the road either, so he couldn't figure out what it could be, but it was eerie.
>
> "Who is it?" said Per, because he felt it moving.
>
> "Oh, it's that Bøyg," was the answer. Per wasn't any the wiser for that, but he walked alongside of it for a ways, since it had to end some place, he thought. Suddenly he was right close up against something again, and when he touched it, it was big and cold and slimy.
>
> "Who is it?" said Per Gynt. "Oh, it is the Bøyg," was the answer again.
>
> "Well, whether you are straight or bowed, you'd better let me through," said Per, because he understood that he was going around in a circle, and that the Bøyg had encircled the cabin. With that, it shifted a little, so Per got through to the cabin. When he got inside, it wasn't any lighter than outside, and he fumbled around the walls and was going to set down his gun and take off his knapsack; but suddenly as he was feeling his way forward, he again felt that big cold slimy thing.
>
> "Who is it then?" yelled Per.
>
> "Oh, it is the big Bøyg," was the answer, and wherever he touched and wherever he tried to walk, he felt the ring of the Bøyg around him. This isn't a good place to be, thought Per, since this Bøyg is both inside and out, but I should be able to

let this lout have it. So he took his gun and went out again and fumbled around until he found its skull.

"So who are you then?" said Per.

"Oh, I am the big Bøyg Etnedal," said the big troll.

Then Per Gynt quickly shot three times right into its head. (A 2: 66–67)[21]

It is enlightening to compare Asbjørnsen's story of the Bøyg with the same character as portrayed in Ibsen's famous play:

(pitch dark)
(Peer Gynt is heard slashing around himself with a large stick.)
PEER GYNT: Answer me! Who are you?
THE VOICE: Myself!
PEER GYNT: Get out of the way!
THE VOICE: Go around, Peer! The moor is wide enough.
PEER GYNT: (Tries to get through at another place but can't.) Who are *you*?
THE VOICE: Myself. Can you say the same?
PEER GYNT: I can say what I want, and my sword can hit! Watch out! Ha! Now it is falling crushed! King Saul slew a hundred; Peer Gynt slew a thousand! (slashes away.) Who *are* you?
THE VOICE: Myself.
PEER GYNT: You can forget that dumb answer; it doesn't clear up anything. *What* are you?
THE VOICE: The big Bøyg.
PEER GYNT: Well then! Before the puzzle was black, now it seems gray. Out of the way, Bøyg!
THE VOICE: Go around, Peer!
PEER GYNT: Through! (thrusts and slashes.) He fell! (moves forward but is stopped.) Ho! Are there more?
THE VOICE: The Bøyg, Peer Gynt! Just one. The Bøyg is unharmed and the Bøyd is injured. The Bøyg is dead and the Bøyg is alive.

PEER GYNT: (throws the stick away.) This protection is hexed; but I have fists!
(punches through.)
THE VOICE: Yes, rely on your fists and your body, Peer Gynt and you will reach the top.
PEER GYNT: (comes back.) Forward and back, it's the same distance; out and in, it is just as tight! *There* he is! And *there*! And around the bend! As soon as I'm outside, I'm back in the ring again. Identify yourself! Let me see you! What are you anyway?
THE VOICE: The Bøyg.
PEER GYNT: (fumbles around.) Not dead. Not alive. Slimy, foggy. No shape either! It is like bumping into a pile of growling half-awake bears! (screams.) Fight back!
THE VOICE: The Bøyg is not crazy.
PEER GYNT: Fight!
THE VOICE: The Bøyg will not fight.
PEER GYNT: Fight! You shall fight!
THE VOICE: The big Bøyg wins without fighting.
(Ibsen [1867] 1991, 302)[22]

But, of course, the *Bøyg* does not win, because, as he tells us, Peer Gynt has women on his side. This comparison of Ibsen's rendition of Peer's conflict with the *Bøyg* with the original story as recounted in Asbjørnsen's version shows how remarkably similar the two versions are, despite Ibsen's poetic re-writing. The conflict starts in the dark, on the road, and the *Bøyg* is as equally slimy, nasty, and impenetrable in Asbjørnsen's source material as he is in Ibsen's famous scene. The dialogue between Peer and the *Bøyg* contains the same snappy retorts in both versions.[23] And in both versions the name *Bøyg* does not enlighten Peer in the least; the oft repeated "Who are you?" is retained from Asbjørnsen's version, and the setting is unmistakably the wild and isolated tracts of the high mountain heaths. The regional landscape of *huldreeventyr* is appropriated by Ibsen into the very character of the dreaming anti-hero Peer, and another layer is added to the national memory and the national narrative.

The Bøyg episode is not the only scene that Ibsen borrowed from Asbjørnsen for his play about the mercurial Peer Gynt. Earlier in "A Reindeer Hunt," the hunting guide Tor tells about the escapades of a certain Gudbrand Glesne, known to have been an excellent hunter:

> One fall he had come across a big buck. He shot at it and couldn't imagine other than that it was stone dead, the way it fell. So he sat down across its back, the way one often does, and was going to loosen his knife to cut the neck bone from the skull. But as soon as he sat down, it sprang up, laid back its antlers, and pressed him back between them, so that he was sitting as if in an armchair, and then away they went, because the shot had just grazed the animal in the head so that it was knocked unconscious. Nobody else ever had a ride like the one that Gudbrand got. Away they went, in weather and wind, over the worst glaciers and terrible rock-strewn slopes. Then he started up the cliff of Gjendin, and Gudbrand started praying to the Lord, because he thought that he never would see the sun or moon again. But at last the reindeer took to the water and swam all the way across with the hunter on its back. In the meantime, Gudbrand had gotten the knife loose, and at the same time the buck set foot on land, he stabbed it in the neck, and it fell dead, and Gudbrand Glesne wouldn't have taken that trip again for all the riches in the world. (A 2: 49–50)[24]

Ibsen's masterful depiction of this wild reindeer ride begins in the very same fashion, and Ibsen even uses the same Norwegian word *skrevs* as Asbjørnsen did to describe how the hunter straddles the reindeer; the hunter is pushed backwards by the horns, and a wild ride begins. In Ibsen's poem, Peer Gynt is telling the story to his mother and he speaks in a torrent of descriptive language. The ridge of Gjendin he describes like this: "Have you ever seen the Gjendin ridge? It is three miles long, sharp as a scythe along the top. Over the edge are glaciers, rock-slides and the mountain side, gray herbs clinging down below. From both sides you can see the dark heavy water more than 2,600 feet below" (Ibsen, 287). In Ibsen's version, the reindeer escapes with his life, since Peer is lying about the entire adventure. Shortly after Peer's story, his mother realizes that he is telling a tall tale and exclaims, "That happened to Gudbrand Glesne, not you—!" (288). In Asbjørnsen's story, several other tales are told of the legendary Peer Gynt, and finally one of the hunters says, "That Peer Gynt was one of a kind. . . . He was a story-teller and a teller of tall tales that you would have enjoyed hearing; he always made himself a character in all the stories that people said had happened in the old days" (A 2: 72).[25] William Archer wonders if this sentence suggested the fantasizing character of the Peer Gynt of the play to Ibsen. At any rate, does it not seem appropriate that Ibsen placed this terrific story of the reindeer ride, appropriated from an oral legend, *back* into a format in which the legend is retold by a gifted oral storyteller, Peer Gynt, to another incredulous audience, his mother?

Peer Gynt has been called the most complex and multifaceted drama in Norwegian literature, and its hero is hailed as both the prototypical Norwegian and Everyman. Certainly this would have been a far different work, probably never written at all, if not for the themes and motifs that Ibsen found in *Norske huldreeventyr og folkesagn*. Ibsen continues to work in the critical spirit of Asbjørnsen as he emphasizes the mendacity of Peer Gynt and creates a semi-official national hero whose very being suggests the utter futility of self-identity, and hence, by implication, of a national self-identity. The irony, of course, is that while Ibsen shows in *Peer Gynt* the futility of the chauvinistic notion of nation, *Peer Gynt* has become the national literary work *par excellence,* and the reindeer ride a kind of nationalistic "It was the Night before Christmas and all through the house."[26] In some respects, does it not seem that the continuing Norwegian search for *norskhet,* or for what the Norwegian considers uniquely Norwegian, bears a parallel to Peer's search for the uniquely Gyntian in his own personality? Does not the introspective focus suggest a national narrative that has shaped such a focus? "Literature was endowed with the capacity to mirror both the individual and the general, binding in this way private moments with public truths" (Jusdanis, 164). And what of a nation whose public truth as reflected in perhaps its greatest national literary work is in its very essence antithetical to nation building? We should not be surprised that the continuing attempt at definition of a Norwegian national identity is fraught with paradox.

As a final commentary on how *Norske huldreeventyr og folkesagn* did its cultural work, consider that between the years of 1814 and 1848, only one book was published in five editions in Norway: *Flora eller Blomstersproget* [Flora, or the Language of Flowers.][27] This suggests that the interest in the natural world was certainly already widespread in the Norway of the early nineteenth century, and that Asbjørnsen, in the remarkable *huldreeventyr*, claimed this natural world both literally and symbolically so that it could become part of the national collective narrative. Should one require, for whatever reason, to consult the entry for *Bjørnsjøen* [Bear Lake] in Norway's largest and most prestigious encyclopedia, *Den Store Norske Leksikon*, one would read:

> Bear Lake, Oslo, one of the most lovely lakes in Nordmarka, 16 km. north of Oslo center, 334 meters above sea level, 1.2 square kilometers in size, wooded shores; in the north, Kikut, one of Nordmarka's tallest hills at 611 meters above sea level. The outlet at the south end is by the Bjørnholt dam building. At the northeast end of the lake lie the farm Bonna and the ski lodge Kikutstua. Bear Lake is the scene of Asbjørnsen's "A Night in Nordmarken." (Den Store Norske Leksikon 1978, 175)

It is clear that Bear Lake, like the Gjendin ridge where Peer Gynt rode the reindeer, has become, like so many other physical sites in Asbjørnsen's stories, more than just a lake: it has assimilated Tuan's "repository of meanings" and has become a concrete representation of a collective narrative possessed by a people through the shared experience of a national literature. It is a long journey from the irrational terror of the natural world felt by medieval man to the modern Norwegian's relationship with nature. Part of that long journey surely winds along the trails and paths of the forests and hills of eastern Norway, along the rushing rivers and rambling streams, and over the high mountain plateaus that Asbjørnsen immortalized in *Norske huldreeventyr og folkesagn*.

CHAPTER 4

Oral Narrative in Its Performance Context:
The Created Informants and Contexts of
Norske huldreeventyr og folkesagn

> *Stories live in native life and not on paper, and when a scholar jots them down without being able to evoke the atmosphere in which they flourish, he has given us but a mutilated bit of reality.*
>
> —B. Malinowski

THE CREATION OF THE FOLK NARRATOR IN CONTEXT

There is no natural existence for folklore beyond the performance" (Honko 1989b, 330). Contemporary folklorists realize that in collecting any oral narrative, as well as objects of material culture, it is essential to include as much complete information as possible not only about the informant him/herself, but also about the entire performance event. Who is the audience? What are the circumstances in which the item of folklore is related or used? What about the physical surroundings, the time of year, the type of language? Is anyone excluded from the audience for a particular performance? "How does the lore function in the lives of the people who possess it? What needs does it meet in their lives?" (Wilson 1986, 231–32). These and others are all questions with which modern collectors of folklore concern themselves.[1] But many collectors of the nineteenth century were not as often interested in other considerations than transcribing the stories they were told as carefully and scrupulously as possible before the living memory of the particular item "died out," a recurring fear among those collectors of that century who saw the tales and stories as a treasure-trove from a magnificent past, or as remnants from an ancient mythology. The "lore" was for them the important thing, because it contained the supposed traces of the beliefs and customs of the "ur" folk, and the tradition bearers were merely the vessels through which the lives and beliefs of the glorious ancient ancestors could somehow be recovered.

Often the name of the informant may be included in these older collections, sometimes the place and date, but in many national collections, the archives are full of thousands of stories, tales, riddles, and other texts that are in many cases virtually useless for study simply because not enough is known about the contexts in which the texts were recorded or how the items were used. When Moe and Asbjørnsen collected their tales and stories, they often made reference to where the item was collected and also to the informant. Ørnulf Hodne has made a full length study of Jørgen Moe's informants in *Jørgen Moe og folkeeventyrene: en studie i nasjonalromantisk folkloristikk* [Jørgen Moe and the Fairy Tales: A Study in National Romantic Folkloristics]. Although Jørgen Moe may have tried to be scientific in his collection methods, Hodne found that he was more likely to note the place than the date, that he never noted where his informant had heard the story and that he usually transcribed the dialects into Danish as he wrote the stories down. Despite many documents that are barely legible, Hodne reached several interesting conclusions from his study of the archival documents. For example, male informants were more likely to tell humorous stories, and females more likely to tell gruesome ones. Hodne explains that Moe selected tales for inclusion in *Norske folkeeventyr* based on how *særnorske* [distinctively Norwegian] they were. Traits that Moe considered *særnorske* included a humor that is often grotesque; the understated Askeladden-type hero who, like his ancestor in the sagas, is quiet and bides his time, and usually ends up succeeding, unlike his German counterpart, *der Dümling*; a *bygdemiljø* [country local color]; and elements from Norwegian nature. Also of great importance to Moe were ethical considerations. Befitting the future bishop, Moe looked for tales that stressed a religious/ethical worldview, in which faithful, unselfish and compassionate behavior is ultimately rewarded. Hodne shows that one of

Moe's favorite informants was Lars Svendserud, the son of a *husmann* [tenant farmer] in Ringerike, precisely because Svendserud's stories reflected the ethical and religious character that Moe felt should be encouraged. While no similar full-length study has yet been made of Asbjørnsen's informants, there is still a considerable amount of information available on his methods of collection, and it is known that he considered the authenticity of his transcriptions to be of paramount importance. In 1853 he wrote to the English philologist Benjamin Thorpe about the *huldreeventyr*:

> I have heard and recorded most of the legends from the people themselves; under no circumstances have I allowed myself to make any changes, improvements, or embellishments of the material or content. On the other hand, when I have had a poor or mediocre informant, I have considered myself justified in altering the language and the way it is presented to reflect how a *good* storyteller would have told it; now and then I guess the language and presentation have also gotten a color of the personality in whose mouth I have placed the legend. (cited in Liestøl 1947, 111)

When Moe and Asbjørnsen published *Norske folkeventyr* the original informants were not much of a consideration. Despite the masterful way in which they were able to give the folk tales a broad Norwegian cast, through language and characterization, most of the stories in the joint collection are fairy tales, derived from oral wonder tales, with the familiar *"Det var en gang"* [Once upon a time] opening and with all the functions of Propp, securely intact, with no autonomous identity remaining of the actual storytellers from whom Moe and Asbjørnsen heard the tales. The method of presentation of the traditional material in Asbjørnsen's independent work is vastly different, with elaborately constructed contexts for the transmission of the legends, which reflects his personal worldview of the folklore he was collecting and preserving, and which affirms this collection as a true creative literary text and not simply as a compilation of legends, such as Faye's earlier work. The text is a literary one, with folklore as its subject matter, and in many ways it exhibits a use of language which Bakhtin has identified as the language of the novel.[2]

Asbjørnsen was part of the movement during his time to enlighten the common people and improve their situation. And despite the enjoyment he assuredly felt in collecting and telling the stories of the people, in their own voices, he also deplored some of the folk beliefs which he knew were actually injurious or, at the least, ineffective. As late as 1874, he writes in a newspaper article, "The superstitious common people, from the cradle to the grave, try to acquire a greater power and increase their own welfare or to hurt and hinder someone else's through the utilization of an almost unbelievable number of precautions, remedies, and occult tricks which are tied in every conceivable way to a person's entire family life, his possessions, and activities" (Asbjørnsen 1874). For Asbjørnsen, as for the other educated men of his time, the folk beliefs which ruled the lives of the common people had to be exposed and debunked in order for everyone to assume his position as a full citizen in an enlightened society. It was Asbjørnsen's intention to write an overview of the folk beliefs: their origins, occurrence, distribution, and meanings. He wrote, "It was my original intention, after the legend material was more or less collected, to publish an overview of our folk beliefs in an appendix or supplemental volume to the *huldreeventyr*" (Liestøl 1947, 158). He gave up this idea at that time because the work would have been as large or larger than the *huldreeventyr* volumes themselves. However, he did not give up the idea of completing such a work at some time. Two years before Asbjørnsen's death, Henrik Jæger wrote that he had always wanted to write about the legends' relationship to Nordic mythology and that "he has been occupied with this scheme so strongly and for so long, that it must be considered his life's main and favorite project" (Jæger 1883, 158).

In the *huldreeventyr* Asbjørnsen faced a dilemma. How could he preserve the rich heritage of stories and folklore, which after all were a great national treasure, without seeming to condone or even strengthen the beliefs which were so integral to the stories he would be repeating? As was noted earlier, Asbjørnsen may have chosen the narrative frame device to tell his stories because of the absence of an established written tradition; but this was by no means the only reason the frame story was such a fortuitous choice. Jæger explains that "to tell the legends separately, as short, disjointed, and fragmentary as they were, would not be successful. He could not bring himself to communicate them in his own name, as though he believed them. But to allow them to be told through a folk storyteller? There was the solution" (64).

The twenty-seven independent stories which comprise *Norske huldreeventyr og folkesagn* contain over a hundred narratives related by ostensible "folk" informants, mostly in the form of legends and memorats,[3] in contexts created by Asbjørnsen to approximate the environment in which the narratives could be expected to be told "naturally." The stories are characterized by a polyphonic discourse, a dialogic language of statements and responses from a variety of characters within a carefully structured oral performance context. Often the stories are told at the end of a day of hunting or fishing, or when people gather in homes in the evenings, or at other times when action is suspended, perhaps because of the weather: all times when story-telling would seem to be a natural occupation. An exception are in those instances when the frame narrator is actively searching for a storyteller, such as in "The Grave Digger's Stories." In this case, the grave digger eventually has to be bribed with tobacco to get him to "talk."

While at least some of Asbjørnsen's created informants are based on the actual informants who told him the tales originally, most are created composites.[4] By allowing these fictionalized "folk" to tell their own stories within the framework he constructed, Asbjørnsen was also able to incorporate Norwegian dialect forms into the written language, something that had been paramount in the joint folk tale collections as well. Most importantly, by situating his created informants within a structure encapsulated by the urban frame narrator, Asbjørnsen exercises an encompassing and subtle control not only over the reader's response to the folkloristic material, but also over the reader's attitude toward the folk informants, through the editorial remarks of the frame narrator, who is, as we have seen, a boon companion of the reader, and hence a reliable narrator, or the other members of the audience, who also frequently comment upon the veracity of specific stories.

If *Norske huldreeventyr og folkesagn* did not make a contribution to the nationalistic construction of the Norwegian *bonde* as a type of "noble savage" and repository of all that was admirable from a glorious national past, perhaps it was because the *bonde* as he is represented in *huldreeventyr* bears little resemblance to the idealized construct that the elite were so busily trying to formulate. It is, of course, simplistic to speak of the *bonde* as though he were a homogenous creature. There was a vast difference between the *bonde* of small holdings as a fisherman farmer of western Norway and the *storbonde* [well-to-do farmer] of eastern Norway, who sometimes had control over thousands of acres. In addition, there was a third group of the *bonde*-type comprising the *husmann*, who farmed land belonging to the large landowner in exchange for a small plot of his own; the hired hand; and the forestry worker.[5] It is this third class of *bonde* that is presented most frequently as a storyteller in *Norske huldreeventyr og folkesagn*. The following description of one such *bonde*, as seen by the urban frame narrator, from the story "A Summer Night in the Krok Forest" may give an indication of why contemporaneous historians and literary critics, anxious to posit the *bonde* as the embodiment of the young Norwegian state, may be forgiven for having found Asbjørnsen's version of the subject slightly less than imitable:

> While Tor Lerberg was telling his story, a person who had been lying there sleeping came out of the lean-to. I didn't know what to think of him, because he really came closer to the image I had imagined of a gnome or a mound dweller than anything I had seen up to then. He was a thin, dry little man with his head cocked to the side, red eyes, and a nose like a big parrot beak. He had an expression around his mouth like he wanted to spit in your eye. (A 2: 164)

It should not be assumed from his often unflattering depictions of the rural residents that Asbjørnsen necessarily held them in distain. His biographer Hans Hansen is quick to point out that Asbjørnsen's family was not far removed from the countryside. "Sound, vigorous Norwegian *bonde* blood flowed in his veins. Asbjørnsen's national instincts were all right, and he was never one of those city people who looked with contempt at the farmer's traditions and customs" (Hansen 1932, 24).

Of the twenty-seven independent stories in *Norske huldreeventyr og folkesagn*, most contain three or four legends, a very few fairy tales, and ostensible memorats. Over a third of the experiences related by the folk narrators are represented as memorats, contemporary experiences. By choosing the memorat so consistently, Asbjørnsen is signifying to his authorial audience that the folk tales of both the rural and the uneducated urban dweller are not just remnants of an earlier mythical system, as the Grimms and other romanticists may have believed, although they may or may not have been based on these earlier beliefs, but evidence that these folk beliefs were still exerting influence in the lives of his contemporary countrymen. The dialectic between the frame narrator and the folk narrators of the stories is the dialectic between the enlightened urban educated class and the still extant and often primitive belief system of large segments of the populace.

Asbjørnsen was convinced that only by bringing these folk beliefs to light could they be eradicated, but at the same time he thoroughly enjoyed a good story. His dilemma is reflected in the very title he chose for his collection; it illuminates the tension between the believer and the skeptic in one word: *huldreeventyr*. This term was, according to Moltke Moe, coined by Asbjørnsen himself, and Knut Liestøl considers it an unfortunate one: "If one could take the word 'fairy tale' in its broad original meaning as 'event, wonderful occurrence,' then 'huldreeventyr' would have been very appropriate. But when one defines 'fairy tale' as folklorists now do, and as Asbjørnsen himself did, then one cannot tie huldre and eventyr together, because people don't believe *eventyr*, but they figure all stories about the hulder to be true; hulder is not a fairy-tale figure" (Liestøl 1947, 166).[6] However, seen in the light of the relationship between the frame and the stories within, we can see that *huldreeventyr* is exactly the right name, a blending of what was believed and what was not in mid-nineteenth-century Norway.[7] Liestøl goes on to explain that Asbjørnsen never really understood the difference between *huldreeventyr* and *sagn*, which Liestøl defines as the difference between memorat and legend, but it seems more probable that Asbjørnsen knew exactly what he was doing when he chose his title. The voice of the frame narrator in this respect can be seen as the authorial voice, stating that *huldre* do not exist, despite what the unenlightened rural populace may have thought. The title reflects the dialectic between belief and disbelief, the mediation of which is embedded in the narratives.

A great deal is known about how Asbjørnsen composed the *huldreeventyr*. His narratives, including the frame stories, were freely composed from composites of his own experiences and from legends that he himself collected from informants or that were sent to him by collaborators. He was also not above borrowing legends from written texts; the story about the mill-spirit, for example, which Asbjørnsen places in the mouth of the frame narrator in "Legends of the Mill," was undoubtedly taken from Faye's *Norske folkesagn* (Liestøl, intro to A 1: 197). It is known that he received editorial advice from many literary figures of his time. In addition to Camilla Collett, both Ivar Aasen and Johan Welhaven assisted Asbjørnsen, as well as others whose names are not well-known today. By comparing the finished products with journal entries and other sources, scholars have determined that Asbjørnsen created his contexts freely, using the best storytellers as a model. Since Asbjørnsen omitted certain types of legends and picked certain variants over others, he was acting as a selective editor as well as a creative artist. His realistic, rationalistic endeavor to capture folk beliefs is, of course, itself a construction. His choice of variants reflects this all-encompassing concern with the composite whole.[8]

In the construction of his fictionalized informants, Asbjørnsen, with few exceptions, was careful to create characters whose veracity or judgement are susceptible to contradiction by the frame narrator, or even sometimes by themselves. While it is the task of the frame narrator to keep a firm grasp on reality, lest the reader mistake legend and personal experience accounts as evidence of the supranormal, this task is sometimes shared by other members of the listening audience. Something or someone *always* subverts the storyteller's claim to a supranormal experience. In only two stories does the frame narrator allow himself to share in the folk beliefs of the common people, in "An Evening at the Neighbors," where the frame narrator reflects back on his own childhood, and in "A Summer Night in the Krok Forest," where the narrator is a fourteen-year-old boy who has taken a false turn, gotten lost in the woods and hears a noise in the underbrush:

> I was gripped by an indescribable terror, my veins turned
> to ice at these noises, and the fear was intensified by the
> dark eeriness between the tree trunks, where all objects
> were distorted, moving, living, thousands of hands and arms
> stretching out to grasp the faltering wayfarer. My frightened
> imagination evoked all the fairy tales of my childhood, and
> they manifested themselves in all the shapes around me. I saw
> the whole forest full of trolls, and elves, and hoaxing dwarfs.
> (A 2: 150)[9]

Only in childhood, or in memories of childhood, can the frame narrator cross the bridge and share in the belief system of the peasants.

Throughout the *huldreeventyr*, the frame narrator, who is not the same person in each story, maintains a somewhat condescending and slightly supercilious attitude towards the characters he meets and listens to. This distancing, with its consequent lack of in-depth characterization, is one of the reasons many literary critics have not found the *huldreeventyr* worthy to be considered creative literature. "There is something superficial in the descriptions of the characters, with a tendency towards schematization; sometimes we only get a loose outline. [Asbjørnsen] gives us a distinct side of their personalities. He sees them from the outside, he sees them from one angle—sometimes from slightly above" (Liestøl 1947, 130). Liestøl admits that it would have been difficult for Asbjørnsen to characterize the informants otherwise, since they are described by a frame narrator who is not omniscient and not able to enter into the thought processes of the people he meets. But, most importantly, by creating frame narrators who view the informants from outside and above, Asbjørnsen creates characters whose actions speak for themselves, much as their glorious ancestors in the sagas did; he also assures himself the distance from the oral narrators the frame narrators require in order to interpret the stories and beliefs for the reader.

Asbjørnsen then, first creates a performance context for storytelling, complete with informants and an appreciative audience; then he deconstructs and negates the supranormal stories with rational explanations through a variety of narrative techniques. In three important stories, Asbjørnsen presents the traditional material without a mediating frame narrator at all, as short stories, in each case because the protagonists and traditional material are so far removed from the enlightened sphere that the very presence of the frame narrator would seem improbable at best. As we know, the effect an outside observer can have on the phenomenon under scrutiny is always of concern to the folklore collector.[10] A series of examples from the text will illustrate the narrative strategies that are utilized to undermine the created oral informants in most of the *huldreeventyr,* and then in the next chapter two of the atypical stories will be examined to show how they represent the folklore of a marginalized Other within the Norwegian society of its time.

"I DO BELIEVE YOU'RE LYING, PER!"

Nearly all of the *huldreeventyr* begin with a first person introduction by a frame narrator, who describes the locale and the circumstances in which he finds himself. Generally the narrator meets an individual or individuals who, at an appropriate time of repose in the narrative, are encouraged by the frame narrator to tell stories. These "tellers of tales" will be referred to as folk narrators, to distinguish them from the frame narrator. Only a few of the *huldreeventyr* have only one folk narrator, and these are evident by the title of the story, for example, "Matthias the Hunter's Stories" or "Berthe Tuppenhaug's Stories." Most often, individuals are both audience and narrator in turn, as a story will often remind one of the audience members of a similar tale. There is a marvelous "give and take" in the dialogue between the narrators and the audience members, who often interrupt the storyteller to offer corrections or comments. By structuring the stories around a performance context, Asbjørnsen is able to filter the traditional material through a series of "reality checks" which virtually guarantees that the reader will not be tempted to believe that the stories could be true. As mentioned briefly earlier, this question of truth status is pivotal in the legend genre. "It seems to be a rule that general reference to belief is an inherent and the most outstanding feature of the folk legend" (Dégh and Vázsonyi 1976, 119).

Normally the legend will deal with supranormal events, an encounter with the supernatural Other.[11] In Norwegian folklore, this Other will often be the *nisse* [pixie], the *hulder* or the *underjordiske* [underground dwellers], or sometimes an animal which has been "hexed" in some fashion so that it has obtained extraordinary powers of one kind or another. The actual folkloristic content of the folk-narrated tales will be the focus of a later chapter.

One of the most representative *huldreeventyr* for the purposes of examining the method by which Asbjørnsen constructs his performance context, and then how he undermines his created informants, is perhaps "A Summer Night in the Krok Forest." This story first appeared in the fall of 1847. Liestøl explains that much of the material for the legends in the story was sent to Asbjørnsen from a school-teacher in Ådal, J. M. Kristofersen, whom Asbjørnsen had met on a collecting trip in the early 1840s. Asbjørnsen included an epigraph to this story from Geijer's poem, "Den lilla Kolargossen" in which a little boy also believes he sees trolls and bears.

In this frame story, the narrator is the fourteen-year-old boy who becomes lost in the woods and becomes so frightened when he hears a noise in the underbrush. The story begins as most of the *huldreeventyr*, with a setting in a specific locale: "When I was fourteen, I came one Saturday afternoon shortly after Midsummers Eve to Upper-Lyse, the last farm in the Sørk valley. I had so often kept to the beaten track, walking and driving the road between Kristiania and Ringerike; so this time, after a short visit to my home, I had for a change taken the road past Bogstad to Lyse, from there to take the short-cut through the northern part of the Krog forest to the waterwheel in Åsa" (A 2: 142).[12] The boy finds no one at home at Lyse, except a black cat and a rooster; tired from the heat of the day and his wanderings, he lies down on the grass and falls into a half doze, only to be awakened by an old woman pacifying a litter of piglets whom she is about to feed. Interjected between remarks to the pigs, the old woman gives directions to the boy, who has inquired about the route to Stubdal in Åsa. Concerned that her directions are rather vague, the boy asks if anyone is available as a guide. No, she says: "They are so busy with the harvest that they hardly have time to eat." So the boy sets off alone with the assurance from the old woman that he will "probably find the way" (144, 145).[13] He starts off confidently on a small path which eventually disappears altogether. The boy continues to try to find his way, finally falls asleep on a bed of moss, and is awakened this time by the loud cry of a bird. The boy continues through the forest in a light, misty rain which darkens everything. He becomes frightened by the sounds in the woods, as cited earlier, but is relieved when he realizes that the noises are not made by supernatural creatures but rather by a bear, who scurries off in the brush. It gets darker, but the boy comes out of the thickest part of the forest onto the shores of a large lake as the sun is setting and realizes that he has walked to the northeast instead of to the west. Through the trees in the distance he can discern the flicker of a fire along the shore, and as he approaches, some of his earlier anxiety returns: "A dark figure was sitting in front of the bonfire, and because of his position between me and the flaming fire, he seemed to be of supernatural proportions. The old stories of robbers in the Krog forest flew through my head, and for a moment I thought of running away; but when I saw the lean-to by the fire, the two fellows sitting in front of it, and all the axes in the stump of a newly felled pine, I realized that they were wood-cutters" (153).[14] When the boy overhears a fourth man, who had been to the creek for a pail of water, claim to have heard a bear in the woods, he steps into the clearing and admits that it was probably himself who was heard rustling in the underbrush. After the boy's explanation, the old man by the fire, Tor Lerberg, tells the boy that they will ferry him across the lake in the morning and offers to fry him a fish. When this has been consumed, the men return to the activity they had been engaged in when the boy interrupted: telling stories about experiences of wood-cutters with the supernatural creatures of the Norwegian forests.

The first story is told by a young man of about twenty and is related as a memorat; the story is about the man's father, and it is localized by the folk narrator in this fashion: "Father was clearing for the fellow at Ask in Lier, and he was cutting up in the Ask fields. In the evenings he went to Helge Myra's cottage down towards the village and stayed there" (156).[15] Here the storyteller interrupts his own narrative to ask Tor if he knew Helge Myra. This is a technique used time and again throughout the *huldre-eventyr* to not only add verisimilitude to the events related, but also to approximate what really happens in a storytelling situation with a live audience.

One day the father had taken too long a nap in the afternoon, and when he awoke, the sun was low in the sky. He began chopping at once because he did not want to stop until he had a full cord, but it became darker and darker, and just as he was about to begin on the last small tree, the head flew off his ax. This happened several more times, and then the man heard a call from over by the face of a cliff, "Halvor, Halvor! You came early and you are leaving late." Terrified, the man quit work for the day.[16] But this is not the story Tor wants to hear. "I have heard that before . . . but that is not the one I meant; it was that time he was in a wedding at the spring cow-barn in Kilebakken." A member of the audience has requested a different story, which could easily happen in a performance situation, and the young wood-cutter is happy to oblige, this time not only constructing a place but also a time: "It was in the spring, right before Easter in 1815, when father lived at Oppen-Eie, and the snow wasn't gone yet" (158, 158, 158).[17] Just as Asbjørnsen is able to create a sense of place in his descriptions of the Norwegian countryside through the voice of the frame narrator, he is able to create a corresponding sense of time and place for the legends related by the folk narrators by using real place names and dates. The interplay between the frame and the internal legends is constantly being adjusted and negotiated by Asbjørnsen's awareness of what real storytelling events are like.

A superb example of Asbjørnsen's skill at creating the performance context and a particularly sophisticated interplay between storytellers and audience is found in the story "An Old-Fashioned Christmas Eve." It is one of the oldest of the *huldreeventyr*, first printed in the newspaper *Den Constitutionelle* right before Christmas in 1843. In this story the frame narrator is a young officer spending Christmas Eve in Christiania instead of home with his family in the country, because he was recently released from the hospital. Still recuperating, he looks forward to a lonely Christmas, but is then invited to spend the evening with the owners of the rooming house in which he lives, two old spinsters named Mette and Cecilie. When he steps into their big old-fashioned living room, he finds that old Ma Skau has also been invited, and several young nieces and nephews of the spinsters are busy in the kitchen with the old housekeeper Stine. The children soon discover the officer and beg him to tell stories. It is of interest to show how skillfully Asbjørnsen shifts the narratives among the various storytellers, as for example, from the young officer to Aunt Mette:

> I had to tell about "Butterball" and the dog Goldtooth and then add a couple of *nisse* stories about the Vager *nisse* and the

Bure *nisse* who took hay from each other, and met with loads of hay on their backs, and fought until they disappeared in a cloud of hay. I had to tell about the *nisse* at Hesselberg, who teased the farm dog until the farmer threw him over the barn bridge. The children clapped their hands and laughed. "That serves him right, the nasty *nisse*," they said and demanded more. "No, now you are pestering the lieutenant too much, children," said Miss Celcilie; "now I am sure Aunt Mette will tell a story."

And Aunt Mette does tell a story, a story about another *nisse*, but a menacing one, and when she is finished one of the young children protests, "I'm scared, now it's your turn, lieutenant; when you tell stories I am never scared, because you tell them so funny" (A 1: 112, 115).[18]

Then the lieutenant is asked to tell the one about the *nisse* who dances the halling with the girl, a request typical of real audiences who often know the repertoire of storytellers and enjoy hearing the same tale again and again, but the frame narrator does not want to tell that story, because

> it was something I didn't like to embark upon because there was a song with it. But they wouldn't let me get out of it, and I had already started to clear my throat to prepare my exceedingly inharmonic voice to sing the Halling dance, when I was saved by the arrival of the aforementioned attractive young niece, to the joy of the children. "Now children, I will tell the story, if you can get cousin Lise to sing the Halling for you," I said as she sat down, "and you will all dance, isn't that right?" (115).[19]

The constant flow of interruptions and comments, requests and questions masterfully recreate actual storytelling events; and this story illustrates how well Asbjørnsen understood a real narrative performance context. Just as the audience reacts to a story, the skillful storyteller must also react to the audiences' reactions and adjust his tale accordingly. After the frame narrator tells his story about the *nisse* who dances with the selfish girl until she is more dead than alive, old Ma Skau tells two stories, first another *nisse* story which was supposed to have been experienced by Stine, the old housekeeper, and then the widely spread legend about the midnight mass of the dead.[20] Ma Skau had been told the story by her mother; it had happened right there in Christiania, on a Christmas Eve. "I know it is true, because she never spoke an untrue word," she says. Ma Skau continues:

> When my mother was a girl, she once in a while worked for a widow, whom she knew, called — now what was her name again? Mrs. — No, I can't think of it, but it doesn't matter, she lived up in Møller street and was a woman a little past the prime of life. It was a Christmas Eve, just like this, and she thought to herself that she would go to the early service on Christmas morning, because she went to church diligently, so she set out some coffee, so that she could have something warm to drink and not go fasting to church. When she woke up, the moon was shining in on the floor, but when she got up and looked at the clock, it had stopped, and the hands showed half past eleven. She didn't know what time it was at night, but she went over to the window and looked out at the church. Light was shining from all the windows. She woke up the girl and had her make coffee while she got dressed and then took her hymnal and went to church. It was so quiet on the street, and she didn't see anyone. When she got to church she sat where she usually did, but when she looked around, she thought the people looked so pale and strange, just as if they were all dead. She saw nobody she knew, but there were many she thought she had seen before, but she could not remember where she had seen them. When the minister came into the pulpit, he wasn't any of the pastors in the town, but a tall pale man, whom she also thought she should know. He preached pretty well, and there wasn't any of that noise and coughing and throat-clearing that you usually

hear at Christmas morning service, but it was so quiet that you could hear a pin drop; it was so quiet that she actually became anxious and apprehensive.

When they started singing, a woman who was sitting beside her leaned over and whispered in her ear, "Pull your coat loosely around you and go, because if you stay until it's over, they will kill you. It is the dead who are holding this service."

"Oh, I'm afraid, I'm afraid, Ma Skau," whimpered one of the little ones, and climbed up on a chair.

"Shush, shush child, she'll get out of it, now just listen," said Ma Skau. "But the widow was also afraid, because when she heard her voice and looked at the woman, she recognized her; it was her neighbor who had died many years ago."
(119–120)

The folk narrator in this passage must validate the fear of the child; she does this by interjecting an aside that the old woman will escape the mass of the dead, but then integrates the fear into the story in the next sentence by saying that the old woman *also* was afraid. The storyteller does not miss a beat. This reaction and mediation of the storyteller to the audience reaction is extraordinarily well-crafted.[21] And when it is remembered that "En gammeldags juleaften" was one of Asbjørnsen's early *huldreeventyr*, appearing in *Den Constitutionelle* in late 1843, his stylistic competence should no longer be an issue.

SUBVERSION OF THE FOLK NARRATOR IN NORSKE HULDREEVENTYR OG FOLKESAGN

In "A Summer Night in the Krok Forest," the young man has finished his stories about his father's encounter with an *underjordisk* bridal party, when Tor Lerberg admits that he too has seen a thing or two, right there in the Krok forest, and if no one is too tired, he will tell his stories too:

"I guess it was about ten, twelve years ago," he began, "I had a charcoal kiln in the woods by Kampenhaug. During the winter I was sleeping in there, and I had two horses that I used to carry coal to the works at Bærum. One day I stayed a little too long at the works, because I met some fellows I knew from Ringerike; we talked a little bit, and we had a few drinks — spirits, you know[22] — and so I didn't get back to the kiln until almost ten o'clock." (A 2: 160)[23]

With this introduction, the story which follows about Tor's difficulties with his horses, who disappear during the night, accompanied by large broad footprints, supposedly those of the *underjordiske* who were angry about being disturbed, can be seen as the result of his own immoderate behavior, rather than caused by the ire of the disturbed inhabitants of the mountain. Alcohol affecting the imagination is one of Asbjørnsen's favorite devices used to undermine the veracity of the storytellers he creates.

Tor Lerberg is by no means the only folk narrator who has a fondness for drink. An altered state of mind induced by alcoholic beverages is a characteristic of many of the created informants: the blacksmith in "An Evening in the Squire's Kitchen," old Elias from "A Night in Nordmarken," the schoolmaster in "A Sunday Evening at the Mountain Dairy," and the father in "An Evening at the Neighbors," to name the most memorable. Without stereotyping, it could nevertheless be said that the class of *bonde* from which Asbjørnsen drew his model informants seemed to have an unfortunate propensity towards over-indulgence whenever the opportunity presented itself.[24]

After Tor Lerberg tells his second memorat, experiences with otherworldly events after another late stay in town, the little gnome who looks as though he would like to spit in your eye comes out of the lean-to and confronts Tor, "How in the hell dumb do you think we are, that we [don't] understand that these are lies and old wives' tales? . . . I cannot for the devil understand how you can sit here and lie and say that you have seen these things yourself" (A 2: 166).[25] And "A Summer Night in the Krok Forest" concludes with a story told by this narrator, who by his words has already undermined his own veracity, as well as that of Tor Lerberg.

This direct confrontation in which one member of the audience accuses another of lying is another device Asbjørnsen uses to control the response of the authorial audience. Not only are the stories untrue, but one would have to be stupid in order to believe them. If someone as disreputable and unsavory as the little fellow who steps out of the lean-to can understand that the stories are not true, then certainly the reader should have no difficulty! In the story, "An Evening in the Squire's Kitchen," the squire comes into the kitchen where the blacksmith is telling stories and addresses him, "Are you here again with your nonsense and lies, smithy?" (A 1: 78).[26] The border between truth and fantasy is constantly being mediated and guarded. And if someone in the audience does not challenge the storyteller, it is not uncommon for him/her to discount his or her stories him/herself, either directly or by volunteering that people do not believe such things any longer. For example, in "A Grouse Hunt in Holleia," one of the hunters teases another by suggesting that he was not so ugly a fellow that he could not have become rich in his youth by being taken into the mountain by a *hulder*. Their subsequent conversation illustrates how Asbjørnsen sometimes offers disclaimers even before a story is told:

> "Ha, ha, ha," Per laughed in his beard, perceptibly satisfied with the captain's jocular remarks about his prepossessing appearance. "I have not believed in such things, because I have never seen a troll or a *hulder*."
>
> "But there lived a *hulder* over in Holleia here in the old days?" said the captain.
>
> "Oh, that's nothing but an old fairy tale. I have heard the talk, but I don't believe it," answered Per.
>
> "Yes, but you must know all about it, since you have been around these parts for so long? Tell what you know, because this city slicker is a fool for such stories."

> "Is that right? Well, I will then, but I don't believe it's true," asserted Per, and started. (A 2: 114)[27]

In the discourse between folk narrator and audience, the frame narrator walks a delicate line between the created context and the reader. Literally and figuratively he walks through the stories as both participant and observer. In order to gain the confidence of the storytellers, the frame narrator must feign belief, or, at the very least, be receptive to the traditional material. On the other hand, in his function as final arbitrator of truth for the reader, it must be clear that in these efforts he dissembles. The frame narrator stands as a true Janus, with one face towards the old world of the tradition bearers and their stories, and the other towards the new world of the enlightened reader. The frame narrator mediates by addressing the reader in narrative asides and explaining his actions and remarks on the one hand, while his spoken conversation is always directed to the performance context. Here is an example of this technique from "The Grave Digger's Stories," in which the frame narrator actively seeks out the grave digger because he has heard that the grave digger knows many stories, and finally finds and approaches him as he is at work in the churchyard:

> "Good evening, grave digger," I said.
> He measured me from top to toe, spat in his hands, and went back to his work.
> "This is heavy work for such wet weather," I persevered.
> "It's not any easier in the sunshine," he answered with a vinegary grimace, and continued to dig.
> "Who are you digging the grave for?" I asked, in the hope that maybe this question would lead to a conversation.
> "For the devil and the church," answered the grave digger. At this I had to request an explanation.
> "The devil takes the soul and the church gets the money," he said.
> "No, I meant, who is going to lie in the grave?"
> "A dead woman," answered the grave digger.

> That was that. I realized that this wouldn't lead to the desired result. Impatient with the rain, it had started to drizzle again, and annoyed with what seemed to be a futile expedition, I told the grave digger how I had sought him out to hear fairy tales and stories from the old days, explaining that he certainly wouldn't tell them for nothing, that it should even make him happy to tell them to me, who believed in such things, which people in general didn't anymore, etc. (A 1: 162–63)[28]

The use of etc. signals the reader that here is a set script, statements that the frame narrator makes as a matter of course in his efforts to find informants which are not at all reflective of his true feelings towards the traditional material.

Yet another example, from "Legends of the Mill," indicates how convoluted the dialectic between the frame narrator, the folk narrator, and the reader can become. The frame narrator and the young boy who is afraid of the dark, and who has been on an errand in the countryside, find themselves at a mill on the river. Here they encounter an old mill worker, and the young boy nervously admits that he has heard from his mother that trolls like to frequent sawmills and the mill house:

> "I haven't noticed anything, I can't say that," said the old man. "Of course, the water has been turned off and on now and then, when I have dozed off at the saw some nights, and once in a while I have heard a rustling in the sawed logs. But I have never seen anything. People don't believe in such things any more either," he kept on, with a questioning look at me, "and so they don't dare venture out; people are too smart and widely read these days."
>
> "You may be right about that," I said, since I was well aware that there was something hidden behind that look he had given me and would rather have him tell old stories than attempt to get me to discuss his doubts and his claim that enlightenment was a threat for pixies and the underground

dwellers. "You may be right about that in a way. In the old days people had a stronger belief in all kinds of magic and witchcraft; now they *pretend* that they don't believe in it anymore, so they can appear smart and enlightened, as you say. But in the mountain villages you still hear that the underground ones show themselves, take people into the mountain, and similar things. Now you shall," I continued, in order to get him started, "now you shall hear a story that is supposed to have happened somewhere, but where and when it happened, I can't quite remember." (A 1: 24. Italics mine)[29]

The frame narrator effectively disassociates himself from those who *pretend* not to believe by his use of "they" as opposed to "us," the initiated. The old man is likely to think that here is a person who can be depended upon to take what he says seriously; at the same time, the frame narrator has made it clear to the reader that all his efforts are merely to get the old man to tell his stories, and that the story the frame narrator is about to relate can be taken with a grain of salt, since the events are *supposed* to have happened, but no one seems to know quite when or where. Here the frame narrator breaks the conventions of the legend form, the "intimations of authenticity" (Ingwersen 1989, 305), expectations that the audience would normally have of a legend.

The frame narrator is not always so devious. In the story "Matthias the Hunter's Stories," Matthias, who is guiding the frame narrator on a short-cut across Nittedal to Gjerdrum, relates his experiences with the *hulder*. Matthias explains that one moonlit night when he was walking on a country road, he saw a beautiful woman walking through a marsh oblivious to the willow scrub and puddles. "I watched her, as I went along the road, but when I had gone a little farther and there was a mountain ridge between us so I couldn't see her any longer, I thought, 'It isn't right, that a person should be trudging through the marsh; you go up on the ridge and tell her that she has gone off the road.' I went up there, but there was nothing else to see but the moon shining on the puddles in the marsh, and then I understood that it had been the *hulder*." The frame narrator then interpolates his observation that "though it seemed to me that it would take more than this to discern that this was a *hulder*, I kept my doubts to myself, since I foresaw that my objections would not shake his belief, but only shut him up; therefore I only asked if he hadn't seen things like this several times" (A 1: 44, 44).[30] In at least one instance, the frame narrator subverts his folk narrator's story by a rational explanation based on his knowledge of the geography of the area. In "The Halling with Angelica Root," a Hallingdal native searches out the frame narrator in town in order to sell him some angelica root. Eager to hear the Halling's stories, the frame narrator buys a little of the root and asks the old man if he knows any stories about the *hulder* or the *underjordiske*.[31] Indeed, the old man has heard a tale from his aunt, who had been one summer at the mountain cabin with the cattle, in Ål in Hallingdal. The frame narrator is familiar with the area because he had been there on a grouse hunt. In a heavy Hallingdal dialect, the old man tells of several experiences he had heard from his aunt and concludes,

> Then there was a day soon after this, when Birgit was tending the cows over by Nysætknippe. Suddenly, she heard horses neighing, cows bellowing, the ringing of bells, the chatter of girls, and the sound of a buck horn, just like when you are taking the cows to or from the mountains. She searched around her in all directions, but saw neither people nor animals, so of course she knew it was the hill trolls who were bringing their herd to the summer pasture. Now she hurried to drive the cows back to the *seter* and to tell them what she had heard. Then they hurried to take the cows home because they didn't dare stay longer at the summer pasture; they were afraid that the hill trolls would be angry if they stayed past their time, you see.

Then the frame narrator immediately offers the only possible explanation,

> I was careful not to confuse the old man in his belief by giving a very natural explanation of the story he had just told me. From my knowledge of the area's valleys, hollows, and steep hills, it was clear to me that a homeward-bound cattle herd had passed through one of the distant small valleys, and that the sound waves from the neighing horses, the bellowing cows and bells, and the girls' talk and playing of the horn had not immediately reached Birgit's ear because of the intervening heights and hills, but only after having been echoed back from the steep side of the Nysæt cliff; and that she, when she couldn't see anything, believed it was the *huldre*. (A 1: 99–100, 100)[32]

In another huldreeventyr, "Berthe Tuppenhaug's Stories," an old wise woman treats the frame narrator's sprained ankle with a magic incantation, while pouring aquavit on his foot. That he later ridiculed her efforts is evident from the conclusion to the tale:

> Berthe told many more stories. Finally snow was creaking under a sleigh, and the horse was snorting at the door. I gave Berthe a couple of coins for care and treatment, and within a quarter hour I was home. A vinegar compress and cold water soon took care of my foot; but when Berthe came up to the kitchen on the farm, and asserted that her arts had the credit for my quick healing, the children couldn't restrain themselves; they chanted her incantation, which I had taught them, and asked if she thought that a drop of spirits and such nonsense could cure sprains. (A 1: 62)[33]

In addition to undermining the folk narrator's tales by rational explanations, ridicule, or questions of veracity, the frame narrator resorts to yet another technique of subversion in many of the *huldreeventyr:* irony. It is indeed possible to say that most of the frame narratives are permeated with a slightly supercilious attitude that can swiftly become ironic. But by his use of irony, the frame narrator is solidifying his relationship with the reader. "Recourse to irony by an author carries an implicit compliment to the intelligence of readers, who are invited to associate themselves with the author and the knowing minority who are not taken in by the ostensible meaning" (Abrams 1988, 92). In some instances the irony is playful, as in the concluding paragraph of "Matthias the Hunter's Stories," in which the frame narrator has been regaled by stories as they walked and

> in this manner Matthias continued to tell about dwarfs, *huldre* and pixies, until we came out on the Kulsrud ridge, from where one looks out across Upper Romerike's wide expanse, which now lay before us in the clear moonlight; towards the north Mist Mountain rose up dark blue with a few patches of snow; right below me I could see Heni and Gjerdrum churches; from this I could set my course, and since I was familiar with the region from earlier hunting trips, I said good-by to my guide, and was lucky enough to reach my destination without being teased by the *nisse* or tempted by the *hulder*. (A 1: 50)[34]

At other times, the irony is more pointed. Asbjørnsen appears to have been particularly concerned about how the actions of unenlightened parents could affect their children. In "The King of Ekeberg," the narrator explains that the *underjordiske* of Ekeberg no longer get the blame for dull-witted children in the Oslo districts of Grønland and the old city because:

> In the first place, enlightenment has reached so far, that instead of beating the changelings on the garbage heap for three Thursday evenings, or pinching their noses with a red-hot tong, as the custom used to be, now they let old Mrs. Torgersen or another wise woman diagnose rickets and illnesses due to witchcraft by casting, or they send one of the

child's diapers to Stine Bredvolden, who is so smart that she can read the child's illness and fate from it, and determine whether it will live or die. (A 1: 39)[35]

And in the second place, the *underjordiske* King of Ekeberg has moved to Kongsberg, because he could not tolerate all the noise in the skirmishes of 1814.

CHARACTERIZATION OF THE FOLK NARRATORS IN THE HULDREEVENTYR

It has been noted that lack of depth in characterization is one criticism that has been leveled at *Norske huldreeventyr og folkesagn* by the majority of modern literary historians who mention the work in the literary histories. But this criticism indicates a fundamental lack of understanding of the function of the folk narrators in the work and a bias towards the type of characterization one has come to expect, for example, in a complex psychological novel, where the characters change, evolve, and develop. As discussed previously, it is precisely in stereotypes that enormous amounts of cultural information can be condensed. In fact, thanks to Asbjørnsen, "the real Norwegian farmer has appeared in our literature" (Christensen 1905, 230). The created folk narrators of *huldreeventyr* represent the thousands of storytellers who have told their tales in front of fires and out in the fields throughout Norwegian history; they are, in one sense, not individuals, they are the *folk*. Had the characterizations been too psychologically individualized, the representative function of the folk narrators would have been compromised. In Norway's first literary history from 1862, writing of Asbjørnsen, H. Olaf Hansen writes, "His *folkesagn* contain . . . a series of typical figures" (Hansen 1862, 106). It is precisely because they are typical that the text can do its cultural work.

But if the folk narrators are typical of their class and lack psychological depth, they are nevertheless often depicted in their outward physical appearances and in their speech patterns in a highly idiosyncratic manner. Asbjørnsen is a master at creating a character by the use of the small distinguishing detail. The characters may be two-dimensional, but they are not flat, and they may still be memorable and believable as part of the created performance context for the stories they tell. "His characters sparkle with life, they are drawn with a few strokes which reproduce the emotions of the moment, and the original tone of the language lives in the conversations. He is matchless in his ability to draw an original, a droll figure, and to render all of his verbal characteristics, and to fuse him into the mood of nature and of the surroundings" (Elster d.y. 1924, 262). A good example of this ability to render verbal characteristics is found in "An Evening at the Neighbors," in which the frame narrator is remembering the stories of his childhood. One of the folk narrators is a neighbor, who, fortified with spirits from the corner cupboard, tells stories to the children. The narrator uses a habitual "filler" as so many people do in their real idiosyncratic speech:

> "It was someplace in Solør, yes it was a wedding. They ate and they drank there—they always drink at weddings—, and while they drank and ate, they heard a sound from the corner of the room. Yes, it was like laughter, *of course*, a hoarse laughter from several people—, but when they couldn't see anybody, and it came from a corner they could see, then the opinion was that there were uninvited guests at the party. It was the underground dwellers, *of course*, because in the old days when something was going on that they didn't understand, it was always the underground creatures who were about and doing things. . . ." Then he drank a glass of beer and continued, "It was confirmed that it had been the underground dwellers, who had been laughing in the corner, *of course*, because later a woman who had connection with these underground ones, was talking to a *hulder*, who lived close by in a mound, *of course*, and who sometimes borrowed butter and milk and such and who always paid it back—when

women start chattering, we know how it goes, *of course.*" (A
2: 212–13. Italics mine)[36]

And again in a second story:

> It was in the old days, *of course,* but it was a long time
> after the time when they built the mountain cabins for
> the travelers over Dovrefjell. There was a fellow who was
> traveling over the mountain at Christmas time on his way
> to Kristiania. He was going to celebrate Christmas there, *of
> course,* and that was stupid of him, because *of course* they
> drink both more and better all times of the year in Trondheim
> than they do in Kristiania . . . when he came to one of the
> mountain cabins—I think it was Kongsvoll—, he was going
> to spend the night there, and it was Christmas night. He
> came in, and there was a fire burning, *of course,* and it was
> snug and good and warm. (214. Italics mine)[37]

The portrayal of verbal idiosyncrasy is one way in which Asbjørnsen creates a realistic depiction of his oral narrators in many of the stories; but he is also a master at description of physical characteristics. A few examples have already been noted in other contexts, such as the man who would like to spit in your eye, but there are others. His description of the appearance and manners of the schoolteacher in "A Sunday Evening at the Mountain Dairy" is one of the most well-known caricatures in Norwegian literature.[38] The frame narrator and the milk maids at the mountain dairy are awaiting the arrival of one of their party along with several young people and the schoolteacher:

> It wasn't long before the company from Tor's cabin showed
> up. The girl was healthy to the core and red and white; she
> had a lively face and a plump figure. Fresh, uncorrupted
> nature, an open frankness shone from the boy's face too. The
> third person was the schoolteacher; even though he wasn't
> much over thirty, his face was full of creases and wrinkles,

which principally seemed to be due to a continual endeavor to give himself a dignified expression. His clothing also seemed designed to support this effort, or to distinguish him from the others: he was wearing brownish evening dress with monstrously long, sharp coat-tails; around his neck he had a white neckerchief and a huge tight collar; and on the edge of this there was located a kind of embroidered edging of points and notches. A monstrous bulge, which I at first thought originated from a growth, protruded from the right side of his vest; later I learned that it was a big inkwell which he always carried with him. This man's whole appearance made a very unpleasant impression on the stranger; especially distasteful was the affected manner in which he pursed his lips when he spoke. The mountain dweller's curiosity and interest in the strangers he meets, his direct, naive, even offensive and awkward questions are well known. But here appeared an importunate curiosity and inquisitiveness under the guise of culture, and every time he asked a question, he looked around with an expression, as if he were standing among Vågå's unwashed youth, and there was an expression on his face, and a smile on his pursed lips, which seemed to ask his listeners, "Wasn't that well said? I can sound out fellows like that!" (A 2: 14–15)[39]

Many examples could be given of Asbjørnsen's ability to create droll and interesting exteriors for his created folk narrators, but in some respects, taking a storyteller, even a fictional one, out of his or her performance context is like taking a tale out of context. It is truly within the stories themselves, and in the situations Asbjørnsen creates, that his folk narrators come to life.

As was the case with Asbjørnsen's appropriation of the Norwegian landscape, others would come after him who would populate the countryside with much more complex, and certainly more idealized, characters than those found in *Norske huldreeventyr og folkesagn*, but it was the cultural work of this text to offer a model. Already in 1866 the literary historian Lorentz Dietrichson could write that

> if Asbjørnsen as a portrayer of Norwegian folk life was precluded from moving into the psychological domain of the national novella, if he drew more outlines than actual character images, it is nonetheless certain that various of these are already *typical*, so that he is unconditionally the creator of the ambulatory teacher and tourist *types*, as we have later so many times seen them appear in literature and on the stage. (Dietrickson 1866, 177. Italics mine)

"When," as Tompkins notes, "literary texts are conceived as agents of cultural formation rather than as objects of interpretation and appraisal, what counts as a 'good' character or a logical sequence of events changes accordingly" (Tompkins 1985, xvii). The characterizations inspired imitation precisely because they *were* typical. "Asbjørnsen's descriptions of the life of the people elicited more imitation and autonomous efforts than the nature descriptions. The realistic portrayal of the farmer's life, which demanded a thorough knowledge of the material, made men who were interested in literature, and who had lived among the peasants, to feel that 'I could have written this myself!'" (Elster d.y. 1924, 264).

While there may have been many who tried their hands and skills at describing the *bonde*, one of the "addressees" of *huldreeventyr* was, of course, Bjørnstjerne Bjørnson, one of the giants of nineteenth-century Norwegian literature and cultural life, and a darling of the literary canon builders. His *Bondefortellinger* [Stories of the Farmers] was the most widely read text of the 1890s (Vannebo 1984, 44) and one whose portrayals of the *bonde* was much more to the liking of the nationalists, and to the shapers of the literary canon, than the often "raw" characterizations of *Norske huldreeventyr og folkesagn*. Of course Bjørnson had drawn an idealized picture of the *bonde* much earlier, in works like *Synnøve Solbakken* from 1857. He is one of the "Big Four" in the Norwegian literary canon of the nineteenth century (along with Ibsen, Kielland, and Jonas Lie) and was a player in the nation-building process as few others, but he (in contrast to Ibsen), always admitted his debt to Asbjørnsen.[40] Bjørnson advises a friend in a letter to read Asbjørnsen if he wants to "become familiar with modern Norwegian literature" (Hansen 1932, 330).[41]

Throughout the pages of *Norske huldreeventyr og folkesagn* wanders a rather motley collection of old men and women, farmers and dairy maids, hunters and fishermen, the occasional bookkeeper or schoolteacher, wood-cutters, sailors, lumber haulers, blacksmiths, a grave digger, and many others. They tell their marvelous stories through a myriad of voices: mumbled incantations, loud oaths, whispered warnings, and raucous laughter. They are dirty and sweaty and cunning and real. They are the folk narrators of the legends of the Norwegian mountains, farms, and forests, representative of hundreds of storytellers down through the centuries who have tried to interpret the events of their lives by sharing their stories, and they are as exuberantly alive today as they were when Asbjørnsen created them over 150 years ago to tell the legends of *Norske huldreeventyr og folkesagn*.

CHAPTER 5

From the Supernatural to the Human Other: The Marginalized Storytellers of *Norske huldreeventyr og folkesagn*

> *They come, one knows not whence;*
> *they go, one knows not where.*
>
> —Eilert Sundt

THE CHANGELINGS: LEGENDS OF A WISE WOMAN

A few *huldreeventyr* in *Norske huldreeventyr og folkesagn* deviate from the established pattern of a frame narrator, a performance context, and internal folk narrators to whom are assigned the tasks of disseminating the traditional material. While all of the tales in the collection of 1845, except "The King of Ekeberg," conform to this pattern, several important stories in the collection of 1848 are written as short stories, without the interaction of a frame narrator with a created informant. While there may be several reasons why Asbjørnsen chose to vary the format which had been so successful, it may be possible that in two cases he did so because he did not want the reputation of his fictional frame narrator, that urbane and supercilious fellow who is the reader's boon companion, to be sullied by association! It simply would not have been believable to insert the enlightened personage of the frame narrator into the context of a dim and dark hovel where a peasant woman waits for a wise woman to perform lead casting to diagnose her baby's illness, or into a county jail where Gypsies are planning their escape. Asbjørnsen was simply not able to *imagine* his frame narrators in this context, because, in addition to dealing with the supernatural Other of trolls and *nisser*, the frame narrator would have to descend into the world of the *human* Other, the Gypsy wise woman.[1]

This character, Gubjør Langelår, is a central figure in the two *huldreeventyr* to be discussed in this chapter, "A Wise Woman" and "The Gypsies," both of which will be examined in turn to reveal how Asbjørnsen uses the widely held beliefs about the magic of an ethnic Other to elucidate practices in the Norway of his time. It is obvious that "from the very first, notions of ethnicity and social boundaries have been associated with the supernatural. . . . People tended to ascribe supernatural abilities to those who were different" (Lindow 1995, 11–12). Lindow traces the relationship between the supernatural and the ethnic Other from the earliest Old Norse literature to show how "the supernatural is assigned to the ethnic others." Lindow suggests that early Scandinavians selected certain "emblems of contrast" to differentiate themselves from "Others" of ethnic origin, the most obvious of which being skin color. "The supernatural beings of folk belief constitute social groups created by tradition participants and marked with the same emblems of contrast" (22, 22). Some of the emblems of contrast that Lindow discusses include shape-changing, an animal characteristic such as a cow's tail, and Christianity.

In the stories "A Wise Woman" and "The Gypsies" the reader is confronted with two Others, a created ethnic Other who narrates the legends and acts within the assigned established realm of magic and folk belief, and the supernatural Other, the stories of whom the ethnic Other can manipulate. I would suggest that the elements of contrast between these two are deliberately blurred by Asbjørnsen to demonize the Gypsy and form a "breakdown of the distinction between ethnic and supernatural beings" (Lindow, 21). That this is highly relevant to the cultural work of *Norske huldreeventyr og folkesagn* goes without saying, because the stories not only reflect stereotypes about an ethnic minority who had long been seen as possessors of supernatural powers, but also codify these same attitudes for the mid-nineteenth-century reader. In discussing the need for stereotyping Sander Gilman explains: "Stereotypes, like commonplaces, carry entire realms of associations with them, associations that form a subtext within the world of fiction. In the case of works claiming to create a world out of whole cloth, such a subtext provides basic insight into the presuppositions of the culture in which the work arises and for which it is created" (Gilman 1985, 27). The ostensibly homogenous Norwegian society has always had an ethnic Other, and in these two *huldreeventyr* it is possible to read the subtext of racism and fear which existed for the society in which Asbjørnsen lived and wrote.[2]

While "A Wise Woman" and "The Gypsies" do not contain a frame narrator, they nonetheless feature the same enlightened urban voice with which the reader has become familiar. "A Wise Woman" begins:

> Several years ago there was a shack on a hill a short distance off a country road in one of the mid regions of Gudbrandsdal—Maybe it's still there. There was mild April weather outside; the snow was melting; brooks were rushing down the hillsides, bare spots were showing on the ground; the thrushes were scolding in the woods; the groves were full of the peeping of birds, signs of an early spring. . . . Inside the closed-up smoke-filled shanty it was dismal and gloomy. A middle-aged peasant woman of a very common and slow-witted appearance was in the process of breathing life into some branches and green wood she had laid under the coffeepot on the low hearth. (A 2: 128)[3]

This story, in marked contrast to most of the *huldreeventyr*, is not localized except in a very general sense. The events of "A Wise Woman" can and do take place anywhere a gullible and undereducated mother worries about a sick child, and there can be no doubt that the folk beliefs that dealt with child care were very slow to lose their power over the people. In a history of medicine in Norway, Fredrik Grøn notes that "a great many situations from our medical reports throughout the nineteenth century testify to the unbelievable tenacity by which traditional child care remained unchanged" (Reichborn-Kjennerud and Grøn and Kobro 1936, 118). Grøn mentions particularly the many deaths of infants due to the belief that they should be baptized as soon as possible after birth. Too early baptism is cited as a cause of infant mortality in a report from Ryfylke in 1863. Of course Christian baptism was seen as a defense against evil powers of all kinds.[4]

The narrator of "A Wise Woman" immediately establishes the contrast between the fine spring day outside and the mood inside the shack. The sinister atmosphere is reinforced by the mother's first words, spoken to her visitor, a traveling wise woman healer, "People say that it's no use casting, because the child doesn't have rickets, they say, but is a changeling; there was a blanket maker here one day and he said the same thing, because he had seen a changeling in Ringebu when he was little, and it was as weak bodied and loose jointed as this one" (A 2: 128).[5] The mother is speaking to a wandering Gypsy, who survives by moving from *bygd* to *bygd* treating the ailments of the peasantry with a variety of methods, including casting, incantations, and an assortment of folk medicines. The narrator's description of this woman indicates a meeting with the ethnic Other:

> The one she spoke to was a big-boned woman of nearly sixty. She was unusually tall in stature, but while she sat down, she looked small, and to this peculiarity she owed her nickname, since to her given name, Gubjør, people had added Longthigh. In the band of Gypsies she had rambled around with, she went by other names. Grey hair stuck out from under the scarf, which surrounded a dark face with bushy eyebrows and a long, irregular nose. The original dim-wittedness, intimated by the low forehead and by the width of the face over the cheekbones, was in contrast to the unmistakable expression of cunning in her small sparkling eyes and to the incarnate shrewdness which was marked by the wrinkles and play of the muscles of her face. Her clothing characterized her as an emigrant from a more northerly village; her face and her whole appearance suggested the wise woman, or at the very

least, a wandering Gypsy woman, who could be impudent and brazen or humble and ingratiating, depending on the circumstances. (129)[6]

It is clear that Gubjør is a wandering *signekjerring* who survives by moving from village to village treating the ailments of the peasantry with a variety of methods, including casting, incantations, and the dispensing of various folk medicines; hence, she is also a member of the feared ethnic Other. Her dark face and wide cheekbones clearly show that Asbjørnsen intended to cast her in this role, and the fact that her clothing marks her as coming from a more "northerly" village is, of course, highly significant, since the north was the realm of the Finn. As Lindow points out, "The 'Finns' are the outsiders and the dangerous ones. In fact, the 'Finns,' imbued with magical powers, are stock figures of Old Norse-Icelandic literature" (Lindow, 11).[7] The older Borgarthing law flatly prohibited belief in "Finns."

The peasant woman, Marit Rognehagen, is afraid that her child may be a changeling, but the wise woman assures her that such is not the case. "I know about changelings because I have seen enough of them" (130).[8] And then Gubjør tells two legends about changelings, which she relates as memorats, even including the names of the mothers, Brit Briskebråten from Fron and Siri Strømhogget. In both cases, the mothers are able to get their own children back by following the established procedures to deal with this calamity.

The belief that trolls or evil spirits are capable of exchanging human infants with their own offspring is a widely held belief in primitive societies and is certainly not confined to Scandinavia. In his notes to "A Wise Woman," Knut Liestøl summarizes the characteristics of a changeling and the methods believed to protect a child from this fate and also what could be done if an exchange had already taken place:

Commonly it is the male children that are exchanged.
The changeling always lies in the cradle and won't stand

up, doesn't learn how to talk, but cries all the time and is
insatiable. It is very ugly with a large head and skinny limbs.
The descriptions which Gubjør gives of changelings in the
narrative corresponds to the usual conception of them. The
child is in danger of being exchanged so long as it is unnamed
and unbaptized. The exchange preferably takes place at
night, most often when the mother falls asleep without
taking the necessary precautions. . . . As protection against
an exchange, one leaves a lit candle or an open fire. Or one
should place steel in the cradle, especially effective would
be a pair of scissors, which forms a cross when left open. . . .
To rid oneself of a changeling, it is necessary to get it to
talk or to laugh by presenting it with something strange or
extraordinary to excite its astonishment. When, by these
means, one knows for certain that it is a changeling, then one
can get the correct child back by mistreating the changeling.
(Liestøl, notes to A 2: 336)

That the belief in changelings to explain stunted growth in seemingly normal children was a true folk belief is documented in many sources. There are Swedish court records of a case from a trial in Gotland in 1690 in which parents set their ten-year-old child, who had always been sickly and frail, out on the garbage heap on Christmas Eve, in the belief that the *underjordiske* would return the rightful child and take the changeling. The child froze to death, and the parents were sentenced to a month in jail on a diet of bread and water (Arens and Klintberg 1979, 91). Martin Luther's advice when he saw a supposed changeling in Dessau was that it should be thrown into the water and drowned (Liestøl, notes to A 2: 337). Certainly a child who did not develop in a normal fashion would be a frightening example of Otherness within a family who believed the folk beliefs about changelings.

But in "A Wise Woman," Gubjør concludes her legends of changelings by remarking that "this child here is no more a changeling than I am" (131) and how could the exchange have taken place anyway, as careful as Marit has been with the child?[9]

Then the wise woman is reminded of another story, which she relates, about an attempted theft of a child which was unsuccessful due to the precautions which were taken.

But if the child is not a changeling, then he is suffering from *svekk* of which there could be as many as nine different types. This illness, which we know is actually rickets and caused by a vitamin D deficiency, was believed to take several forms and be caused in several ways. Throughout the recitation of the tales by the *signekjerring* and in the subsequent preparations for the casting of lead to determine the type of *svekk*, the peasant mother exhibits nervousness about the probable return of her husband, who does not believe in the efficacy of the wise woman's actions and has, in fact, offered to send the child to the doctor. "'To the doctor? Ha!' said the wise woman and spit . . . 'no, going to the doctor for such a child who has *svekk* would be a hell of a thing'" (134).[10] Gubjør continues by telling Marit that doctors do not understand treating *svekk* because it is not in their books, and that casting is the only solution for diagnosis and treatment.[11]

The *signekjerring* has been at Marit's on two previous Thursdays to perform her magic diagnosis. She recapitulates the results of the previous efforts:

> "The child has *svekk*, but there are nine kinds of *svekk*.
> Well, I have told you before, and you saw yourself, that he was exposed to troll *svekk* and water *svekk*; because the first Thursday it came up a man with two big horns and a long tail. That was troll *svekk*. Last time it came up a mermaid. Well, you saw it as plainly as I described it. That was water *svekk*. But now it's Thursday again, and now I wonder what it will be, when we cast now. As you know, it's the third time that counts. Here is the child," she said, and handed it to the woman, "Just let me have this last sip of coffee and I'll get started." (134)[12]

There is a certain chilling normalcy in Asbjørnsen's description of Gubjør as she goes about her daily routine of separating the incredulous peasantry from their meager savings by performing her magic. As she prepares her equipment for the casting, the conversation with the peasant woman illustrates the strict procedures to which the gullible peasants adhered at the advice of the *signekjerring*:

> "Since last Thursday," she said, "I have been in seven parishes and have scraped lead from the church windows at night, because the lead was used up the last time. That is nerve racking for both soul and body," she mumbled to herself as she shook out some of the toilsomely obtained lead from a snuffbox into the casting ladle.
>
> "You have, of course, gotten the north-running water at midnight?" she asked.
>
> "Yes, I was at the mill stream night before last; that is the only water that runs north anywhere around here," answered the crofter's wife and took out a tightly covered pail from which she poured water into an ale bowl. Over this was placed a piece of barley flatbread, which had had a hole made in it with a needle. When the lead was melted, Gubjør went over to the door, looked up at the sun, picked up the casting ladle and slowly poured the molten lead through the hole into the water as she muttered some words. (135–36)[13]

The results of the third casting for Marit Rognehagen's child are disastrous. The wise woman studies the lead figures in the water for quite some time, then exclaims, "Corpse *svekk*, Corpse *svekk*! — first troll *svekk*, then water *svekk*, then corpse *svekk*. One of them would have been enough!" She goes on to explain, "Yes, now I see how it happened. . . . First you traveled through a woods and past a mountain, while the trolls were out; you said Jesus' name there. Then you passed over a body of water; there too you said Jesus' name over the child; but when you came past the churchyard, it was before cockcrow, and you forgot it, and there the child caught corpse *svekk*" (136, 137).[14] There is but one possibility to save the child. Gubjør will make a doll replica of the child and bury it in the churchyard. Then the dead will believe that the child is dead, but "they ask for inherited silver. Do you have any inherited silver?" The mother searches for two old silver coins she had gotten from a godparent. She had not had the heart to use them before, but "when it's a matter of life and death, then . . ." (138, 138).[15]

The wise woman quickly sews a doll from some rags and then announces that she will return again in three weeks, but that the mother will be able to tell if the child will live by looking into its eyes. "If the child is going to die before the leaves fall, then you will see only black, and nothing else but black" (138).[16] The *signekjerring* then tells another changeling story, but it is evident that Marit Rognehagen is becoming more and more anxious that her husband will return to find the wise woman there. In the story as it appears today, and in all editions except the first edition, the *huldreeventyr* ends in this fashion:

> During this story, the housewife showed unmistakable
> signs of anxiety. Towards the end of the tale this became
> so conspicuous that even the storyteller, who seemed to be
> caught up in her own account, became aware of it. "What's
> the matter?" asked the wise woman. "Oh, it's your husband
> who's coming," she went on with a glance out the door, and
> then she added formally, "Gubjør cannot be staying here
> on your bench; but don't be afraid, I will go down past the
> churchyard, then he won't see me." (141)[17]

It has been noted before that very few actual changes in content were made in the three editions of *huldreeventyr* which Asbjørnsen himself edited, except for a continual Norwegianizing of the language and rephrasing. But "A Wise Woman" is an exception. In the first edition, the story does not end with these words of the wise woman. After she promises to leave so the husband will not see her, there follows an exchange between Marit and her husband:

> Shortly afterwards the husband came in. He wiped the sweat
> from his brow on the sleeve of his shirt, looked searchingly

around the room, his eyes followed his wife, who was misleadingly busying herself at the hearth; then the casting ladle, which had been left lying under the table, caught his attention.

"Is there any food, woman?" he asked.

"Oh, God help me," she answered, "I had fried a little pork, but this thieving cat stole it while I was taking care of the baby."

"Well, I never!" said the man, "Pork for a poor man on Thursday? God knows we're lucky to have it on Sunday. No, I suppose it's gone with Gubjør Long-thigh; I thought I saw one of her long legs behind the church wall."

"I thought she would be back with that casting of hers, but let me tell you this, if she comes back again, I'm going to have her thrown in jail! And you, woman, you will hear a tale of a different color!" (Liestøl, notes to A 2: 248)[18]

One can assume that the desperate mother will pay for her disobedience with a black eye or worse. Why did Asbjørnsen remove this ending from the editions of 1859 and 1870? It seems clear that artistically the narrative is more balanced without the entrance of the crofter. His presence, in a sense, undermines the sinister mood of the story, and the almost fatalistic chain of events that end when the wise woman scurries off to avoid meeting the disapproving husband. His entrance is anti-climatic, and there is no doubt that the story is a better one without the original ending. However, I would argue that the original ending was, in effect, a failed mediation attempt between the world of the superstitious housewife and the enlightened worldview of the narrator.

Not content merely to describe the procedure of casting, and dissemination of the changeling legends, Asbjørnsen wanted to leave the reader in no doubt about the sometimes dire consequences which the old folk beliefs could have. That the crofter was to represent the enlightened worldview is foreshadowed early in the story when the housewife admits that her husband has offered to have the child see a doctor. His actual appearance confirms his superiority over the rustic women. No mention here of the low forehead or shrewd little eyes of the peasant.[19] "He wiped the sweat from his brow . . . and looked searchingly around the room." A hard-working, alert and enlightened fellow, seemingly. But then he speaks, and his language is the language of the peasant. In the final analysis, Asbjørnsen cannot turn a sow's ear into a silk purse. "A Wise Woman" can and does have to stand on its own as an example of the existing folk beliefs of a large segment of the populace without the comforting frame narrator or an inauthentic enlightened peasant to offer explanations. The magic world of the ethnic Other is simply too far removed from *us* to be successfully mediated by Asbjørnsen's usual narrative devices.

DECEIVING THE BURO: THE LEGENDS OF TATERE

"The Gypsies" was one of the last *huldreeventyr* written for the collection of 1848. In this story Asbjørnsen creates a context in which his urbane frame narrator would have been distinctly uncomfortable. The setting is a small and cramped country jail, really just an appendage to the sheriff's house. It is February and the snow is flying outside, but inside the glow from embers of a fire throw illumination on two quite disreputable personages:

> In a shadowy corner on the innermost bed or stall of the barrack a man lay stretched out on a sheepskin blanket. Behind the low forehead, which leaned against a swelling muscular and hairy arm, coursed thoughts whose shadows played over a face as dark as the sooty wall, and which flashed out in glances so piercing, glaring, and sinister that even the apathetic watchman felt uneasiness when they chanced to fall on him. But no word betrayed the turmoil within. His wiry, coal-black hair, sharp features, the long face, whose lower part was covered by a short black beard, and this distinctive cast of eye showed that he belonged to the itinerant Gypsies or long-tramps, as the peasants in some parts of the country call

them. His eerie appearance had given him the name Black-Bertel. He was a horse gelder by profession, but also dabbled with varying success in curing horses.

The other man seemed to be of a more carefree nature, and had a lighter skin color; but the low forehead, sharp face, deep-set eyes of the Gypsy race, and this indescribable cast of the eye, at once searching, staring, stabbing with its unpleasant phosphorus glance, marked him too. (A 2: 171)[20]

The sheriff soon brings several more Gypsies to the jail, among them Gubjør Long-thigh, but the Gypsies pretend not to know each other, the better to plan an escape.

Asbjørnsen met a group of Gypsies on one of his collecting trips and even learned a few words of their language, which he includes in snippets throughout the story; but most of his information about the Gypsies was supplied by Eilert Sundt, who in 1850 would publish his comprehensive study of the Norwegian Gypsies and itinerant travelers.[21] There can be no doubt that there was considerable fear of these *tatere* among the rural peasantry, and it appears that at least some of these fears were founded on experience. An excerpt from Eilert Sundt's work indicates the difficulties which the small, isolated landholder had with some of these roving bands of Gypsies:

> One must follow the Gypsy bands into the houses to see the excesses of brutality and violence with which they disrupt the people's peace! In Værdal, right at the point where the Jæmteland road swings off from the main road along the Trondheimsfjord, lies a neat crofter's cottage. There, I thought, one probably had a good opportunity to observe the journeys of the "wanderers," and I was not deceived. The crofter, supplemented by his wife, told the following story, which was corroborated by some neighbors who happened to be there: Late one evening—it was early in the spring, right after the Levanger market—there was a pounding on the door, which was naturally opened in a

hurry by the inhabitants, who were awakened from a sound
sleep, and a Gypsy company of two men and a woman asked
and threatened and forced their entry and demanded night
lodging. The inhabitants could do nothing else but stay awake
and pay heed. The contents of a bottle of spirits soon brought
the ferocity of the travelers to the highest level, and the two
men started fighting with each other. The crofter did not dare
restrain them; everything, both living and dead, had to give
way for their kicks and punches. Finally the man put his wife
and children in a side room, shoved a bed against the door
and ran—one can imagine how fear and anger hastened his
steps—for "the King," the village watchman, who lived quite
far away. (Sundt 1852, 228)

Although the Gypsies broke the door and knocked over a cabinet, when the sheriff was consulted the next day he advised it best to let them go, since they had not committed violence against the inhabitants of the house. According to Sundt, this was by no means an isolated incident. And, although begging was illegal, farmers and small landholders continued to give food and other items to the itinerant Gypsies, partly from a conviction that it was the Christian thing to do, but perhaps more because of a lingering fear of what the Gypsies might do in revenge if their requests were not met. Most probably the majority of these traveling bands of Gypsies were peaceful and wished only to be left alone to live their nomadic lives, but there is no doubt that they did nothing to dissuade the general populace from the belief that they were "Finns." Sundt, summarizing the various theories on the origin of the Gypsies writes that

> most often one hears the opinion of the common people,
> that the Gypsies are Finns . . . since they have not only made
> the practice of magic arts a main occupation, as shall be
> demonstrated later, but have also found it advantageous being
> taken for Finns, inheriting all of the superstitious prejudice
> against them, that was already rooted in the people. This has

also been very successful for them in many places, as shall be seen, and maybe partly explains that in Lister and Jæderen, for example, where a Finn has certainly not been seen for hundreds of years, the memory of the Finns and belief both in their helpful and revengeful power is quite fresh and alive to this day. (8–9)

Sander Gilman explains that "when a group makes demands on a society, the status anxiety produced by those demands characteristically translates into a sense of loss of control. Thus a group that has been marginally visible can suddenly become the definition of the other." Writing about this created image of the Other, Gilman observes that "various signs of difference can be linked without any recognition of inappropriateness, contradictoriness, or even impossibility. Patterns of association are most commonly based, however, on a combination of real-life experience (as filtered through the models of perception) and the world of myth, and the two intertwine to form fabulous images, neither entirely of this world nor of the world of myth" (Gilman 1985, 20, 21). In "The Gypsies," Asbjørnsen links reality with myth to create characters and stories that reflect the perceptions of the ethnic Other in the Norway of his time.

The Gypsies begin to tell stories. Their intent is to engage the watchman to win his confidence and to keep him occupied while two members of the group plan an escape and also a burglary at a neighboring farm. The stories revolve around the methods used by the Gypsies, in this case Gubjør, to fool the farmers into payment of goods or money. It was widely believed that the Gypsies had a power over the health of the farm animals and could either heal or harm them. Gubjør relates one such encounter which involves the construction of a "troll-cat."[22]

> "Wicked neighbors have sent out a troll-cat to suck the blood and marrow out of your cows," I said, "I see that; but if I am allowed to, I will uncover it and I will help you, so that it doesn't get the power to hurt other cows."

"If you can do that, my dear woman, then I will pay you generously, and you will get food and clothing too," said the farmer. "Come along to the barn and I will show you the one who sucks blood and breaks bones," I said to the farmer; "but bring along your hoe and shovel." He took his hoe and shovel, and his wife followed after him like a dog. "I have never been here," I said, "but I have a good sense of smell and am familiar with hidden things; go to the black and white cow," I said.—"There has been digging here before," said the farmer. "Dig again!" I said, "that which is hidden shall be revealed." "The man dug, and as he was digging, a cat sprang out of the stall and across the floor, shrieking terribly. At the same time the eyes of the farmer and his wife were sparking like fire."

Here she nodded meaningfully to her listeners and a secretive expression appeared on her face. . . . "For this I got coffee and tobacco, wool and linen, pork and cured meat, six silver spoons, and lots of money." (A 2: 180–81)[23]

In "The Gypsies," as in "A Wise Woman," it is evident that Asbjørnsen is not only relating legends but also describing actual practices and belief systems that were still extant in the countryside of his time. It does not seem likely that the elaborately staged deception described by Gubjør in this story could have been a common occurrence, but it seems evident that for the majority of people in the countryside, it seemed best to be safe rather than sorry in dealings with the Gypsies. Obviously, by the time Eilert Sundt made his study of the life and habits of the Gypsies, there had been a weakening of the belief in supernatural agents; but Sundt's investigations make clear that much remained to be done. On this very issue he writes that

> When one bends the ear low to hear the thoughts of the people, one must often be startled over how prejudice and superstition still in the nineteenth century guards itself against the clearer light which is advancing everywhere.

> Superstition can be clever in its battle with common sense. A farmer's wife confessed to me her belief in the magic power of the Gypsies' words; she related an incident as proof and transgressed thereby; a Gypsy woman—so went the myth—came late one evening to a farm and asked to spend the night, but was turned away. She left then, but with these words, "If you will not house people, neither shall you house cattle," and since that time some of the farm's cows and horses died every year, a misfortune that continued even after the owner sold his farm to another man for this very reason. "Is it still like that?" I asked, "Oh no," was the answer, "it is now over thirty years since Big-Serina died, so by now her bones must be rotted in the ground, and with that the witchcraft ends." —It is certainly true that such stories about the people's reliance on the Gypsies' magic help in all kinds of trouble as I mentioned above is more rare than it was, but the belief that they can cause harm by their evil eye and wicked words has held up better and one considers it most advisable to gain their friendship by charity or other willingness. "I don't believe in their power, but it is probably best to give them something anyway, when they ask," is a common expression used particularly by the farmer's wife, concerned for her animals, as a justification for her great indulgence of the Gypsies' impudence. It is therefore a kind of half belief, which rests on what the ancient Dogmatics would have called *argumentum de tuto*. (Sundt 1852, 278–79)[24]

After Gubjør's story about fooling the farmer with the troll-cat, another Gypsy tells a story about a character named the wooden-legged Finn, who was able to travel by flying through the air. This tale engages the watchman, who relates a story of his own. While this is transpiring, Black Bertel and another Gypsy named Svolke-Per complain bitterly about the treatment of the Gypsies at the hands of the *Buro* (the Gypsies' term for non-Gypsies), and continue with plans to escape, rob a neighboring farm, and flee to Sweden, where things are said to be more peaceful.

The sheriff stops by to check on his prisoners and to confiscate any alcohol they may have hidden but is unable to find any contraband, since Gubjør has concealed the flasks carefully. The sheriff refuses to lend the Gypsies a deck of cards and tells them they may return to their stories, which they do, telling two very uncomplimentary tales about the clergy, whom the Gypsies found to be extremely meddlesome. These stories, as most of the stories in *huldreeventyr*, deal with subject matter consistent with the worldview and interests of the storytellers, but in "The Gypsies" as in "A Wise Woman," the stories are not localized to the extent that they are in most of the *huldreeventyr*, and the traditional material is often more fantastic in many instances. The gruesome tale of the skinned bailiff could perhaps not have been related by any other narrator than the despised Gypsy:

> There was a bailiff, north in the valley, he was so grossly depraved that he didn't care what he did, and he got a restless death. At the viewing of the body, he lay still when nobody was there, but when people came in, he would stand up and take their hands and greet them. When he was going to be buried, they put him in the mausoleum under the church floor. Then he was quiet for a while, but then suddenly he started to walk again every single night. One day a shoemaker came to a farm close by the church; he didn't believe in ghosts, so he bet he could sit in the church by the coffin the whole night and sew a pair of shoes. They agreed to this. They took the coffin out of the cellar and the shoemaker sat down on the floor, but first he drew a circle around himself with chalk. Late in the night, the very devil came flying in, tore the lid off the coffin, knocked the head off the bailiff and started flaying the skin off him. He was so occupied with this that he didn't see the shoemaker, who pulled the skin into the circle as the devil was removing it from the bailiff, and when the last piece came loose, he pulled it all inside the circle. When the devil was going to pick it up, he couldn't because of the circle. Then he got so angry and furious that he could

have committed both murder and fire, and he screamed and swore. He wanted the skin back.

"You shan't have it," said the shoemaker.

"What in the devil do you want with the worthless skin?" asked the devil.

"I want to tan it and make shoes from it," said the shoemaker. (196)[25]

The storytelling continues and as the night wears on, the Gypsies are able to ingratiate themselves with the watchman, little by little; finally they are able to convince him to swallow Gubjør's concoction to aid his upset stomach. "Before an hour had passed, the watchman felt overcome by an overpowering heaviness and drowsiness. The fire died down; finally it only glowed in the embers of the big pine root, whose resinous remains sometimes burst into flames, which for an instant cast a dark red light over the Gypsies' sly faces. Finally the watchman's heavy breathing and deep snores proclaimed that he could not hinder their flight" (198–99).[26] The Gypsy faces lit by fire to a dark red hue continue the demonization of the ethnic Other. Asbjørnsen reinforces the connection between the supernatural Other and the ethnic Other in the conclusion to the story. The neighboring farm is indeed robbed while the inhabitants are away at a wedding celebration, and the Gypsy company cannot be found. "It was as if it had sunk into the ground" (200). The Gypsies *become* the *underjordiske*.

Of course, Asbjørnsen cannot allow the Gypsies to profit from their nefarious dealings. In the last paragraph of "The Gypsies," the narrator explains that much later certain facts came to light about some members of the company. One was killed in a fight, another is in prison and

> there is a trace of the wise woman Gubjør Long-thigh. Last autumn a reindeer hunter, who was following a wounded deer in a remote region of Illmann Mountain, where you can see over to the wild peaks of Rondane, found the remains of a human skeleton, which had been gnawed to pieces by

wolverines and mountain foxes. Between the rocks lay a
copper snuffbox, filled with small pieces of lead. In addition
was found a rolled up row of skate teeth, some skulls of a
venus mussel and different other sea animals—odds and ends
that no one in the valley had seen or knew the use for, but
things that the Gypsies make use of in their potions,—plus
some small bottles, one of which contained a brownish or
golden-red liquid which the district doctor said was opium.
(201)[27]

Gubjør is severely punished with a gruesome death for her sins against the incredulous common people, and the lesson is clear for the nineteenth-century reader as the ethnic Other blurs into the supernatural Other, both of whom pose a threat to the well-being of the insider group.

THE SCANDINAVIAN WORLDVIEW OF THE OTHER IN *NORSKE HULDREEVENTYR OG FOLKESAGN*

In the pre-industrial Norway of the mid-nineteenth-century and long before, the inside group, the "us," would have been a very small one indeed in many cases. People speaking various dialects from valley to valley, even within fairly close proximity to each other, would be likely to view anyone even slightly different with suspicion. It is evident that "the line between the supernatural and merely ethnically different enemies must have been difficult to draw and difficult to keep" (Lindow, 16). Writing about particularly Scandinavian conditions of an earlier time, Lindow says:

> By populating the mountains and forests, the rivers and
> streams, even the land under their farms and the days long
> ago with supernatural beings and by assigning to them
> the same emblems of contrast they assigned to the human
> groups and individual strangers they encountered, I submit
> that people *created* other social groups and categories

> and thought about them in the same terms they used to think about the other outside groups we would term ethnic groups. Let us make no mistake about this point: supernatural beings enjoyed an empirical existence and were probably—we can only guess about this—more real to many than, say, Hottentots or Bushmen or the King of England would have been. Similarly, the supernatural aspects of such ethnic groups as Saamis and Finns and of such disadvantaged individuals as those accused of witchcraft were also empirically demonstrated. In other words, the distinction on which we insist, between "natural" and "supernatural" or "human" and "supernatural" was not terribly important in the relatively fixed stable system of Scandinavian (here we could probably just as easily say "European") worldview. (20–21. Lindow's italics)

Lindow goes on to argue that what mattered was simply the distinction between one's own group and everything outside of it, and that "the logical consequence of this line of thought is a breakdown of the distinction between ethnic and supernatural beings" (21).

Assuming that Lindow's argument is essentially correct, it may be intriguing to juxtapose his conclusions with an observation of Julian Kramer, the South African immigrant to modern Norway, who states that

> one problem faced by many foreigners in Norway, is the Norwegian's lack of understanding of the possibility of people being multicultural. That is to say, that it is possible to master several cultures, and "shift" between them depending upon the situation. For example, being Vietnamese at home with the family but Norwegian out among one's co-workers. It seems like it is difficult for Norwegians to accept that this is possible without the concerned party becoming schizophrenic. I think that Norwegians experience this as problematic because they have been raised to believe that one

is either Norwegian or something else. That it is impossible to be "in-between" or "two things at once." (Kramer 1984, 90)

Kramer believes that this "either-or" axis of Norwegian ethnicity is due to Norway's long anti-colonial struggle, in which it became necessary to value similarity and disdain differences, as well as a tribal mentality, where one is Norwegian because one is from Trøndelag or Telemark, for example. Therefore, it is impossible for foreigners as ethnic groups to be accepted as Norwegians: "There have also not developed any so-called 'hyphenated identities' in Norway either, as the case is in countries where the largest part of the population consists of immigrants. The Norwegian counterpart to Irish-American, Afro-American, Italian-American would be an absurdity. One is either Norwegian or not. There is nothing in-between" (96). Although one could point out to Kramer that hyphenated identities are most probably uniquely American (and perhaps Canadian) phenomena, it is nevertheless true that his observations are intriguing. But if Norwegians are raised in the belief that one is either Norwegian or not Norwegian, as Kramer says, with no possible multicultural gradations, then is this not a reflection of the Scandinavian worldview as it developed over hundreds of years? If Lindow is correct about the blurring of Otherness in the historic Scandinavian worldview, then it becomes evident that no possible compromise *can* exist since a plurality of cultural identity would be conterminous with the supranormal, a situation which will be discussed in greater detail in the next chapter. Of course, it could be argued that it is a giant leap from Lindow's analysis of an archaic worldview to the modern Scandinavian conception of the world, but it must be remembered that modernization came late to Norway; it is perhaps not surprising, as Tord Larsen asserts, that Norwegians are not yet comfortable living in the city (Larsen 1984, 36–37).[28] Urban Norwegians have brought the rural to town, and can they not have brought a rural worldview as well? A worldview is shaped by so many factors; is it so easily reformulated by industrialization and urbanization?[29]

But what do the Scandinavian worldview of the Other, the difficulties of assimilation of contemporary immigrants to Norway, and a contemporary Norwegian either/or reaction to ethnicity have to do with the cultural work of *Norske huldreeventyr og folkesagn*? I would suggest that the blurring of the supernatural Other with the ethnic Other as represented in "The Gypsies" and "A Wise Woman," and to a lesser extent in other of the *huldreeventyr*, more or less accurately illustrates the prevailing Norwegian worldview of ethnic minorities at mid-nineteenth century; and that this portrayal, when committed to print, helped to legitimize this worldview for the generation of Norwegians who were forming the new Norwegian national identity. It has been noted that *Norske huldreeventyr og folkesagn* has not been considered a creative literary text, despite its obvious literary characteristics. If "the literary and philosophical canons . . . cannot tolerate pluralism" (Jusdanis, 58), then these liminal characters, the Gypsies of "A Wise Woman" and "The Gypsies," with their blurred identities, were as truly marginalized out of a literary canon that demanded the homogenous as they were out of the society that they moved through, wandering from place to place, as demonized in life as they were in the pages of *Norske huldreeventyr og folkesagn*.

CHAPTER 6

Spirits of the Woods, Fields, and Mountains:
The Tradition Content of
Norske huldreeventyr og folkesagn

> *Eg kjenner deg, du Trollheim graa,*
> *du Skugge-Natt!*
> *Eg rømte rædd; men stundom maa*
> *eg sjaa deg att.*
> —Arne Garborg

LEGEND AS A REFLECTION OF WORLDVIEW

If the boundary between the ethnic and the supernatural Other is blurred in stories such as "The Gypsies" and "A Wise Woman," the majority of the stories in *Norske huldreeventyr og folkesagn* do not deal with Gypsies or Finns, but with the supernatural, and here, also, the line is often difficult to draw and difficult to keep. "Every ethnic group defines itself by positioning itself in opposition to an Other which, in turn, is always attributed nonhuman characteristics" (Tangherlini 1995, 60). The negotiation of this boundary between the insider group and the Other is the primary theme of the stories of *Norske huldreeventyr og folkesagn*, and it is a negotiation that is fraught with ambiguity. A study of the human/Other relationships in some of the stories may very well offer an insight into the ongoing process of Norwegian self identification because it is probable that the egalitarian worldview of contemporary Norwegian society, with its roots in a long non-hierarchical tradition, may itself contribute to that society's difficulty in self-definition.

When one considers the vast array of possible legendary material which Asbjørnsen could have incorporated within the repertoires of the fictive storytellers in *huldreeventyr*, it may be enlightening to briefly survey the types of legendary material he chose *not* to include, since such a comparison offers an illustration of the very different focus of this text compared to many nineteenth-century legend collections. Rather than recovering the splendor of an heroic past, *Norske huldreeventyr og folkesagn* examines the negotiation of identity in a more prosaic present.

Legends have traditionally been subdivided by folklorists for purposes of classification into categories of mythical, historical, and etiological, but these are by no means hard and fast divisions. In fact, legends have been "one of the most difficult" genres to define (Kvideland and Sehmsdorf 1988, 18). Often, the belief factor is cited as an identifying element of legend: legends are supposedly believed to be true by either the teller and/or part or all of the audience. In his introduction to *Folktales of Norway* Reidar Christiansen divides the Norwegian legends into only two subcategories, the historical and the mythical. It is intriguing to realize that one can search the *huldreeventyr* in vain for any example of the vast corpus of legends which Christiansen terms historical, those concerning St. Olaf, Norway's patron saint, or any of the legend cycles that describe the ravages of the Black Death of the fourteenth century. Missing also are the popular stories about Sinclair, the mercenary Scot whose troops were killed by the legendary exploits of the brave Gudbrandsdal farmers during the Kalmar War of 1611 to 1613, or, for that matter, legends of war of any kind. Since it is unlikely that Asbjørnsen would have failed to collect such legends on one or more of his numerous collecting trips throughout a long life, it becomes clear that in *Norske huldreeventyr og folkesagn*, as the title indicates, Asbjørnsen consciously and consistently selected those tales which Christiansen would term mythical legends, those dealing with human encounters with the inexplicable, legends in which "non-human elements play a decisive part" (Christiansen 1964, xxiv. Trans. Pat Shaw Iversen). Included in this category must be the dozen stories dealing with the *trollkjerring*, in which human *becomes* the Other. In addition to his omission of historical legend within the stories of *Norske huldreeventyr og folkesagn*, Asbjørnsen also omitted two *huldreeventyr* from the 1870 edition, the last which he personally edited; these omissions have been perpetuated in later editions of the work up to and including the definitive 1949 edition edited by Knut Liestøl. Asbjørnsen felt that "A Forest Valley in Western Norway," which was first published in 1869, was artistically weak. "A Christmas Visit to the Parsonage" appeared in the second edition of the first collection in 1859, but because it was still his intention to write an overview of the folk beliefs of the people, Asbjørnsen omitted this story in its original form from the 1870 edition because it "really contains more reflections over legends and fairy tales than actually recounts them" (Asbjørnsen 1870, iii). Two narratives which were originally part of "A Christmas Visit to the Parsonage," "The Goblins on Sandflesen," and "Trolling for Mackerel" appeared as independent *huldreeventyr* in the 1870, and subsequent, editions.

By his almost exclusive selection of legends dealing with the human encounter with spirits of the woods, fields and mountains, and by his technique of casting these stories into a contemporary milieu, Asbjørnsen was creating a picture of the mid-nineteenth-century Norwegian peasant that was far from flattering, not at all historical, and out of step with romanticism's infatuation with great deeds of antiquity. While Asbjørnsen was certainly not consciously trying to create a national narrative in our modern sense of the term, as explicated by Jusdanis and others, he was elucidating for the educated how very far many rural Norwegians had to progress before they could take their place in a modern society. Although he was primarily interested in the legends for their own sake, he was very much aware of the scope of the problem that those who wished to "enlighten" the peasant would face and was throughout his life concerned by the tenacious hold that the old beliefs continued to exert among the *almue*. Even as late as 1874 he would lament that lives were being lost because "people mistake the cries for help of a drowning man for the alluring, deadly call of the *nøkk* and the *draug*" (Asbjørnsen 1874).[1] His hope was that the publication of the folk beliefs within the legends of *huldreeventyr* would help lead to eradication of beliefs and practices that were injurious to the people.

The legends Asbjørnsen retells in his text belong mostly to an agrarian population struggling to define the boundaries between the inner and outer realms, the self and the Other. A history of past greatness or events, as might be fitting in construction of a national narrative in Germany or Sweden, could not define identity for the Norwegian on several grounds, primarily because true political independence was not yet a reality. Could not this colonial consciousness in some respects have forced the nineteenth-century Norwegian to identify himself by what he *was not*, rather than by what he was? It should be remembered that the Norwegian constitution of 1814, which did give more autonomy to Norway in her union with Sweden than she had had under Danish rule, still expressly forbade certain religious groups in Norway: "§ 2. The Evangelical-Lutheran religion shall remain the official religion of the State. The inhabitants professing it are bound to bring up their children in the same. Jesuits and Monastic Orders must not be tolerated. Jews are still excluded from admission to the Realm" (Andenæs 1989, 125. Trans. Ronald Walford).[2]

Perhaps it is not surprising that a colonial population with such a terror of others' beliefs would have to begin its own self-construction of an identity with an attempt to clarify its relationships with the metaphysical, with an evaluation of its worldview, and with an evaluation of its position with respect to the Other. I would suggest that the modern egalitarian, non-hierarchical nature of Norwegian society can at least partly be traced back to this nineteenth-century society, which had little to define itself against. After all, if Jews and Jesuits are not allowed and ethnic minorities are marginalized into a shadowy quasi-supernatural realm, then it is easy to see how the ubiquitous tenets of the "Jante Law" could have been codified as a type of societal "Ten Commandments" of identity (or lack thereof).[3]

But, in fact, the Norwegian *bonde* had been negotiating the boundary between self and Other for hundreds of years, and his folklore is a reflection of that ongoing process. It is my premise that the line between human and Other has *always* been difficult to determine in Scandinavian tradition, as is evident from the numerous examples of complicated shape-shifting, human/Gods interactions, and returns from the dead that are staples of Scandinavian mythology, and that this very ambiguity with respect to identity, in which the humanlike *huldrefolk* (so difficult to recognize) came to represent the ambiguity of Otherness, has evolved into a modern worldview which still struggles with identity.[4]

Since the folkloristic content of the stories in *Norske huldreeventyr og folkesagn* reflects a nineteenth century representation of how that worldview interpreted events of the inexplicable, a study of this content will reveal not only how the mid-century peasants viewed the Other, but also how they viewed themselves. In this scrutiny of the traditional material of the narratives, the schism between the constructed, idealized picture to be presented by the Norwegian literary canon of the proud and independent *bonde*, as typified by the work of Bjørnstjerne Bjørnson, and the representation of *huldreeventyr*, where the belief systems of this *bonde* are consciously critically evaluated and mediated by the frame narrator, should become even more evident.

It would certainly be possible to identify the traditional stories told by the folk narrators of *Norske huldreeventyr og folkesagn* by their tale type or motif index, as developed by Aarni/Thompson, and for the Norwegian migratory legends, by Reidar Christiansen, and many studies of Scandinavian texts which deal with traditional materials take precisely this structuralist approach; classifying by tale or motif type can be a helpful tool, however: "Without a clear understanding of the literary context in which these motifs function, such listings remain empty bits of information" (Bottigheimer 1987, x). If one agrees that Asbjørnsen was recreating narratives which reflected a worldview prevalent at his time, then a more useful approach would seem to be one in which the legendary material is examined to determine the integration of legend into the daily lives of the people to whom the folklore belonged.[5] Simply, why and how were these legends useful for the people who told them and listened to them? Reidar Christiansen echoes two of William Bascom's classic "four functions of folklore" elements when he writes about mythical legends. "They were told not as entertainment but as constantly renewed proof of the necessity not to deviate from the traditional code of behavior" (Christiansen, xxxv. Trans. Iversen). If this is so, which traditional codes of behavior did the legends reinforce for the mid-nineteenth-century Norwegian?[6]

While it could legitimately be argued that it is not possible to determine the content or function of the legendary material in *Norske huldreeventyr og folkesagn* precisely because Asbjørnsen recast the materials within a literary frame, it must be remembered that any telling or rendition of an oral narrative is simply *one* rendition, which will nevertheless conform to the basic skeletal structure of the story, the tale-type. Asbjørnsen, for example, however he may have embellished the style of a legend, or fused variants together for a better story, would never have changed a *nisse* to a *hulder*. "Folk narratives tend to exist in multiple versions" (Oring 1986, 123) and therefore a study of the manner in which Asbjørnsen utilizes the traditional material he collected can also reveal a great deal about the attitude of a representative of his station towards the *almue*. In the descriptions of the human interaction with the Other as recorded in *huldreeventyr*, it should be possible to isolate elements of a worldview, and while few would disagree with Lauri Honko's assertion that "tales cannot be used as primary material for the study of folk beliefs" (Honko 1989a, 105), it should nevertheless not be necessary, paraphrasing an old saying, to throw the changeling out with the bath water! Stories are remembered and told for a reason or reasons, and since legends change in response to history,[7] then the legendary material within *Norske huldreeventyr og folkesagn* represents tradition that was current in the mid-nineteenth century, and will reflect, if not a unified worldview, at least elements of an orientation to the world that can be studied both through the traditional material itself and through Asbjørnsen's use of it.

WHO TELLS THE STORIES?
DO CLASS AND GENDER MATTER?

In his article on supernatural and ethnic others, which was cited earlier, John Lindow concludes that, in Scandinavian legend tradition, "two of the major factors of intellectual discourse of the last century, class and gender, were apparently not much of an issue." Lindow continues:

> I cannot see that the supernatural beings or ethnic others of Scandinavian rural legend tradition or folk belief highlighted their social class or a class system or showed any particular interest in gender roles. This is not to say that these matters were not at issue. As Bengt Holbek verified (1987), they were probably central to fairy tales. How then could they be so absent from the emblems of identity? The reasoning followed here would suggest that crofters and peasants, day laborers and housewives, found in their situations more in common than in contrast. Only in the psychologically more expressive form of the fairy tale could they ventilate their differences. (Lindow, 27–28)

Could Lindow's conclusions apply to the stories of *Norske huldreeventyr og folkesagn* as well? Most of the *huldreeventyr* contain more than one legend, many contain three, four, or more. Since the narratives are retold by internal folk narrators, fragments also appear occasionally, much as in real storytelling situations, in which members of an audience may already be familiar with a story and only require hearing certain parts. As Kvideland and Sehmsdorf point out:

> Legends and folk beliefs were shared by everyone and were told and talked about under many different circumstances as an integral part of everyday life. This meant that stories were usually referred to or told only in an abbreviated

> form—everybody knew what they were all about.... It
> is often said that the legend has a firm, stereotyped form,
> but in fact the complete form is transmitted only in certain
> situations, for example, when the legend is told to someone
> who is not familiar with it, as mentioned earlier. More often
> the legend is referred to only summarily. According to Linda
> Dégh, the recital of the legend usually takes the form of a
> conversation. (Kvideland and Sehmsdorf 1988, 14, 18)

But because *Norske huldreeventyr og folkesagn* is a literary text, by far the largest number of legends in the stories are complete narratives, with a beginning, middle, and end. They are told by the created oral informant for the outsider, the frame narrator. Based on this criterion of a beginning, middle, and end, the twenty-seven *huldreeventyr* contain 117 distinct narratives, and when these narratives are examined based on selected criteria, several patterns emerge and questions of class and gender can be addressed.[8]

When he created the frames for the stories he had collected, Asbjørnsen selected characters and a milieu that would correspond to the type of legendary material that was being presented. Lauri Honko writes that

> tradition is not maintained by individuals but by social roles.
> The tradition of a fisherman is different from that of a cattle
> breeder; in learning a profession or role, people also learn the
> supernatural tradition connected with it. The same individual
> can occupy several social positions and roles, but only one
> is active at a time while others remain latent. Similarly a
> person can know various kinds of supernatural traditions, but
> the tradition that comes to mind in a situation is determined
> by his or her active role at the moment. (Honko 1989a,
> 105–106)

Asbjørnsen created folk narrators to tell the stories in the context in which they would be told naturally, and because the majority of the frame narrator's experiences take place in the world of the

Norwegian countryside, in a masculine world of hunting, fishing, and outdoor life, it is not surprising to find that the majority of the folk narrators Asbjørnsen created are male. Of the 117 narratives studied, eighty-five (seventy-three percent) are told by male folk narrators, and the protagonists of these stories are also overwhelmingly male. Do male folk narrators tell stories about male protagonists? Of the eighty-five stories told by male folk narrators, eighty-six percent deal primarily with male protagonists. Male folk narrators tell only seven stories with a female protagonist.[9] Of the twenty-seven stories told by female folk narrators, seventeen are about female main characters, while ten are about men. These are only statistics and do not in and of themselves offer any interpretive information because many of the stories, as previously indicated, take place primarily in the traditionally male-dominated environment of hunting and fishing. When stories are given an indoor setting, there is more likelihood of a female narrator. Some stories, such as "A Wise Woman" and "Berthe Tuppenhaug's Stories" include only female folk narrators. Legend shows that the woman's sphere is often, although not exclusively, in the private realm of the home. But what is of more interest is the relationship, or lack of one, between Asbjørnsen's created folk informants and the original source material, either oral or written, and the interrelationships between the human and the Other as reflected in the legends.

In his notes to *huldreeventyr* Knut Liestøl often discusses the provenance of legends included in each story, particularly if there is a question about the origin or if the legend is a compilation of several variants, which is sometimes the case. Liestøl's notes show that Asbjørnsen did not seem to be overly concerned with gender differentiation when creating his folk informants. The story "Legends of the Mill," contains three legends, all of which are narrated by male folk narrators. One of these legends, the story about a miller who defeats a mill spirit who has stopped his waterwheel by throwing hot pitch and tar into its mouth, is actually derived from a printed version which appeared in Andreas Faye's collection of Norwegian legends in 1833, while the second and third legends were told to Asbjørnsen by, respectively, "a girl from Drammen" and Camilla Collett. The story of a witch's daughter forced to demonstrate her dark powers by a Gudbrandsdal minister, related by the gravedigger in "The Gravedigger's Stories" was actually one that Asbjørnsen had heard from his mother, and the last legend in "A Summer Night in the Krok Forest," about a man who had been to the Bærum plant to pick up an enormous iron griddle, told by a lumberjack in the story, was transmitted to Asbjørnsen in one variant by Jørgen Moe's sister, Maren. Liestøl relates that Asbjørnsen was never able to record it exactly as she told it because "before she got halfway through the story, he was laughing so hard that he lost both the pen and the paper" (Liestøl, notes to A 2: 349). Lest one believe that Asbjørnsen was in some way deliberately marginalizing the women in his stories, or "silencing" the female voice, there is also an example of a story in "From the Mountains and the Dairies" that Asbjørnsen places in the mouth of Brit, a milkmaid, although he actually heard the tale from a Jakob Pladsen Brække (Liestøl, notes to A 1: 261). Examples abound of legends which Asbjørnsen heard from male informants that he attributes to different fictional male characters in the text. There are also other examples of legends that Asbjørnsen may have read in various written renditions, including one that appears in a play by Holberg (255). If Asbjørnsen was not particular about changing the gender of the storytellers, neither did he care much about class differences so far as the chain of transmission of the legends was concerned, so long as they had ultimately originated with the broad and encompassing "folk." While the overwhelming number of legends in Asbjørnsen's literary text are told by folk narrators of the working classes — although even this term hardly seems appropriate to a pre-industrial society such as Norway was — some of the legends were actually told or sent to Asbjørnsen by friends in the same literary circles as himself. What seems evident is that Asbjørnsen was primarily concerned with creating a plausible performance context for the legends he was preserving and creating a literary unity within each *huldreeventyr;* he was not particularly interested in class or gender issues except for the very clear contrast between the frame narrator and the folk narrators, a division that was actually based more on educational differences than on economic factors.[10] Does the folklore itself reflect a similar disinterest in class and gender?

"MAY GOD HELP US, IT'S THE PIXIE!"

If the crofters and peasants, day laborers and housewives, of *Norske huldreeventyr og folkesagn* found more in common than in contrast in their lives, it may have been because they were conscious of inhabiting one side of a sort of parallel universe with the folkloristic creatures of the Norwegian woods, fields, and mountains, the *huldre*, *nisser* and *underjordiske* inhabiting the other side. In his introduction to *Folktales of Norway*, Reidar Christiansen gives concise and helpful background information on the Norwegian "invisible" folk. Some of his observations may be helpful in understanding the various types of supernatural entities with which the people of *huldreeventyr* have to contend.

Christiansen explains that the legends which deal with man and unseen powers comprise the largest number of legends recorded in Norway and continues:

> Some kind of systematic arrangement is necessary for a survey of this mass of legends, and usually these beings—the term *spirits* may be misleading, as there is very little that is spiritual about them—are grouped according to the sphere of their activities, as spirits of the sea, of the air, of the hills and wilderness, and household spirits. An arrangement of this kind is similar to a zoologist's classification of animals, but does not take into sufficient account the fluidity, the interchange, of stories and motifs among these groups. . . . The classification of such "spirits" according to the sphere in which they operate is open to the qualification that the classes often overlap, so that one is left with the impression that all these beings belong to the same family. In the

> Norwegian tradition this family group is covered by the term *huldre*-folk, meaning the "hidden people." Equally common is the term *underjordiske*, meaning "those under the ground." They are also called *hauge*-folk, "people of the mounds, *berg*-folk" . . . meaning "people of the hills" and by other names as well. (Christiansen 1964, xxix, xxxiii. Christiansen's italics. Trans. Pat Shaw Iversen)

Although he stresses that there never was a systemization of beliefs, Christiansen also discusses the various theories of origin of these "invisible ones" such as that they

> were the children of Adam and his first wife or they were the children of Eve. Once, when our Lord came to see her, after they had been driven out of Eden, she had only washed some of her children. She hid the rest away. Our Lord knew this and decreed: "Those not revealed shall remain concealed." (*huldre*, from the verb *hylja*, meaning "to cover or conceal"). A third explanation is that they belonged to the party of angels that rebelled against our Lord and were driven out of Heaven. Some of them were not as bad as the rest and remained in the air between Heaven and Hell. Their ultimate salvation is an open question, but they are also said to have churches and clergymen of their own, and some of them are said to be so strict that they cannot stand to hear cursing or swearing. (xxxviii. Trans. Iversen)

It is evident that these explanations are of relatively recent date, as Christianity arrived in Norway around the year 1000, and they do not resolve the ultimate origin of belief in the spirits of the woods, fields, and mountains. Christiansen resolves this dilemma nicely by stating that "the problem is very difficult; no attempt can be made here to enter upon this discussion" (xxxviii. Trans. Iversen). And, indeed, neither need it concern the present one since we are interested in the nineteenth-century Norwegian rather than his pagan ancestor.[11] But one clue to the origin of the nineteenth-century view is clearly enunciated by Matthias in "Matthias the Hunter's Stories" when he responds to a question by the frame narrator regarding his belief in the *underjordiske*, " 'Well shouldn't I believe what can be read in the Scriptures?' he answered. 'When Our Father cast out the fallen angels, some fell to Hell, but those who hadn't sinned as badly, they are in the air and under the ground and in the sea, I know. And besides, I have often both heard and seen such in the forests and fields' " (A 1: 42). The belief in the *underjordiske* is, ironically enough, authorized and sanctified by the church![12] Complicating the cast of characters of the Otherworldly, or perhaps we should say under-worldly, inhabitants—is, as Christiansen notes, "the persistence of the ancient pagan conception of the nature of man. He is not conceived of as consisting of two elements, the one surviving on the destruction of the other, but remains himself, continuing in some way to live on and on, to remain live and active" (xxxviii. Trans Iversen). But in only a few legends of *Norske huldreeventyr og folkesagn* are humans confronted with these "living corpses." The men and women in Asbjørnsen's texts are much more likely to encounter a *hulder* or a *nisse* than they are ghosts. Who are the participants in these human versus Other encounters, and what are the outcomes of the interactions for both human actant and Other?

Of the 117 narratives told by the created folk informants in *Norske huldreeventyr og folkesagn*, all but eleven deal with some type of encounter with either an *underjordiske* of one kind or another, a magical item belonging to an *underjordiske*, shape-changing animals and humans, or the "living corpse."[13] Asbjørnsen, of course, was aware that all of these liminal creatures were called by various names throughout different parts of the country, and this is reflected in the stories. He makes no attempt to classify these beings at all, content to let the folk narrator simply tell the tale, using terms which would be used in the locale where the story is placed; hence, some tales will refer to *underjordiske*, others to *haugfolk*. Regardless of name, their situations are similar: they live under or in the stable, in a mountain, or under a farmhouse; they move with their livestock into the mountain dairies in the fall when the humans leave. They have, for the most part, a similar family structure as the human (except for the *nisse*, who lives alone in close proximity to people, either guarding the stable animals or making sure that proper schedules are kept in the house); they have parties and weddings and church services, reflecting the interests and occupations of the human as if in a mirror. But there is something "not quite right" about them. And, traditionally, they are normally unseen unless the human in some fashion violates their "space" or in some other way interferes with their activities, or, conversely, when the Other deliberately tries to lure the human into his world, for there is evidently nothing more desirable for the Other than a sexual relationship with the human, and the human in turn is often fatally attracted to the lures of the beautiful *hulder*.

As has been noted, the vast majority of the human beings who encounter the supernatural in the stories of *huldreeventyr* are the rural, relatively uneducated men of the fields and forests, workmen of all types. The creatures they encounter, however, are a more varied assortment. Gender designations of the Other are very specific in most instances. A *nisse* is always male, while the term *hulder* generally refers to a female. The devil and *troll* are male, but the *trollkjerring* is female. The *underjordiske* or *haugfolk* as a collective comprise both male and female members, and, in some cases, the human encounter is with an entire group of *underjordiske*, either on their way to a mountain pasture or a wedding. Sometimes the *underjordiske* are encountered inside the mountain or under the ground where they have their dwellings.

Fully a third of the encounters between the human and the Other in the 117 narratives of *Norske huldreeventyr og folkesagn* result in an escape from danger by the human, or no particular outcome at all; a man may see a *hulder*, or a milkmaid may see the *nisse*, but *nothing happens*, except for this human recognition that the Other has been in his/her midst. The recognition is not usually instantaneous. On the other hand, when harm of one kind or another is inflicted, the Other is equally as likely to be injured in some fashion by the encounter with the human as the human is to suffer at the hands of the Other. Usually the injury is of a minor nature; a person may be *huldrin* [driven half-witted] for a period of time, or a *hulder* may have her tail pulled off. In many cases, a symbiotic relationship seems to exist between the human and the Other, with benefit to both parties.

The truly serious consequences are visited upon the human-turned-Other: the witch or *trollkjerring*. Transgressing this boundary is one which must be severely punished, and this group of legends distinguishes itself by the dire consequences faced by the *trollkjerring* when her true identity is made known.[14] It is evident that these stories rely on the memories of the witch trials of the seventeenth century, since the witches are often burned. What is particularly interesting in the *trollkjerring* stories, however, is the identity of the witch; she is nearly always a woman of some consequence in the community, often the wife of the minister.[15] This feature of the witch legends illustrates the ambivalent attitude in Norwegian tradition towards the teachings of the Lutheran church; the minister himself may very well have learned how to exorcize the devil, according to legend, from the "Black Book" school in Wittenburg.[16] While there appear a certain resentment and suspicion within the legend tradition on the part of the *almue* towards any members of the government-appointed *embets* class, which would include the clergy, this suspicion and resentment are greatly outweighed by the primary concern, which is outwitting the Other.

Because of the sheer volume of stories in *Norske huldreeventyr og folkesagn* it is not feasible to consider more than a few narratives in detail, and since one of the most intriguing elements in the Scandinavian legend tradition is the remarkable fluidity of the boundary between the inner and outer groups, the difficulty which the human often has in recognizing the Other in his midst, we will concentrate on several examples that illustrate this characteristic, some related stories that show the integration of the Other into the inner group, and finally on what behaviors these stories may have reinforced for the nineteenth-century population. If the modern Norwegian has difficulty in defining what it means to be *norsk*, it may be because his national narratives, including *Norske huldreeventyr og folkesagn*, have taught the Norwegian that making the distinction between self and Other, the inner and outer realm, is fraught with complexity, and that things are never quite the way they may seem.

The boundary between the human and the Other is remarkably fluid in Norwegian legend tradition, due to the ability of the *underjordiske* to shape-shift, even taking on the semblance of the human, and the corresponding ability of the human *trollkjerring* to change her shape as well. In addition, changelings and marriage with the *hulder* bring the Other into the inner realm, just as *bergtakning* brings the human into the realm of the Other. In one of the legends told in "Berthe Tuppenhaug's Stories," a young man arrives just in time to save his intended bride, who is at the mountain dairy, from being married to an *underjordiske* man. As

> she was sitting in the cabin one afternoon, it seemed to her that her sweetheart came and sat down with her and started to talk about that it was time to have the wedding. But she sat quite still and did not answer at all, because she felt rather queer. By and by more and more people arrived, and they started to set the table with silverware and food, and bridesmaids carried in a crown and finery and a fine wedding gown, which they dressed her in, and they put the crown, which they used at that time, on her head, and they put rings on her fingers.

But, just in time, the proper bridegroom arrives, "'What is the meaning of all this?' he said, 'Why you're sitting here dressed as a bride!' 'Why would you ask me that?' said the girl. 'You've been sitting here all afternoon talking about the wedding.' 'No, *I* just came,' he said, 'but it must have been someone who assumed my appearance'" (A 1: 59, 60, italics in original).[17] This legend is widespread in Norway. In this variant, the young man is alerted by the girl's dog that something is amiss. Animals were thought to recognize the Other more easily than humans could do so, but, at the same time, the Other, particularly the devil and witches, could appear in the guise of animals as well. Most often the *underjordiske*, however, *looks* just like everyone else. It is in its *actions* that the Other is recognized. In "Legends of the Mill," a poor woman is allowed access to a mill at night in order to grind a small amount of grain. As she is sitting there, another woman arrives and greets her. There is no indication that anything is amiss until the *underjordiske* woman begins raking the coals around on the hearth to put out the fire. Even ghosts, which appear rarely in *huldreeventyr*, are not immediately recognizable. The old woman in "An Old-fashioned Christmas Eve" observes the other worshippers and thinks that "the people all looked so pale and strange, exactly as if they all could have been dead. There wasn't anyone she knew, but there were many she thought she had seen before, but she couldn't remember where she had seen them. When the minister climbed to the pulpit, it wasn't any of the ministers in the town, but rather a tall, pale man, whom she also thought she should know" (A 1: 118). Only when the woman beside her on the pew speaks to her does the old woman recognize her as a neighbor who had died long ago.

If the supernormal creatures can be difficult to recognize, they nevertheless sometimes carry Lindow's "emblems of contrast" by which they can be identified by the alert human being. The *hulder* normally has the tail of a cow, which she tries to conceal beneath her skirt;[18] the *nisse* usually wears a red stocking cap and has furry hands with no thumbs; the devil wears gloves to hide his claws. Sometimes the human is able to recognize the Other in time to avert calamity, at other times elaborate tricks are involved in order to get the supernatural to show his true colors. The changeling legends, for example, often stress the difficulty of determining whether or not an infant is truly a changeling. Only when this has been proven beyond a reasonable doubt, usually by getting the creature to talk or to laugh by means of some trickery, can the proper steps, involving mistreatment of some kind, be taken to gain the return of the real child.

If the changeling legends illustrate situations of an unwilling human/Other relationship, the opposite is true in those legends in which the human falls in love with a *hulder* and marries her.[19]

While the *hulder* is often very beautiful at first sight, this illusion does not usually persist after the wedding, at least in the variants that Asbjørnsen utilizes. The *hulder*, however, has another and more permanent attribute: she is terribly strong. In "An Evening in the Squire's Kitchen," the last story told by the blacksmith concerns a young man who has heard of the great beauty of a *hulder* girl who moves into his family's mountain dairy in the fall, after the people leave. One year he determines to see the girl and rides back to the *seter* after the *underjordiske* have moved in. He is mesmerized by her beauty and is determined to have her, so shoots a shot over her head, which should put her in his power. Her beauty disappears at once, but he is ordered by her parents to take her and marry her, and promised that he shall not want for anything. They are married and whenever her parents visit, he always finds a great quantity of money, but "ugly she was and ugly she stayed, and he was fed up with her, and it can't be denied that he was a little mean to her once in a while, in that he hit her and gave her a thrashing" (A 1: 80).[20] One day the man is attempting to shoe a horse, but try as hard as he may, he is unable to get the shoe to fit, and most of the day passes by. Finally his wife says that she will fit the shoe, and if it is too big or too little, he can correct it. The story concludes:

> She went to the smithy, and the first thing she did was grab the shoe with both hands and straighten it out.
> "Look here," she said, "This is how you do it." Then she bent it together, as if it had been made of lead. "Hold up the foot," she said, and the shoe fit so perfectly that the very best blacksmith could not have done it better.
> "You've got pretty strong fingers," the husband said, and looked at her.
> "Do you think so?" she said, "What do you think had happened to me, if your hands had been as strong? But I love you too much to use my strength against you," she said.
> From that day on, he was a different man towards her. (81)[21]

Another story of marriage to a *hulder* is told in "The Hulder Clan" when the frame narrator attempts to woo the young folk narrator. She discourages his advances by claiming descent from the *hulder*; as she exclaims, "'What do you want of me? My God! Do you know what you are risking?' she said. 'You know my family! Surely you know that I am descended from *hulderfolk*, and that the blood of trolls runs in my veins?'" The girl then begins her story, "My great grandmother or great-great grandmother was a real *hulder*, you know" (A 1: 88).[22] Again in this story, the husband has not always treated his *hulder* wife as well as he could have, and he also receives a demonstration of her remarkable strength:

> When it was almost autumn and the cabbages were big, then the wife was going to chop and prepare for slaughtering, but she didn't have a chopping board or a chopping trough. She asked her husband to take the axe and go up the mountain and chop down the big pine tree that stood beside the bog on the way to the mountain dairy; she wanted it for a chopping trough.
>
> "I think you're nuts, woman," the man said. "Should I chop down the best tree in the logging woods to make a trough? And how would I get it down from the mountain at this time of year, it's so enormous that no horse would be able to drag it?"
>
> She asked him to do it anyway, but when he absolutely refused, she took the axe, went up into the woods, chopped down the tree and carried it home on her back. When her husband saw this, he was so frightened that he never again dared to oppose her, or do anything other than what she asked, and from then on there was complete harmony between them. (91–92)[23]

These stories illustrate the need to be cautious in dealings with the Other, whether known or unknown; this is a trait which some might claim to recognize in the modern Norwegian, but do they not also reflect a typically Nordic sensibility of gender equality and egalitarian ideals?

The amorous advances of the frame narrator in this story are effectively quelled when the girl concludes her story, "You can figure out what to expect if you really make me angry" (92).[24] The frame narrator is unable to enter into the magic world of the *hulder* and the *nisse* except as an observer. The negotiation of the boundary between the human and the Other must be constructed by those to whom the stories belong, and since this boundary is so fluid and flexible, it must be vigilantly guarded. It can be argued that the *hulder* marriage stories indicate situations where the Other holds the upper hand over the human, but I would suggest instead that in a society where the Other is often hard to identify, and where the boundary between human and supernatural is fluid and shifting, legend serves as a cautionary device. When one considers that in legend the Black Death is often personified as an old woman sweeping or raking, it is certainly not too far-fetched to conjecture that the hulder with her cow's tail but great strength can also represent the forces of a nature domesticated but still dangerous and unpredictable. The hulder bride's emblems of contrast are contradictory. Her tail is that of a domestic animal generally considered to be gentle and unthreatening. Here is nature at its most tranquil. When the hulder demonstrates her other emblem of contrast, she takes the man by surprise with her great strength. A cautionary reminder to the human that one must be ever vigilant in dealing with the natural world, even when domesticated. So the *hulder* marriage legends exert a reinforcement of the non-hierarchical Norwegian worldview and maintain harmony in a society where the division of labor and community stability depends on a cooperation between the physically stronger and the "keeper of the keys."

Øystein Holter writes of the comparative lack of authoritarianism in personal relationships in Norway and traces this lack to the fact that Norway was never a feudal country with a feudal social order. He writes that

> Norwegians lived spread out across the land, with each farm or *gård* as a self-owned and (to a great extent) self-governing

unit. This had been the case also in Viking times, and in other Germanic areas as well, but in Norway the pattern survived. Local political authority retained the sense of "first among peers" typical of kinship societies—again very different from the feudal sense of authority deriving from pope or king.... The relatively "public" character of the Norwegian family can probably be connected to the relative importance of the household, compared to other institutions of society. In one sense the household was everywhere the main institution, up until the industrial revolution, since it was the primary producing unit.... In the Norwegian tradition, the power of the household and of women as main producers within the household was symbolized by the *gård* wife's key to the *stabbur* [store house]. This power was usually connected to a comparative lack of strong male institutions surrounding the household. Here is another pattern with modern-day connections: German men visit the Bierstube, the British go to the pub, etc.—Norwegians, however, go home. (Holter 1993, 151–52).

It appears that the behavior being reinforced in the legendary material in *Norske huldreeventyr og folkesagn* for the most part is that which stabilizes the rural society, particularly through emphasis on the importance of the institution of marriage and the rite of baptism. Several examples illustrate how legend underscores the importance of the home in pre-industrial Norwegian society.[25] After the farm girl was rescued by her boyfriend from the mountain dairy wedding, "he took her right down to the settlement, and so that she wouldn't be subject to any more foolishness, they had the wedding right away, while she was still wearing the wedding finery of the underground people. The crown and all the other finery was hung up at Melbustad and it is said to be there to this day" (A 1: 61).[26] A new family is formed and the stability of the community against the wiles of the Other is restored. Women were in danger from other-worldly forces at any time they were on the boundary between one stage of life and another, especially in the liminal states of engagement, pregnancy, and birth. A legend in the story "The Lund Family" reinforces the importance of a public and concrete manifestation of intention on the part of a man when he has decided to marry. In this story, the woman was taken by the *underjordiske* during childbirth:

> It was the underground people who took her, and they had been after her for a long time before that too, because when they had the engagement party for her at Lier, they took her and set her head-down in a water vat, but there were so many people out in the farmyard that she didn't come to any harm; and then a voice from the mound over by the storehouse said that it happened because she didn't have an engagement ring. But since that time, every worthless wench who has a fellow walks around with an engagement ring. (A 1: 104)[27]

Ostensibly a symbol of protection against the Other, in actuality an engagement ring takes a private agreement into the public sphere, thereby reinforcing the stability of the community.

As has already been noted in the discussion of "The Wise Woman," it was considered imperative that a child be baptized as soon as possible. While legend reinforces this rite as a safeguard against a child being exchanged by the *underjordiske*, it had long been a requirement of early Scandinavian church law. An unbaptized child was a heathen, and, in times of high infant mortality, it was imperative that an infant not die in this state. Baptism was considered so critical in the early church that in the Christian Laws section of the early laws of Iceland, the *Grágás*, the first section gives detailed instructions on how, when, and by whom baptism can be performed, with penalties of outlawry if the baptism is not performed correctly. But whether as a defense against the powers of the Other or as a church ritual, *what really happens* with baptism, of course, is a public and official recognition of paternity—a critical stabilizing factor in most societies. It appears likely that Lindow is correct when he says that class and gender were apparently not much of an issue in rural Scandinavian legend tradition; of importance was "resolution of conflict, the elimination of the threat and restoration of the status quo" (Lindow 1995, 28). In the legends of *Norske huldreeventyr og folkesagn* what was important was the recognition of, and negotiation with, the Other.

THE MODERN NORWEGIAN AND THE LEGEND TRADITION

Can we draw any conclusions about modern Norwegian society, and the difficulty Norwegians have defining *norskhet*, from this brief survey of the problems nineteenth-century rural peasants sometimes had in recognizing friend and foe? Is there a continuity in worldview?

In his study of the modern Danish urban legend as it has evolved from earlier legend tradition, Timothy Tangherlini asserts that the distinction between inside/outside was easily made in agrarian nineteenth-century Denmark. Outside consisted of areas outside the immediate farm house and buildings, and community membership was easy to ascertain. I would suggest that, in agrarian Norway, nothing could be further from the truth, and that Tangherlini's assertion bears reconsidering in Danish legend tradition as well. In a time when natural forces were poorly understood, living conditions quite primitive, and things were often not quite what they seemed, it must have appeared as though the Other was never far away, and that the boundary was not nearly so easily determined as Tangherlini says. A child would fall ill, a woman would disappear, a man would perhaps go "berserk" and the frightened on-lookers would find themselves looking into the eyes of the Other.[28] It would seem evident, contrary to Tangherlini's observation, that the distinction between the insider and the outsider is far easier to make in modern society than in a time when the supernatural was an integral element. Tangherlini shows how the supernatural Other has been replaced with the ethnic Other in contemporary Danish urban legend:

> With the advent of scientific scepticism, universal education and the move away from rural lifestyles, folk belief concerning trolls, elves, and witches declined. Concomitantly, the need for actants to assume the newly vacated legend functions appeared. With the marked change in Danish demographics, primarily the influx of large numbers of Asians and southern Europeans in the 1960s and 1970s (Danmarks statistik 1961–1984), the immigrants and minority populations were the logical culturally relevant replacement. (Tangherlini 1995, 34)

It is likely that a similar process is occurring within the Norwegian legend tradition. The ethnic Other has also replaced the supernatural Other in contemporary Norwegian society: "Today a Norwegian living in Oslo is likely to ride to work in a tram-car driven by an Indian man, buy fruit for lunch from a Vietnamese woman, have his office cleaned by an Albanian family, and shop for daily provisions from his local Pakistani grocer. In many ways, it can be said that immigrants are integrated in Norwegian society" (Long 1993, 191). Integrated, perhaps, but not considered really *norsk*, if Julian Kramer is correct in his assessment that Norwegian identity depends on regional origin, a type of tribal identity marker in a society with a long colonial history where it is impossible for ethnic groups of foreigners to be accepted as Norwegian especially if

> they insist upon cultural symbols which emphasize their non-Norwegian origins. It has become possible for individual Sami to be accepted as quasi-Norwegian despite their Sami background. But being Sami will never be a variant of being Norwegian along the same lines as being a trønder, a hedmarking, a telemarking and so on. This is even more forcefully so for ethnic minorities with a skin color that identifies non-Norwegian ancestry. In other words, there cannot exist a category of black Norwegian—at least not the way Norway is today with Norwegian identity tied to origin. (Kramer 1984, 95–96)

But Kramer sees reason for optimism: more people are growing up in cities and seeing them as their hometowns, it will soon be possible to speak of a generation of Norwegians who have not experienced a colonized or occupied Norway, more third-world children are being adopted and brought up as Norwegians. A more cosmopolitan definition of *norskhet* is possible.[29]

It is intriguing to consider that had the Norwegian nineteenth-century literary canon tolerated pluralism, perhaps the national narrative could have grown to include all the voices, the voices of the Other inhabitants who have always occupied Norway along with the Norwegian *bonde*: the Sami and the Finn, the wise-woman and the Gypsies, the Germans of the Hanseatic League, the immigrants in the mines, Danes and Swedes, and other early immigrants. Norwegian identity need not have been the narrowly defined construct it somehow became, based on a tribal regionalism, because the *real* Norwegian is, after all, not a *bonde* in a *lusekofte*, a mythical figure created by a small group of nation-builders, but rather a complex human being who has struggled with his harsh natural world and with its demons, real and imagined, for hundreds of years. If the modern Norwegian is facing an identity crisis, it may very well be because he is finally confronted with the Other, against whom identity is shaped, in a concrete *human* representation, with readily recognizable emblems of contrast, rather than by the often murky illusiveness of an ambiguous supernatural Other as represented by the *hulder* and her relatives that one meets in the Norwegian legend tradition and in the pages of *Norske huldreeventyr og folkesagn*.

CHAPTER 7

From Danish to Dialect:
The Myriad Voices of
Norske huldreeventyr og folkesagn

> What the eye is to the lover . . . language—whatever language history has made his or her mother tongue—is to the patriot. Through that language, encountered at mother's knee and parted with only at the grave, pasts are restored, fellowships are imagined, and futures dreamed.
>
> —Benedict Anderson

THE SHARED WRITTEN LANGUAGE

In August of 1858, when she was twenty-two years old, Elise Aars noted in her diary the visit to the Lom parsonage, where her father was pastor, of a party of gentlemen including a young man from Copenhagen named Trier. Before the development of the modern roads and railroads, and the tourist industry of modern Norway, the country parsonages were often almost hotels for various travelers who would arrive with letters of introduction from a shared acquaintance. The travelers would be housed and fed, and, in turn, would bring welcome news from the outside world to those living the restricted and quiet country life. Trier was a lively conversationalist who regaled the assembly with stories of life and people in the big city. And although Elise, whose journals and letters reveal a great deal about mid-century Norwegian life amongst the *kondisjonerte*, thoroughly enjoyed hearing about H. C. Andersen and Ingeman, Hertz and Christian Winther, she could not but lament, "Alt dette kunde været meget moersomt om vi blot ikke havde faaet det at vide paa Dansk; men o Himle, hvilket Sprog det dog er! Saa blødt, saa vammelt, saa smagløst, saa ganske uden Kraft og Kjerne, at det i en Herres Mund formelig tager sig eekelt ud!" (Aubert 1921, 68) [All this would have been hugely entertaining if we just had not had to hear it in Danish; but oh, heavens, what a language it is! So soft, so nauseating, so tasteless, so completely without strength and tonal quality, that in a gentleman's mouth it is actually revolting].[1]

There is a delicious irony in Elise Aubert's words, of course, since the written language she used—had to use—to express these very Norwegian words, was none other than the despised Danish. The English speaker is familiar with the variations in pronunciation between, for example, Oxford and American English; but those differences pale in comparison to the way a Dane and a Norwegian would read the passage cited above. The linguist Einar Haugen explains the various linguistic changes Danish has undergone in comparison with the other Scandinavian languages. These changes have caused Danish to "reduce the 'body' of its words," replaced the tongue-trilled *r* with an uvular one, and "When we add to this that the central Scandinavian tones of Norwegian and Swedish have been replaced by glottalization, leaving what sounds vaguely like a hiccup in a word like *mand*, it is not surprising that other Scandinavians find Danish difficult to understand when spoken" (Haugen 1976, 39). To the Norwegian, a Dane speaks as though he has porridge in his mouth, words disappearing into undifferentiated sounds in the throat, so it is perhaps not surprising that Elise Aubert would have been repelled by the speech of the visitor from Copenhagen; nonetheless, in their written forms Danish and Norwegian *bokmål* are virtually the same language, even today.[2]

The story of centuries of this shared written language, and subsequent attempts to shape a truly Norwegian written language after 1814, can be said to constitute the loom on which the threads of Norwegian national identity are woven, because without a written language there can be no national identity at all, nor any way to express its narratives. "The most important instrument for the creation of a national consciousness is the vernacular" (Jusdanis 1991, 41). But what happens to a national consciousness if its vernacular is a babble of various dialects, or a created language, rather than a true regional dialect accepted as the norm? Does not the Norwegian search for *norskhet* reflect a splintered national personality, as reflected in its splintered language situation? Does Norwegian national identity depend so much on the "place" of a physical geography because the symbolic "space" has not yet been completely appropriated through one unified written language? Certainly the complexity of the Norwegian language situation both historically and in the present must be seen as a contributing factor, probably the critical factor, in the modern Norwegian's identity crisis.

A complex of historical circumstances in the late Middle Ages led to the virtual disintegration of the old written Norwegian language after 1370:

> In Norway, the strong fermentation in the language in the 1300s and 1400s coincided with a political, economic, and cultural depression. In other Germanic countries, the foundations for the modern written languages were laid in this linguistic age of conflict. Norway did not have such a development; the unifying factors were too weak to allow a new official language to grow out of the Norwegian dialects.
>
> Had the written language been allowed to develop in peace and quiet, it is reasonable to suppose that it would have incorporated the new characteristics in the spoken language to the extent that we would have gotten a new, modern *Norwegian* written language. But development went a different way: the Norwegian written language came to an end, Danish crept in as the written language and took root here. (Leitre, Lundeby, and Torvik 1975, 80. Italics in original)

In 1380 Norway entered into a union with Denmark in which the former country was the weaker party. The seat of government was Copenhagen, and the language of the official bureaucracy was Danish. Norway was entering into what some have called its "400-year night," a time of Danish dominance.[3] When this union came to an end in 1814, the task was to build a Norwegian language based on the national romantic idea of a previous golden age of Norwegian language, a Norwegian that was unsullied by foreign corruption. There was disagreement on how the written Norwegian language could best be renewed to reflect the Norwegian pronunciation, rather than Danish. A more conservative, gradual change in the written language towards Norwegian pronunciation was favored by many, including its leading proponent Knud Knudsen. But a brilliant young linguist, Ivar Aasen, *created* a Norwegian language based on the dialects of western Norway, those most closely related to the revered classic old Norse. This *nynorsk* [new Norwegian] language was adopted as an official language in 1885, and since that time Norwegian school districts have been able to choose whether *nynorsk* or the modified Dano-Norwegian *bokmål* [book language] is to be their primary language. The struggle between *nynorsk* and *bokmål* proponents has only in recent years begun to ebb, with the vast majority of Norwegians preferring *bokmål* as their language of choice, but the subject still occasions controversy and is by no means a static one.[4] Whether *bokmål* or *nynorsk* will eventually grow closer together into a kind of *samnorsk* [pan-Norwegian] now seems unlikely. Jørgen Haugan, a proponent of *bokmål*, shows how the "400-year night" myth was created during the nineteenth century as a part of the national romanticism movement as a reaction against Denmark and the Danish language, and how the rise of *nynorsk* was tied to the rise of the political left and its denial of 400 years of shared literary history. Haugan writes:

> Ivar Aasen lived in Christiania, and while he shaped his *landsmål*—in the form of a scientific reconstruction of a spoken dialect-based language with Old Norwegian as the frame of reference—he himself wrote and spoke an affected, bookish Danish his whole life.
>
> Historically speaking, the history of this *landsmål* language is the account of the Norwegian linguistic dispute. It is important to point out that the origin of the *landsmål*

movement was much more peaceful. *Landsmål* is the product of the embets culture, which not only made Ivar Aasen's collection work possible, but also warmly supported it. And this same culture-bearing officialdom welcomed Ivar Aasen's results with joy and with pride because the spirit of the age was national romantic and the style-setters were in the midst of a national collecting of folklore: folk tales, ballads and dialects. The whole effort was a national mobilization to give Norway a glorious historic past. (Haugan 1991, 40–41)

And Norway's glorious historic past was to be chronicled through a new written language! The story of Norway's struggle for this new written language is the story of Norway's struggle for a national identity. The threads of nature, folklore, and ethnicity are interwoven in the language, a complex *gobelin* of Danish, *landsmål*, *riksmål*, and Dano-Norwegian *bokmål*. Of course Norway today does not have a unified written language; it has two: *nynorsk* and *bokmål*, and its citizens learn both, although they select one to be their primary language. Residents of some areas of Northern Norway can also elect to have their instruction in the Sami language. The elite who welcomed the development of Ivar Aasen's *nynorsk* was followed by a strong intellectual and academic faction of Norwegian society which was able to gain the *nynorsk* language an equal footing by 1885 and continued to exert influence far beyond its numbers up to, and including, the present day.[5] This influence was intensified by a number of talented poets and novelists who wrote in *nynorsk*. During much of the twentieth century, to be in favor of *nynorsk* was for many synonymous with patriotism; the defenders of *riksmål* were somehow seen as less patriotic, not as *norsk*, simply because they defended the written language they had always used, the language in which they wrote and the language in which they read many of the classics of nineteenth-century Norwegian literature, the language which was not Danish to them, but Norwegian. Perhaps surprisingly, this faction often included the very element one would expect to favor *nynorsk*: the common people. In the post World War II era,

"Many intellectuals converted to *nynorsk* in solidarity with 'the people,' who, however, preferred *bokmål,* as they always have!" (Haugan, 29).

The view that it is in some ways unpatriotic or elitist to prefer *bokmål* is no longer current, but the result of the struggle between *riksmål* and *nynorsk* is a society with a splintered written tradition, and therefore a society which is a great deal more pluralistic than many may wish to believe.[6] The infancy of this pluralistic language situation, and the controversy of how Norwegian was to be written to conform to its spoken sounds, is illustrated in microcosm in the pages of *Norske huldreeventyr og folkesagn* and in its reception, for "Asbjørnsen begins the development that in quite a short time gives our language a new character" (Christensen 1905, 223).

As has been mentioned, Asbjørnsen himself edited and revised the editions of *huldreeventyr* through and including the 1870 edition, and while the changes in the story content were few (one example is the altered ending of "A Wise Woman"), he did make significant changes in orthography and phrasing, continuing the *fornorsking* [Norwegianization] of the language in both vocabulary and form of expression.[7] A detailed study of particularly the orthographic changes is presented in *Asbjørnsen's Linguistic Reform*. In this work Daniel Popp forms several interesting conclusions which once again point to the importance that *Norske huldreeventyr og folkesagn* has had in the development of a Norwegian national identity, in this case the very essence of that identity, the language itself. Popp analyzes Asbjørnsen's linguistic changes with the aid of computer technology and writes in his concluding remarks:

> On the one hand, it seems necessary to allege that Asbjørnsen's revised orthography played a significant role in the emergence of the first set of orthographic norms for *bokmål*. In fact, until further evidence is gathered, in the first stage of its existence the orthography which developed for *bokmål* deserves to be called Asbjørnsen's own. The more important point is, on the other hand, that here we do have

compelling evidence that the individual writer stood behind much of what took place as orthographically *bokmål* became *bokmål*. (Popp 1977, 96)[8]

While the minute and detailed comparisons necessary for this evaluation are interesting in and of themselves, are valuable contributions to the linguistic study of the development of the modern Norwegian language, and illustrate the importance of *Norske huldreeventyr og folkesagn* in this development, it is not necessary to summarize them here. Popp is not alone in his assessment of Asbjørnsen's importance to the development of Norwegian. Arnulf Øverland, in writing of Bjørnstjerne Bjørnson, says, "He is probably the man, along with Asbjørnsen, who has had the greatest influence on the development of our language" (Øverland 1967, 50). Important though the linguistic aspects of Asbjørnsen's work may be, of greater interest in our context is how he, through opening a written dialogue between the formal Danish and the spoken dialects, actually created a new multi-layered discourse, a step in the development of a truly modern Norwegian prose. Writing of Asbjørnsen's *huldreeventyr* and its place within a national romanticism based on the realism called for by the 1830s intelligentsia, Lilly Heber explains that even Jørgen Moe was not fully aware of the text's importance: "J. Moe was so preoccupied by the poetic and especially the scholarly problems that national romanticism posed for Norwegian cultural life that he did not see the epoch-making work that Asbjørnsen started for the development of Norwegian prose, the short story and novel" (Heber 1914, 252).

Of course Asbjørnsen was not the first to try to write the Norwegian language the way it was spoken. It had been attempted, with greater or lesser success, by a number of writers before him, primarily in the genre of poetry. Norway's first novelist, Maurits Hansen, had even included a few dialect words in some of his short stories and novels. And of course Asbjørnsen and Moe themselves had been very concerned with giving the *Norske folkeeventyr* a truly Norwegian character, and it is the joint follk tale collection that is usually given so much credit for the *fornorsking* of the language, away from Danish to a more Norwegian mode of expression. And certainly the *folkeeventyr* richly deserve their reputation in this regard, but important as they undoubtedly are, the fairy tales, distinctly Norwegian in character as they may well be, still mainly take place in the unlocalized never-never land of atemporality. The voices of *Norske huldreeventyr og folkesagn*, in contrast, are often the voices of the mid-nineteenth century Norwegian farmer, crofter, or dairymaid of a specific locality, voices in a regional dialect, localized in time and place. What was different in the *huldreeventyr* was the realism with which the speech was represented, growing as it did not out of lyric rhapsody, the magic world of fairy tales, or a dark and demonic romanticism, but out of specific situations in the daily lives of the people as they told their stories.

This is not to suggest that the internal narratives in *Norske huldreeventyr og folkesagn* were written in one or another of the Norwegian dialects as we know them today. What Asbjørnsen did do was to attempt to reproduce the speech of many of the created folk narrators in writing, with the aid of others who were more familiar with the speech forms than he himself was. Ivar Aasen, for example, helped Asbjørnsen with the language of western Norway, particularly that found in the story "From the Sognefjord." What Asbjørnsen began in *huldreeventyr* with its polyphonic language of urban frame and internal folk narration was to expand the dialogue between *riksmål* and *landsmål*, and in so doing, he created an open-ended work of multi-layered discourse subject to diverse interpretation. "To allow characters to speak with their own social, regional and individual accents . . . is to make interpretive closure in the absolute sense impossible" (Lodge 1990, 23).

THE LANGUAGE OF THE NOVEL

What was the Norwegian reading public reading when *Norske huldreeventyr og folkesagn* appeared in its first edition in 1845? Religious writings of all types were the most read during the first part of the nineteenth century. Later, many read German novels in translation; but by 1830 Walter Scott was the author whose books were most often borrowed from the lending libraries, and by 1850 translations from English dominated. Dickens was very popular. Most intellectuals and literary critics bemoaned the lack of homegrown creative activity in this genre. "There were few Norwegian novels to choose from, and none of them were good." Norwegians were searching for a modern Norwegian novel, and this appeared first with Camilla Collett's *Amtmandens Døtre* [The Governor's Daughters] published anonymously in 1854. (Beyer and Beyer 1978, 168, 169). Camilla Collett served part of her literary apprenticeship collaborating with Asbjørnsen on several of the *huldreeventyr*.

Camilla Collett and her husband Peter Jonas Collett were friends of Asbjørnsen and that Camilla helped to write parts of the *huldreeventyr* is mentioned by Asbjørnsen himself in the forward to the 1859 edition, in which he acknowledged that Camilla had written most of the introductory frame for "The Gravedigger's Stories" and the introduction to "From the Mountains and the Dairies." P. J. Collett was a strong advocate for the establishment of a realistic and modern Norwegian literary tradition and had encouraged Asbjørnsen in his review of the first collection of *huldreeventyr* to give more attention to the frames of the stories and to give the folk narrators more individuality. He encouraged Asbjørnsen to create a more perfect synthesis between the traditional material and the frame narration. Writing of P. J. Collett's review and of the collaboration between Camilla Collett and Asbjørnsen, Lilly Heber states:

> Here it is the determined advocate for the Norwegian novel and short story, who deflects national romanticism in a realistic direction, so that it will serve the growth of the entire national literature, not just a branch of it. . . . Collett knew what he was doing; he had himself experienced that such a synthesis was possible: where Asbjørnsen's ability to creatively frame the huldreeventyr faltered, his [Collett's] wife had obligingly stepped in, precisely in those years when she

herself was groping for a form for her own creative instincts. In cooperation with Asbjørnsen she found a temporary expression for this and in return she learned Norwegian-ness from Asbjørnsen. (Heber 1914, 254)[9]

Norskhet. What Camilla Collett learned from Asbjørnsen was no less than *Norwegian-ness,* and a large part of this *norskhet* was the representation of the speech of the folk informants in dialogue with the speech of the frame narrator. This is the polyphonic discourse of the novel.

Of course, *Norske huldreeventyr og folkesagn* is not itself a novel; it can more properly be called a series of short stories, connected by common themes and literary structures, with folklore as the subject matter. But the text contains the three elements of discourse which Bakhtin has shown to be particular to the novel: the direct speech of the author, the represented speech of the characters, and doubly oriented or doubly voiced speech that is parody (Lodge 1990, 21). And if the novel genre is itself, as Bakhtin claims, a developing genre of "becoming," then *Norske huldreeventyr og folkesagn* can be seen as part of an ongoing process in the development of the modern Norwegian novel. "The boundaries between fiction and nonfiction, between literature and non-literature and so forth are not laid up in heaven. Every specific situation is historical. And the growth of literature is not merely development and change within the fixed boundaries of any given definition; the boundaries themselves are constantly changing" (Bakhtin 1981, 33. Trans. Emerson and Holquist). Given this flexibility, it becomes permissible to talk about the language of *Norske huldreeventyr og folkesagn* as the language of the novel. In an earlier chapter we saw how the reliable narrator of *huldreeventyr* uses various narrative techniques to control the reaction of the reader to the discourse of the created folk narrators. "It is a characteristic of the classic realist text that in it the narrative discourse acts as a 'metalanguage,' controlling, interpreting and judging the other discourses." However, despite this control, it is Bakhtin's contention that "the variety of discourses in the novel prevents the novelist from imposing a single worldview upon his readers even if he wanted to." In *Norske huldreeventyr og folkesagn* the reader becomes as familiar with the worldview of the peasant and his folk beliefs as he does with that of the enlightened frame narrator. "As soon as you allow a variety of discourses into a textual space—vulgar discourses as well as polite ones, vernacular as well as literary, oral as well as written—you establish a resistance . . . to the dominance of any one discourse" (Lodge 1990, 47, 22, 22).

Readers in every age approach texts with certain preconceived notions of how the texts will conform to elements of style, composition, and other variables based on their previous experience with texts of the same genre. If a text somehow does not conform to the expectations, it can be said to widen the "horizon of expectation."[10] Several examples from *huldreeventyr* will show how Asbjørnsen's use of language widened the "horizon of expectation" for his contemporary readers, because of the relative lack of earlier texts with which the polyphonic discourse could be compared, and how this widening of the boundaries of acceptable literary representation laid a foundation for the future pluralistic voices of the modern Norwegian novel.

While it is impossible for us as modern readers to experience *Norske huldreeventyr og folkesagn* as the original audience would have done, we must try to place ourselves in a time capsule for a moment. It is 1845, and as we open up the first edition and begin reading "Når verden går meg imot," seventeen-year-old Henrik Ibsen is in his second year as an apothecary apprentice in Grimstad, Bjørnstjerne Bjørnson is a thirteen-year-old schoolboy in Molde, Jonas Lie is dreaming about going to sea, and Alexander Kielland will not be born for four years. We are reading before *Amtmandens Døtre*, and long before Amalie Skram, Arne Garborg, Hans Jæger, Knut Hamsun, Hans Kinck, Johan Bojer, Olav Dunn, Sigrid Undset, and *all* the other Norwegian novelists. We are reading at a time when all the connotations of all the words of all the modern Norwegian novels do not yet exist, at a time when *sult* just means starving, at a time when Peer Gynt is a legend figure familiar to a few people, at a time when our conception of a legend collection is that of Andreas Faye's *Norske sagn* of 1833. "The words we use come to us already imprinted with the meanings, intentions and accents of previous users, and any utterance we make is directed toward some real or hypothetical Other" (Lodge, 21). As a contemporaneous reader of *Norske huldreeventyr og folkesagn*, many of the words you will read have no connotation for you in a literary sense. Your "horizon of expectation" is about to be stretched.

In *Norske sagn*, Andreas Faye performed a valuable service in collecting and preserving folk tradition, but as has been mentioned, his method of exposition is far different from that used by Asbjørnsen. It is likely, according to Liestøl, that Asbjørnsen actually appropriated Faye's legend about the mill goblin for his own version in "Legends of the Mill." The two versions show clearly how Asbjørnsen reformulated the essentials of the legend into a style more in keeping with oral narrative. First we will read the stilted Danish account of the mill goblin with which we, as readers of 1845, are probably familiar:

> En Tid lang opholdt han sig i Sandaker-Fos, hvor en Mand havde en Mølle. Saa ofte han vilde male Korn, standsede Qvernen. Manden som vidste, at det var Qvernknurren, som forvoldte denne Fortred, medtog en Aften, da han vilde male, noget Beg i en Gryde, hvorunder han gjorde Ild. Saasnart han lod Qvernen løbe, standsede den som sedvanlig. Han stak nu en Stang ned for at bortjage Qvernknurren, men forgjeves. Endelig lukkede han Døren op for at see, men i Døren stod Qvernknurren med aabent Gab, saa stort, at Underlæben sad ved Dørtærskelen, Overlæben ovenover Døren. Han sagde til Manden: "Har du sett saa stort Gabendes?" Flux greb denne den sydende Beggryde og slog den ind i Gabet med de Ord: "Har du smagt saa hedt Kogendes?" Brølende forsvandt Qvernknurren og siden har man ikke seet ham. (Faye [1833] 1948, 55–56)

> [For a long time he stayed in the Sandaker waterfall, where a man had a mill. Whenever he wanted to grind grain, the mill stopped. The man, who knew that it was the mill goblin

who was causing this harm, took along one evening, when
he wanted to grind, some pitch in a pot, under which he lit
a fire. As soon as he starting running the wheel, it stopped as
usual. He stuck a pole down to chase away the mill goblin,
but to no avail. Finally he opened the door to look, but in the
doorway stood the mill goblin with his mouth open, so wide
that his lower lip was at the threshold, the upper lip above
the door. He said to the man, "Have you ever seen such big
gaping?" Straightway the man grabbed the seething pitch-pot
and threw it into his mouth with these words, "Have you
ever tasted such hot cooking?" Bellowing, the mill goblin
disappeared and has not been seen since.]

Now let us imagine that we are reading Asbjørnsen's version from "Legends of the Mill" where the story is related by the frame narrator in order to encourage the old man at the mill to tell his own stories:

Der var en Mand, som havde en Mølle ved en Fos, og der
var ogsaa en Kværnknur. Om Manden, som skik er paa nogle
Steder, gav ham Levsekling og Juleøl forat øge Melet, har jeg
ikke hørt, men det er ikke sandsynligt; thi hver Gang han
skulde male, tog Kværnknurren fat i Kværnkallen og stansede
Kværnen, saaat han ikke kunde faae malet. Manden vidste
godt, at det var Kværnknurren, og en Aften han skulde paa
Møllen, tog han med sig en Gryde fuld med Beg og Tjære
og gjorde Ild under den. Da han slap Vandet paa Kallen, gik
den en Stund, men saa blev den, som han ventede, standset.
Han stak og slog efter Kværnknurren nede i Renden og
omkring Kværnkallen, men det hjalp ikke. Tilsidst aabnede
han Døren, som gik ud til Kværnkallen og Renden, men da
stod Kværnknurren midt i Døren og gabede, og dens Gab var
saa stort, at Underkjæften var ved Tærskelen og Overkjeften
ved Dørbjælken.

"Har du seet saa stort Gabende?" sagde den. Manden foer
efter Beggryden, som stod og kogede, slog den i Gabet paa

den og sagde: "har du kjendt saa hedt Kogende?" Da slap Kværnknurren kallen løs og slog op et forfærdeligt Brøl. Siden har den hverken været seet eller hørt der, og heller ikke har den hindret Folk i at male. (Asbjørnsen 1845, 8–9)[11]

[There was a man who had a mill by a waterfall, and there was also a mill goblin there. If the man, as the custom is in some places, gave him *lefse* and Christmas beer to increase the amount of flour, I have not heard, but it is not likely because every time he was going to grind flour, the mill goblin took ahold of the waterwheel and stopped the mill, so he could not grind. The man knew very well it was the mill goblin and one evening when he was going to the mill he took along a pot filled with pitch and tar and built a fire under it. When he started the wheel, it went for awhile, but then it was stopped, as he had expected. He poked and hit at the mill goblin down in the channel and around the waterwheel but it did not help. Finally he opened the door that went out to the waterwheel and the channel, but there the mill goblin stood right in the door gaping, and his mouth was so big that the lower jaw was by the threshold and the upper jaw by the doorbeam.

"Have you seen such big gaping?" he said. The man ran for the tar pot, which was boiling, threw it into his mouth and said, "Have you ever felt such hot cooking?" Then the mill goblin dropped the waterwheel and started bellowing. He has neither been seen or heard since, and he has not hindered anyone from grinding either.]

A comparison of the two accounts shows how Asbjørnsen is able to take the elements of the story and keep them virtually intact, while transposing them into another voice, the voice of oral, as opposed to written, narrative, with the simpler forms of vocabulary and syntax which conform to spoken speech. For example, Faye's convoluted phrase, "Manden som vidste, at det var Qvernknurren, som forvoldte denne Fortred." becomes simply "Manden visste godt, at det var Kværnknurren." The formal "forgjeves" becomes "det hjalp ikke." This simplification of the language followed the pattern established by Asbjørnsen and Moe in the *Folkeeventyr* and is an example of how much Asbjørnsen's style in his independent work owed to the collaboration on the folk tale project. Together with the *Folkeeventyr*, *Norske huldreeventyr og folkesagn* stretches the "horizon of expectation" of the readers of 1845 as a new way of storytelling is being formulated in print. Of course, we cannot become readers of 1845, we cannot erase our knowledge of everything that has come after, we can only speculate upon the effect that this text must have had on its contemporaries, when we consider that even today, over 150 years later, the work is eminently readable. It is readable because it utilizes the language of the novel, a language that engages the reader diachronically.

The example from "Legends of the Mill" illustrates the language used by the educated urban frame narrator in relating a legend. But the dialogical language in *huldreeventyr* is as pervasive in the narration of the legendary material as it is in the frame structures. Perhaps the best example in the entire collection which illustrates the dialogic character, multiplicity of voices, and the force of parody—elements in the language of the novel—can be found in the story "A Sunday Evening at the Mountain Dairy," in which language itself is the subject of confusion and merriment. The frame narrator and his companion, the British sportsman Sir John Tottenbroom, and their guides are on a hunting trip and arrive in the evening at the mountain dairy where they will hear stories told by the previously described pedantic schoolteacher and several other local storytellers. The frame narrator gives the reader insight into the Englishman's linguistic capabilities (or lack of them) already in the first paragraph:

> Den unge brite hadde sett seg om i vårt land; han forstod
> og kunne til nød gjøre seg forståelig i vårt sprog, men da
> han som de fleste engelske turister fornemmelig hadde
> pleiet omgang med bønder, talte han et høyst besynderlig
> gebrokkent bondesprog. Dog strakte dette ikke alltid til; når

tankene utfoldet seg livligere, hvilket de undertiden gjorde på en temmelig forvirret måte, slo han plutselig over i sitt morsmål, eller også ble han stikkende i et sådant kaudervelsk, at det ville være forgjeves å prøve på å gjengi det. (A 2: 7)

[The young Brit had been round and about in our country; he understood our language and could make himself understood in a pinch, but since he, like most English tourists, had associated mostly with farmers, he spoke an extremely odd broken peasant language. But this wasn't always sufficient; when his thoughts became expanded and animated, which they sometimes did in a quite confusing way, he would suddenly switch over to his native tongue, or he would start in with such a gibberish that it would be fruitless to try to reproduce it.]

The pedantic schoolteacher is curious about the travelers and also wants to impress the visitors with his knowledge, and the resulting cacophony of babelistic confusion, with its over-riding parody of the schoolmaster can only be appreciated fully by citing the scene in its entirety:

Jeg hadde hittil så godt som alene underholdt skolemesteren og dels besvart, dels avvendt en strøm av disse nysgjerrige spørsmål, der meget gravitetisk fremsattes i den eiendommelige skolemesterstil, en på stylter gående komisk efterligning av et foreldet boksprog, hvori der av og til uforvarende plumpet grove brokker ut av den djerve gudbrandsdalske dialekt; men til sist tapte min reisefelle, som stedse følte seg såre ubehagelig berørt ved nærgående spørsmål, tålmodigheten og utbrøt temmelig bredt i sitt morsmål: "Gud fordømme denne mann og hans øyne og hans munn og hans uforskammenhet!"

"Å," sa skolemesteren med en mine, som om han hadde fått bukt med et reguladetristykke, da han fornam disse fremmede ord, "nå kan jeg sandelé begripe, det er reisende menn fra fremmede lænder! Måskje fra Engeland eller

Frankrige, eller kanskje vel endog fra Spanien; ti her var en greve derfra i fjor."

"Tro bare ikke det, skolemester," svarte jeg, "De kan nok høre, at norsk er mitt modersmål; men min medreisende, Sir John Tottenbroom, er fra England."

"Ja så nu—så denne verdige mann er fra det britiske rige?" sa skolemesteren og så seg om for å gjøre oppmerksom på den kunnskap i geografien, han nu aktet å legge for dagen. "Er han reist hertil vannveien over det betydelige hav som kalles Nordsjøen, eller har han reist landveien gjennem Frankrig, Holland, Tyskland, Danmark og Sverige, og hvilke ærender har han her i landet med forlov, at jeg er så nåsåvis at spørge?"

"Spørr kun, skolemester," svarte jeg oppmuntrende; "Deres første spørsmål kan jeg besvare; han er kommet vannveien over Nordsjøen. Angående hans ærender får De henvende Dem til ham selv."

"Da blir du klok, skulmester," sa hans medbeiler, den dunhakede gutt, som hadde satt seg ned, og behaget seg i å røke tobakk av en liten merskumspipe med sølvbeslag og et hornrør med slange av kobbertråd og langt munnstykke; "han javler væl bare englis."

"Ja, var han enda mektig det tyske sprog," sa skolemesteren med overlegenhet, "så skulle jeg nok tale ham til; ti deri er jeg noget befaren—jeg haver studeret Geddikes lesebog og Hübners geografi i dette sprog."

"Damn you," utbrøt Sir John, der uaktet sin ergrelse dog ikke kunne holde seg fra å le over skolemesterens forlegne miner. "De spørr om mitt ærend, skolemester?" sa han på tålelig tysk. "Blant annet reiser jeg om for å studere menneskenes narraktigheter, og det later til der her er god leilighet til å gjøre studier."

"Das ist inglis, kan nix forstehen," sa skolemesteren, "aber," fortsatte han, snappende efter det første han fikk fatt på i sine kunnskapers kramkiste, "was ist Ihre formeinung anbelangende det faktum, som står geschribet om Det

Euxinske Hav, das udi året 715 frøs soledes att, dass isen var førti ælner tjukk, und da das eis gesmalt, so gestand von derudav sodan ein hidsighet udi luften, dass der uppkom en pestilens, von hvilke alle mennesker bestarb udi Konstantinopolis."

Den latter, vi utbrøt i over dette "faktum" av Hübners geografi, endte den tyske konversasjon, og skolemesteren var en stund temmelig muggen. (15–18)

[Up to this point I had pretty much maintained the conversation with the schoolmaster by myself, partly answering and partly deflecting a stream of questions from this curious fellow, which were very pompously posed in the peculiar schoolmaster style, in a high-flown comic imitation of an antiquated book language, in which there were occasionally interspersed coarse fragments of the frank Gudbrandsdal dialect; but at last my traveling companion, who all along felt himself uncomfortably offended by the tactless personal questions, lost his patience and burst out pretty coarsely in his mother tongue, "God damn this man and his eyes and his mouth and his impertinence!"

"Ah," said the schoolmaster, with an expression as if he had overcome a matter of great complexity, when he heard these foreign words, "now to be sure I understand, they are traveling men from foreign lands! Possibly from England or France, or perhaps even from Spain, since there was a count from there here last year."

"Don't you believe it, schoolmaster," I answered, "You can certainly hear that my mother tongue is Norwegian; but my traveling companion, Sir John Tottenbroom, is from England."

"Is that so now—so this worthy gentleman is from the British empire?" said the schoolmaster and looked around to draw attention to the knowledge of geography he now intended to demonstrate. "Did he travel here by sea across the considerable ocean called the North Sea, or has he traveled by way of land through France, Holland, Germany, Denmark, and Sweden, and what mission does he have here in our country, if I may be so bold as to ask?"

"Just ask, schoolmaster," I answered encouragingly. "I can answer your first question; he came by water across the North Sea. With respect to his mission you will have to ask him."

"You'll be a lot wiser for that," said his rival, the fuzzy-chinned boy, who had sat down and was pleasing himself by smoking a little meerschaum pipe with silver fittings and a horn stem with tubing of copper wire and a long mouthpiece. "He can probably only jabber in English."

"Yes, if only he had a command of the German language," the schoolmaster said with an air of superiority, "then I would certainly speak to him; since I am somewhat conversant with that language—I have studied Geddike's reader and Hübner's geography in this language."

"Just go ahead and talk to him in German, schoolmaster," I said, "I am sure he can respond in that language."

"Damn you," Sir John burst out, who despite his irritation could not keep himself from laughing at the schoolmaster's uncertain expression. You ask about my mission, schoolmaster?" he said in passable German, "Among other things I am traveling around to study the foolishness of men, and it appears that there is a good opportunity to do that here."

"That is English, cannot understand," said the schoolmaster, "but," he continued, grasping at the first thing he could get a hold of in his grab-bag of knowledge, "What is your meaning regarding the fact, which is written about the Black Sea, that in the year 715 it froze solid, and that the ice was eighty feet thick, and when the ice melted, such a heat was released from it into the air that it was a cause for pestilence, from which all people in Constantinople died."

The laughter which broke out over this "fact" from Hübner's geography ended the German conversation, and for a while the schoolmaster was pretty sulky.]

The humor of the above situation is intensified when one reads in Liestøl's notes to this passage that the only German reader written by Friedrich Gedicke, who was a very prolific writer of readers in English, French, Italian, Latin, and Greek, was *Kinderbuch zur ersten Übung im Lesen ohne ABC und Buchstabiren*, and that Johann Hübner's well-known geography book, *Vollständige Geographie* does not include any facts about the freezing of the Black Sea, although it is full of other similar information. Liestøl notes that in Asbjørnsen's hand-written copy of the story, he refers to a work called *Le Bosphore et Constantinople* and includes the information that since the time of Herodotus, the Black Sea has been partially or completely frozen seventeen times and that the year 715 was not one of them (Liestøl, notes to A 2: 303). The depiction of the pedantic schoolmaster is complete: not only is he unable to distinguish English from German, he does not even have mastery over the very topic on which he prides himself.[12]

"MODES OF EXPRESSION ONE IS ASTONISHED TO SEE IN PRINT"

Writing in 1949, in one of his many essays on the topic, Arnulf Øverland, a champion of *riksmål*, defended the old written Dano-Norwegian language against the despised *bokmål*, a created amalgamation, with these Bakhtinian thoughts:

> He who understands what a language is, he will never venture to mess with it. They who want to create a language have simply set about making a soul for us. They are so considerate! While I am speaking about understanding a language—what does it mean to understand just one word? That is something completely bottomless! That is to understand all those people who have used the word; it is to understand all the states of mind, all the shadows of memories, all the shimmering impulses that are connected to it! (Øverland 1967, 62)

So when a writer uses words or modes of expression that his audience is not expecting to see in print, that the audience actually is astonished to see in print, as Andreas Munch and others articulated in the reception of *Norske huldreeventyr og folkesagn*, then it is not surprising that there would be a certain amount of initial resistance to the language even as the "horizon of expectation" would be expanding to eventually include the new vocabulary. It will be remembered that the written language of Norway in 1845 was Danish. Here is how the author of a Danish critique of *huldreeventyr* defended Asbjørnsen's usage:

> There comes to mind the objection that quite a few have actually made to me, when I have asked them to read Asbjørnsen's tales: "There are so many words that we don't understand." For the most part, this objection comes from laziness and because we are prisoners of habit: The particularly Norwegian words are perfectly well understood, as are the provincial Danish ones, but one refuses to take the trouble to admit it, because they have not had a place in our written language before, and one completely forgets to what a degree precisely these shadings of the language contribute to the poetic lucidity. Everyone senses that, when a farmer from Zealand uses the word *øg* for his horse, that this is a closer designation, either disparaging or playfully affectionate, than the word *hest* would be. In the same way, the Norwegian feels differently when he calls his horse *Gampen* than when he says *hesten*. Should one let these fine nuances in conception, precisely these that give life, be dropped for the sake of ease? That would be like translating all the names for gold in Bjarkemål's fragments in Snorri's *Edda* with the one word "gold." It is just the fact that one is always obliged by certain words, by phrases and small particles, to hear the language ring Norwegian which gives a stamp of authenticity and originality to all that is told and on which its refreshing and satisfactory effect for a large part depends. (Rosenberg 1867, 91–92)

Rosenberg goes on to inform his readers that if they are too lazy to use a dictionary for certain words, Asbjørnsen has provided a glossary at the end of the book.

In addition to words of slang and Norwegian phrasing, several of the *huldreeventyr* contain storytellers who speak with a regional dialect, for example the old farmer from Hallingdal in "The Halling with Angelica Root," and the examples of *sognemaal* (the dialect of Sogn) in "From the Sognefjord." That Asbjørnsen was very concerned about the veracity of his transcriptions of dialect is evident from Liestøl's notes to this story. He writes: "It is first mentioned in a letter from Asbjørnsen to Ivar Aasen. The piece is not yet finished, but he sends a part of it to Aasen with the request to give it 'a color of the life of Sogn and the language, which I can't give, since I have not been in Sogn for more than ten to twelve days altogether'" (Liestøl, notes to A 2: 362). That Aasen complied with Asbjørnsen's request is evident from the forward to the edition of 1866, in which Asbjørnsen credits Aasen for his contributions to the story. It is clear that Asbjørnsen took very seriously his responsibility to represent the spoken word as accurately as possible. It will be remembered that he took pains to reproduce some words of the Romany language in the story "The Gypsies," and his rendition of the fractured Norwegian of Sir John is a comic example of the language of a student struggling to master the intricacies of the language: "'Her må vi få urret,' fortsatte han, 'men elven er ikke så klar, som den skudd være; den skudd være så klar som kristall; og ser De hvilket sjeneri det er her, for når jeg fisk' jeg ser ikke efter fisk alene, men på hvert maleriske tre der speile seg i elven, på hver flye der flive, jeg hør' efter hver fugl der singe'" (A 1: 151) ["'Here we must get trout,' he continued, 'but the river is not as clear as it should be; it should be as clear as crystal; and see what scenery there is here, for when I fish I don't look only for fish, but at each artistic tree that mirrors itself in the river, on each fly that flies, I listen to every bird that sings.'"] This approximation of an English speaker's Norwegian is truly masterful, complete with the common word order error, present tense verb form confusion, and Norwegianizing of English words that will be so familiar to language teachers. This careful attention to detail in representation of spoken speech is evident throughout the *huldreeventyr*. In the introduction to the 1881 English translation, Edmund Gosse asserts:

> Here in England, where our poetical language has been repeatedly renewed at the fresh wells of the vernacular, where Chaucer and the Elizabethans, Butler, and Burns, and Dickens, each in his own way, have constantly enriched our classical speech with the bright idioms of the vulgar, we can scarcely realize how startling a thing it is when a great writer first dares, in a ripe literature, to write exactly as people commonly speak. This is what the author of these tales has done in Dano-Norwegian. He has cast to the winds the rules of composition, the balance of clauses, the affected town-phrases, and all the artificial forms hitherto deemed requisite in Danish prose, and he has had the courage to note down the fine idiomatic speech of the mountaineer in its native freshness. (Gosse, intro to Asbjørnsen 1881, xiii-xiv)

Most importantly, the use of new words and new modes of expression would give voice to those who spoke the dialects that Asbjørnsen included in *Norske huldreeventyr og folkesagn*. By his use of a variety of forms of speech, Asbjørnsen created a linguistically pluralistic work which legitimizes the voices of the individual idiomatic variants of spoken Norwegian, of which there are so many. Norwegians are only partly joking when they claim that every *bygd* has its own dialect. There are four primary dialect divisions identified for the country, but the text *Språket vårt før og nå* [Our Language in the Past and Present] gives examples of twenty distinctly different dialect forms, and certainly many others could have been included. This in an area roughly the size of Great Britain or Japan. Of course, this is perhaps not so surprising in a mountainous country where valley communities were isolated and insulated from each other and outside influences for hundreds of years. But one is reminded of Julian Kramer's tribal analogies, as he articulates his experiences in adjusting to life in Norway:

> My primary claim is that Norwegian identity must be seen as a product of a tribal attachment and underdevelopment—important features of Norwegian society until quite recently. . . . Norwegian national costumes with all their local variants can in other words be been as an expression of tribal identity—a social phenomenon one usually considers typical for natives of the third world.
>
> Little by little, as I learned the language and became better acquainted with the native Norwegians, the conception that the Norwegians' identity as "Norwegians" was defined by something that resembles tribal ideology was strengthened—that their origin is anchored in a particular area with its own dialect and local culture. (Kramer 1984, 91)

There can be no doubt that Norway's language situation contributes to the splintering of the Norwegian national identity. Jørgen Haugan suggests that Norway should repeal the law that gave *nynorsk* an equal official standing with *bokmål*, designate *nynorsk* as one of several recognized minority languages in the country and leave *bokmål* to be the only official language of the realm. "Such a decision, which certainly is not immediately imminent, would mean an official write-off of the '400-year night' myth. The resolution would at the same time indicate that Norway is no longer a tribal society, but a modern constitutional state, finally a unified country with one national language" (Haugan 1991, 93). This is a radical suggestion and not one that is likely to be taken seriously. But when Norwegian nation builders in the nineteenth century demanded a break with the Danish written language in order to propose a clearly Norwegian national identity, they helped to build the myth of the "400-year night," a myth which effectively denied a joint Danish/Norwegian literary tradition, and helped to establish the basis for the modern Norwegian language situation of today, in which a country of less than five million people with several official languages and dozens of regional dialects are continuing a national dialogue, a dialogue reflecting the myriad voices and polyphonic language legitimized in print in the pages of *Norske huldreeventyr og folkesagn*.

CHAPTER 8

The Tapestry Woven:
A Gobelin of Nature, Folklore, and Language

> As a collection of narratives, the literary canon contains the tales by which members of a community understand their common links. Literature in a sense is the nation's diary, telling the story of its past, present, and future.
> —Gregory Jusdanis

CONCLUSION: REREADING A CLASSIC

At the beginning of this book, Olaf Bull's poem *gobelin* was selected as a metaphor for the imagined community of Norway, and the blending of the real and the imaginary that is *Norske huldreeventyr og folkesagn*. Olaf Bull imagines himself walking the path into the forest that is represented on a sofa-pillow and discovers a magical world of fairy tales along with his daughter Merete. But not only children and poets wander in imaginary worlds of their own making; the carefully constructed national romantic image of a Norway peopled by noble, independent *bønder*, created as it was to trigger associations with the ancestors of the sagas, is also a construction, part of the diary of the Norwegian people, a diary with a four-hundred-year lacuna. In my construction of a new reading of *huldreeventyr*, the strands of nature, folklore, and language have been integrated to weave an interpretation of this work from a perspective that may be at odds with the prevailing evaluation of this text, a new tapestry which may very well occasion a cry of "Han har jo ikke noe på seg!"[1]

Nearly 120 years ago, Henrik Jæger wrote about critics' responses to *Norske huldreeventyr og folkesagn* that "there have been too few points of view, and those points of view have been too similar. It is necessary to find new points of view" (Jæger 1883, 1–2). Jæger's words are eerily echoed by Jørgen Haugan over a hundred years later when he writes, "It is striking that Norway lacks new readings of its classics" (Haugan 1991, 103). Haugan views this as a symptom of an insular and moribund academic tradition.[2] In the preceding chapters I have proffered a new perspective on *Norske huldreeventyr og folkesagn,* showing that the elements of nature, folklore, and language form a totality that insists on the reassessment of this text as an autonomous literary work, and one that has had enormous influence on the development of not only modern Norwegian prose but on the entire cultural narrative of Norway, becoming part of the nation's collective diary.

The perspective brought forward here is that this text performed cultural *work* at the time of its reception and in the decades following, and that to read the text only as a sacred monument to national romanticism is to ignore the germinal issues of identity and ethnicity that the text addresses. *Norske huldreeventyr og folkesagn* can be seen as a type of cultural barometer which, by its depiction of elements of Norwegian life at mid-nineteenth century, reveals as much about the conditions of its time of inception as it does about the folklore it sought to preserve and the folk beliefs it aimed to eradicate. The strands of nature, folklore, and polyphonic language which are so richly interwoven in the pages of *huldreeventyr* reflect in microcosm conflicts that are by no means resolved in contemporary Norway, issues of identity and ethnicity which have been shown to have a long history in what is often thought of as very much an homogenous society.[3] The intellectuals who formed the Norwegian literary canon, in glorifying the *odelsbonde* [freeholding farmer], continued the process of privileging nature over culture, country over city. This reflects a society that to this day in many ways values the traditional over modernity. That this is the case is evidenced by how Norway chose to represent herself to the world when all the world was watching: the opening and closing ceremonies of the 1994 winter Olympics in Lillehammer. In these highlights of the media coverage the world did not see the modern Norway, an affluent nation with one of the highest standards of living in the world; it saw a world of *vetter* [sprites, spirits], straight out of folklore, a struggle between good and evil, a representation of nature *as* culture. The Norwegian anthropologist Arne Martin Klausen, in his book about the phenomenon of the Lillehammer Olympics, writes, "We were going to show the world who we are and what we have to market in goods, services, and values. This was successful beyond expectations through the media coverage. But as the analysis of the foreign presentations show, the folkloristic and exotic dominated, the common and the modern did not catch the media attention to the same extent" (Klausen 1996, 240). Of course not, since the folkloristic and exotic were highlighted in the ceremonies that most viewers saw. One is tempted to ask if the Norwegian really wants to be modern.

Viewed as an autonomous text, *Norske huldreeventyr og folkesagn* clearly was instrumental as a blueprint for early Norwegian nationalism. With its appropriation of the physical space of eastern Norway and the high mountain plateaus, this work formed a bridge into the countryside for the educated urban *embets* class, a panegyric to the Norwegian physical geography which helped to create place from space. At the same time, the many voices of this text, and its often negative depiction of the rural peasantry, were problematic for the text's positioning within the Norwegian literary canon. "The literary and philosophical canons cannot tolerate pluralism.... The canon serves as a utopian site of continuous textuality in which a nation, a class, or an individual may find an undifferentiated identity" (Jusdanis 1991, 58, 59). It has been convenient for literary historians to view *Norske huldreeventyr og folkesagn* as a static classic of the national romantic past, neatly pigeonholed within certain boundaries of definition and genre for over a hundred years, duly mentioned in new literary histories with virtually the same words again and again, and erroneously included in the "Asbjørnsen and Moe" canonical entity. But "one can always put new questions to old material" (Darnton 1984, 4). Of course, asking new questions is always a selective process. Selecting one question precludes the asking of others, and different questions might well lead to other conclusions. My interpretation of *Norske huldreeventyr og folkesagn* is as much a literary construct as any other literary analysis, and this attempt to place *huldreeventyr* within its cultural context while at the same time reevaluating its literary position is necessarily an incomplete undertaking.[4]

Robert Darnton has remarked that "nothing could be more misleading in an attempt to recapture the experience of reading in the past than the assumption that people have always read the way we do today. A history of reading, if it can ever be written, would chart the alien element in the way man has made sense of the world. For reading, unlike carpentry or embroidery, is not merely a skill; it is an active construal of meaning within a system of communication" (Darnton, 216). How the nineteenth-century Norwegian interpreted his world through his evaluation of his folklore as it is represented in *Norske huldreeventyr og folkesagn*, and how that folklore has helped to shape the modern Norwegian worldview has been the focus of this book. And if the interpretation is necessarily incomplete, it nevertheless shows that this text deserves greater recognition for its role in advancing the national narrative, a national narrative that is not nearly as homogenous as it has been constructed to be, and a narrative that contains 400 missing years of a shared literary tradition. If "Norway is a country which has problems with its identity," then cannot this collective amnesia be a contributing factor? How can you know who you are if you have forgotten your past?

Norwegians have always spoken with many and varied voices, and new readings of the classics of the Norwegian literary canon (or texts not canonized for that matter) may free other voices so that the modern Norwegian can accept that his identity need not be "either Norwegian or something else," but can be more complex and multifaceted, more cosmopolitan. There seems little doubt that a rereading of the classics of the canon, the national diary, from the perspective of a variety of literary and historical research methods, could only broaden the possibilities for the creation of that national identity that has, in Sørensen's words, "not yet been completed."

Notes

Chapter 1

1. Obviously the vocabulary has changed over the years, but when Jørgen Moe wrote to P. Christen Asbjørnsen in 1836 of Adam Oehlenschläger's collection of fairy tales "men *norske* er de naturligvis ikke," [but, of course, they are not *Norwegian*], he was already engaging in the favorite Norwegian pastime of defining *Norskhet* (Moe 1915, 144. Moe's italics).
2. Unless otherwise noted, all translations are my own. I will supply the Norwegian original only when the language itself is the focus of the discussion, as in chapter seven, with the exception of all quotations from *Norske huldreeventyr og folkesagn*, which will be provided in endnotes. All quotations are from the 1949 edition, edited by Knut Liestøl, which was based on the 1870 edition, the last which Asbjørnsen himself edited. Any substantive changes in content from the 1870 edition will, of course, be noted. Readers interested in the changes that Asbjørnsen made in language between the three editions he edited should consult Daniel Popp's *Asbjørnsen's linguistic reform*. While the changes between the editions are interesting, my comparison of the three editions have convinced me that only in rare cases do changes affect the stories in their entirety as literary works. The changes are primarily in spelling, changes in word order, and an increasing usage of "Norwegian" as opposed to "Danish" language. Most of the changes are to the frame narratives, rather than to the internal folk legend narratives. All source references to Asbjørnsen's text will be abbreviated A 1 or A 2, to indicate *Norske huldreeventyr og folkesagn* volumes 1 or 2. In all instances, the capitalization of Danish and Norwegian books and articles appear as they were originally published.
3. Anders Krogvig has an unfortunate tendency to depreciate Asbjørnsen in all of his writings. A glance at Asbjørnsen's publications in all fields and his library record at the University of Oslo library does not substantiate the claim that Asbjørnsen was lazy.
4. Additional information and speculation about Asbjørnsen's domestic life,

much of it anecdotal and sometimes not fully documented, can be found in *Peter Christen Asbjørnsen: diger og folkesæl* by Truls Gjefsen.

5. Ingwersen in "The Folktale as Response to History" (83). The 1983 edition of *Norske Folkeeventyr* published by The Norwegian Bookclub includes all of the stories from *Norske huldreeventyr og folkesagn* interspersed, at random, among the fairy tales. This may be understandable in a popular edition such as this, but it is surprising how many people who should know better continue to treat Asbjørnsen's independent work as part of the "fairy tales" and think of Asbjørnsen and Moe as a set of Siamese twins, instead of as two very different people who each went his own way after the early collaboration. Asbjørnsen himself unwittingly contributed to this blurring of texts and genre by publishing an edition of *Norske Folke- og Huldre-Eventyr i udvalg* in 1879. This was the first volume to be illustrated, and although only Asbjørnsen's name appears on the title page (along with the illustrators) later editions have added Jørgen Moe as author. Part of the object of this book is to separate Asbjørnsen from Moe, as Jack Zipes has separated the Brothers Grimm, one from the other, so that Asbjørnsen's independent work can once again be viewed autonomously with respect to the legend collection.

6. Given the largely negative connotations of the term "nationalism" for many people today, I prefer to use the phrases "national identity" and "nation building" in discussing how cultural artifacts shape a shared sense of nationality. As Anderson says, "In an age when it is so common for progressive, cosmopolitan intellectuals (particularly in Europe?) to insist on the near-pathological character of nationalism . . . it is useful to remind ourselves that nations inspire love" (Anderson, 141). Certainly in the case of Norway, which celebrates its Constitution Day with parades of children, rather than with the ubiquitous shows of military force common in many nations, this distinction between Nationalism with a capital "N" and "national identity" as a sense of shared tradition is an important one. See Nina Witoszek's analysis of the 17th of May celebration in *Norske naturmytologier: fra Edda til økofilosofi* in which she identifies the celebration as an historic rite which has changed character since its inception. Although the original manuscript of *Norske naturmytologier* is in English, it has not yet been published in English. All page references to this work are to the Norwegian text.

7. The distinction is Tuan's in *Space and Place*. He writes, "What begins as undifferentiated space becomes place as we get to know it better and endow it with value" (6).

8. I lament, as others have done before me, that the Norwegian word *bonde* does not really have an English equivalent. "Peasant" presupposes a feudal system, which Norway never really had. As Kåre Lunden explains, the

lack of a Norwegian nobility meant that the Norwegian *bonde* assumed a function of the nobility in other countries with respect to service in the military. Furthermore, Lunden shows that the *bønder* in Norway already had a position in society that other states' citizens received only with democratic revolutions.

9. This quotation and the overview of Herder's ideas are from "Herder, Folklore and Romantic Nationalism" by William A. Wilson in *Folk Groups and Folklore Genres: A Reader* (25). See also *Norske naturmytologier* by Nina Witoszek for an interesting discussion of Norwegian national romanticism. Witoszek believes that because of Norway's lack of an urban culture, European transcendental romanticism had little to say to Norway's reality and that the leading trend-setters in the 1830s more or less renounced the ideals of romanticism.

10. I have paraphrased Østerud's five paradoxical features. See "Nasjonalstaten Norge—en karakteriserende skisse" in *Det Norske Samfunn*. Although beyond the scope of this discussion, a clear example of this postulation and production, among many others which could be cited, is the Norwegian *lusekofte* [Norwegian ski sweater] which has become a national costume of sorts. The search for the uniquely Norwegian national identity is far from over. An ambitious project at the University of Oslo, *Utviklingen av en norsk nasjonal identitet på 1800 tallet* [The Development of a Norwegian National Identity in the Nineteenth Century], recently completed, published a series of studies on the topic. A member of the project, Professor Gudleiv Bø, has stated that the quest is no longer for the uniquely Norwegian, but rather for what the Norwegian *thinks* is uniquely Norwegian.

11. It is necessary to define terminology as it is used in this study. I use "folk tale" generically as an inclusive term to include stories of any genre that have a history of oral transmission. The category can include tales of magic as well as fables, personal recollection stories and legendary material of various kinds. I use the terms "fairy tale" or "wonder tale" interchangeably to refer to stories that contain elements of magic and include standard formulaic fairy tale language such as "Once upon a time" and the classic happy ending. There can be some confusion with the titles of Asbjørnsen and Moe's collections simply because genre classifications do not necessarily translate cleanly. The joint collections of folk tales published by Asbjørnsen and Moe are primarily composed of fairy tales and some fables and jocular tales, but I will refer to them as the folk tale collection or joint collection, although the literal translation would be "Folk Fairy Tales." By contrast, Asbjørnsen's independent work consists mainly of legendary material. I will translate the Norwegian word *eventyr* as "fairy-tale" when translating directly from Norwegian sources, and will consistently translate *sagn* as "legend." See also the discussion of legend sub-types in chapter six.

12. I have translated and, in some cases, paraphrased the following summary from Moltke Moe's work, pp. 42–49 of volume three of his collected works. Moe did not publish much during his lifetime. His biographer Knut Liestøl says of him: "When one is going to describe Moltke Moe as a scholar one runs into the curious and exceptional problem that his writings do not give any adequate expression of what he was and what he did, not to mention what he could have done. He never wrote a great work that was finished, he never published an important book. Most of what he published were popular science accounts in various periodicals, Christmas magazines, almanacs, memorial publications or in introductions to works by others. His largest monograph, "Det nationale gjennembrud og dets mænd," was published as a part of Gerhard Gran's *Nordmænd i det 19de aarhundrede* and was never completed; it was, as a matter of fact, not a folkloristic work in the usual meaning of that term. His work on the *Draumkvædet* was twice partially in proofs but was never published, and the manuscript was never finished. Nevertheless, when he died, the international Folklore Fellows published a large volume of its "Communications" dedicated to his memory: 'To the Memory of Moltke Moe . . . the Greatest of Scandinavian Folklorists'" (Liestøl 1949, 55–56). In that volume see "Personal impressions of Moltke Moe" by Axel Olrik. Olrik writes that Moe was so burdened with his work on spelling reforms in textbooks that he was not able to conduct his research. "It was as if the eagle could not catch the air under his wings" (Olrik 1915, 35).
13. Maurits Hansen (1794–1842) was considered the finest literary talent of his generation by his contemporaries. He wrote mostly short stories, but also some novels.
14. The natural scientist, philosopher, and novelist Henrich Steffens (1773–1845) was born in Norway. His lectures in Copenhagen in 1802–1803 had a great influence on Oehlenschläger. As with Moe's summary, I have translated Hansen's remarks more or less directly.
15. Steen Steensen Blicher (1782–1848), the Danish regional short-story writer whose literary reputation is greater today than during his life. "Blicher . . . through the use of Romantic elements, undermined the Romantic vision and foreshadowed twentieth-century literary developments" (Ingwersen 1996, 67).
16. Of course Asbjørnsen may have checked out the books and not read them, as occasionally happens, but it seems reasonable to assume that he would at least have skimmed those books he was interested enough to obtain, and anecdotal evidence indicates that he was an omnivorous reader.
17. Asbjørnsen must have found Tullin's poetry very much in accord with his own feelings about nature. Compare Tullin's "Majdagen" with some of the frame descriptions in *huldreeventyr*.

Chapter 2

1. Although their friendship lasted until Moe's death in 1882, the two friends had little contact in later years. Their interests and occupations were too divergent
2. It must be noted that the style of *Norske folkeeventyr* has not always been universally admired in Norway. See, for example Rikard Berge's article on "Norsk eventyrstil," in which Berge is highly critical of the *østnorsk* forms used by Asbjørnsen and Moe.
3. Many of the letters from Asbjørnsen to Moe are not extant, so conclusions about the genesis and style of the fairy tales are based primarily on Moe's letters and samples of Asbjørnsen's early writing, which show poor stylistics. At Jørgen Moe's death, his papers were left to his son Moltke. Had Jørgen Moe not destroyed Asbjørnsen's letters, they surely should have been among his effects. Moltke Moe must undoubtedly have told someone what happened to the letters, but I have been unable to locate this reference. All sources I have consulted simply state that the letters are "lost."
4. See the discussion on this issue in Gjefsen's recently published biography of Asbjørnsen. Gjefsen summarizes the points of the controversy and points out moreover that Hallvard Bakken used Moe's submissions to Andreas Faye in 1840 to show that Moe was by no means a sure stylist at that time. With respect to Bakken's example and in the context of Asbjørnsen's first efforts in *Nor,* Gjefsen writes, "Knut Liestøl remarks that Bakken does an injustice to Moe by claiming that the legends show everything the writer was capable of as a storyteller—they were probably adjusted for Faye's dry style. This is the same injustice that Krogvig does to Asbjørnsen with his reference to the fairy tales in *Billed-Magazin for Børn*. Solomon-like, Liestøl assigns equal honor to both parties and amazingly does not address Bakken's main point: Asbjørnsen was in fact the one who first published something that was pretty good, and Moe did not consider himself a participant in it" (Gjefsen, 111).
5. Moltke Moe's work on "The National Breakthrough and its Men" was not completed in his lifetime. Parts of the published text were finished using Moe's notes by Anders Krogvig. It may be possible that the rather harsh critique of *Norske huldreeventyr og folkesagn* in this text may owe as much to Krogvig as to Moe.
6. Moe writes that the Grimms' book "fell into his hands." Is it not more likely that his friend Asbjørnsen advised him to read it? Asbjørnsen checked *Kinder- und Hausmärchen* out of the Oslo University library in January of 1835.
7. See Asbjørnsen's 1843 letter to Moe in the collection of Moe's letters. Asbjørnsen writes, "Your last fairy tales have, in comparison to previous

ones, been extraordinarily carelessly handled; that was especially the case with 'Det har ingen Nød med den' and so on; I have therefore, as you will see, taken the liberty of making a number of corrections and changes in them, which I hope will have your approval" (Moe 1915, 224). Asbjørnsen goes on to say that he showed the fairy tales to several others, who agreed that changes were necessary. On the whole, this letter indicates that perhaps Asbjørnsen and Moe were more equal in stylistic ability than commonly believed.

8. I have made no effort to rhyme this translation: "But then I have something that I want to talk to you about, if you can spare an hour from the punch bowl and the fish pond. . . . As far as I know, our subscription list in this part of the country has added only one name to the chain of subscribers and that is about what we can expect, I think."

9. "Jahn" is Johan Sebastian Welhaven. Welhaven was the aesthetic trend setter of his day and his approval was important. He also helped Asbjørnsen later with the *huldreeventyr*. "Nella" is the abbreviation for the newspaper *Den Constitutionelle*.

10. The first English translation was published in 1858 under the title, *Tales from the Norse* by George Webbe Dasent. Dasent did not acknowledge Asbjørnsen and Moe in any way in this work. Since that time, many translations have appeared in many languages and the Norwegian fairy tales can be said to belong to world literature.

11. Much of the research on Norwegian fairy tales has been structuralist, such as Irene Engelstad's *Fortellingens Mønstre: En strukturell analyse av norske folkeeventyr*, or informant studies such as Ørnulf Hodne's *Jørgen Moe og folkeeventyrene*. A recent interesting interpretation of the Askeladden type, found in many Norwegian folk tales, is by Nina Witoszek in *Norske naturmytologier*, in which she finds great similarities between Askeladden's worldview and that of Zen and Taoism. A full length study that includes references specifically to the character of Scandinavian tales as opposed to others is *Grimms' Bad Girls and Bold Boys* by Ruth B. Bottigheimer, in which Bottigheimer claims that heroines in the Danish tradition are more active and autonomous than in the Grimms' tales. Robert Darnton in *The Great Cat Massacre* includes a discussion of the differences between French, German, and Italian versions of the "same" stories, concluding that "French tales tend to be realistic, earthy, bawdy, and comical, the German veer off toward the supernatural, the poetic, the exotic, and the violent" (50). See also Zipes' criticism of Darnton's characterization of German tales in *The Brothers Grimm: From Enchanted Forests to the Modern World*.

12. Of course there are also examples of skæmteeventyr. See Niels Ingwersen's "Ethics Upheld/Ethics Defunct: The Magic Tale and the Fabliau in Scandinavian tradition" in *Scandinavian Studies* 61 for a compelling discussion

of this subgenre and why Ingwersen believes that the term *fabliau* is to be preferred as more easily understood across language boundaries. The first collection of Asbjørnsen and Moe's fairy tales contained mostly the classic fairy wonder tales, while Asbjørnsen's later editions of the tales contained more of the *skjæmte* or *fabliau* type.

13. Bettelheim's contention that just because fairy tales are not real does not mean they are not true is not relevant to the distinction between fairy tale and legend which is being made here.
14. This does not contradict Bruno Bettelheim's contention that fairy tales help children integrate their personalities, although this may be debatable, but this is "person-building," not "nation-building." That fairy tales have often been used to delineate differences among classes within a society has been shown convincingly by many scholars, among them Jack Zipes, Robert Darnton, and Bengt Holbek, who concludes that the structure of fairy tale tradition could only come into being in a stratified society and that fairy tales have probably always been the voice of the proletariat (Holbek 1987, 605). Jack Zipes has probably done as much as any other scholar to show that fairy tales' universality is in some respects a myth, despite their formulaic character, and that tales need to be studied in their historical contexts. A recent discussion of the importance of this context within Scandinavian Studies is Niels Ingwersen's "The Need for Narrative: The Folktale as Response to History" in *Scandinavian Studies* 67.
15. When Moe says that the fairy tales in the collection *folkeeventyr* are no longer being created, he is clearly speaking of "tale types" as opposed to variants. This quotation also makes clear that by the term *huldreeventyr* Asbjørnsen is not talking about fairy tales, but about legends concerning *huldre*.
16. Reidar Christiansen feels no such compunction. His *Migratory Legends* type-list contains variants given by Asbjørnsen in *huldreeventyr*.
17. In his use of the genre definition "novella," it is likely that Moe was referring to the distinction of his time between the "Erzählung" and the "Novelle" as it was clarified by Goethe, among others. This distinction and a history of the term are discussed in Asbjørn Aarseth's chapter on the novella in *Episke Strukturer* and Aarseth's work in its turn is critiqued by Lars Arild and Jørgen Haugan in their *Edda* article from 1986, "Novellen i teori og praksis."
18. Review of *Norske huldreeventyr og folkesagn* by an anonymous reviewer in *Morgenbladet* 1845, number 258.
19. Of course Asbjørnsen's earlier biographers Hans Hansen and Knut Liestøl discuss the *huldreeventyr*, but there is little of literary criticism in their remarks. The stories are treated as autobiographical insights into Asbjørnsen's life. In his annotated edition of *Norske huldreeventyr og folke-*

sagn from 1949, the edition cited in this study, Liestøl gives detailed biographical background material for each of the stories. Truls Gjefsen in his recent biography does take the cultural context of Asbjørnsen's times into greater account in his discussion of the *huldreeventyr*.

20. Hansen does not mince words in his criticism. Of the unlucky Rolf Olsen he writes, "Rolf Olsen, like his afore-mentioned father Andreas Olsen, had at one time a literary reputation, but he deserved it as little as, perhaps even less, than his father did" (137). A great many other now forgotten, and some not forgotten, authors are similarly summarily dismissed in this remarkable little book. In his discussion of Moe and Asbjørnsen Hansen is, in a footnote, extremely critical of a Danish Professor Flor, who in the most recent edition of his *danske læsebog* had included a story by Bjørnson as the only work by a Norwegian writer after 1814. Hansen writes, "Why hasn't Professor Flor also included Asbjørnsen, since a new era in Norwegian literature originates with him" (103).

21. Asbjørnsen showed no compunction in combining elements from different variants of a legend or tale in order to make a better story. In fact, he carefully selected the variants of each particular legend that could most closely be integrated into the overall effect of the composite story. He was undoubtedly as much a "selective" editor as he was a "selective" novelist in the variants he chose to use.

22. In *Norske naturmytologier,* Nina Witsozek traces the importance of nature in Norwegian society from the time of the Eddic poem *Håvamål* up to and including the present. With respect to nation-building, she writes "I wish to suggest that what gives the period of nation-building its ideological and poetic coherence and integrity is a tradition which might be tentatively described as 'eco-humanist.' Eco-humanism in this case refers to a cosmology based on humanist ideals, but one in which the symbolic referents of identity derive from nature imagery and from a particular allegiance to place" (43).

23. This passage contains literal translations of Asbjørnsen's story titles in order to underscore the point that Jæger is making in his analysis; however, the reader unable to read the stories in the original will be hard pressed to find good translations in English. Precisely because the *huldreeventyr* are localized in time and place, they have not generated much interest outside of Norway, or at least Scandinavia. The most complete collection in English of which I am aware is to be found in the 1881 text *Round the Yule Log: Norwegian Folk and Fairy Tales* translated by H. L. Brækstad. This volume contains these stories with Brækstad's titles: "An Old-fashioned Christmas Eve," "Matthias the Hunter's Stories," "The Cormorants of Udrøst," "A Day with the Capercailzies," "Mother Bertha's Stories," "Legends of the Mill," "Mackerel Trolling," "The Giant and Johannes Blessom," "An

Evening in the Squire's Kitchen," "A Summer Night in a Norwegian Forest," "The Witch," and, strangely, part of "A Reindeer Hunt in the Rondane Mountains" translated as "Peter Gynt." Though not inaccurate translations, these renditions lack the freshness and vigor of the originals and totally fail to convey the difference in language between the frame narration and the narration of the folk narrators. Interestingly enough, the volume is introduced by Edmund Gross, today perhaps best known as an Ibsen critic, in this fashion: "Three names in the living literature of Norway may be said to have escaped from the provinciality of a narrow home-circle, and to have conquered a place for themselves in the general European concert. Two of these,—Ibsen and Björnson,—are borne by professional poets; the third is that of a man of science whose irresistible bias towards literary style may be said to have made a poet of him against his will" (xiii).
24. According to Liestøl, the model for the young woman in "The Hulder Clan" was the daughter of Ole Jacobsen Grinder, Caroline Marianne, one of Asbjørnsen's students when he was a tutor and to whom he was briefly secretly engaged (Liestøl, notes to A 1: 229).
25. Note that Baumgartner too insists on linking Asbjørnsen with Moe, and certainly 1845 would seem to be somewhat late for "declaring a program" and "launching a folkloristic project" since *Norske folkeeventyr* was first published in 1841. In actuality, neither Asbjørnsen nor Moe seemed particularly interested in political issues.
26. As Moe's letters to Asbjørnsen make clear, neither of the two fairy tale collectors seemed particularly interested in political issues of the day. Soelvold was the editor of *Statsborgeren*, a periodical which appeared from 1831 to 1837 and which was influential as an organ for the farmer opposition to the establishment. Asbjørnsen, in so far as he would have had a political leaning at all would most probably have been in sympathy with the views of the *intelligens* party, and the status quo, rather than sympathizing with the farmer's point of view.

CHAPTER 3

1. There is a vast literature on this subject, but see particularly Nina Witoszek's "Der Kultur møter Natur: Tilfellet Norge" in which she argues that the Nature vs. Culture dichotomy doesn't hold for Norway, where Nature *is* Culture, her book *Norske naturmytologier*, and "Nasjon og natur: Eit essay om den norske veremåten" by Gunnar Skirbekk. Of course, Norwegians are not alone in claiming a special relationship to nature. See, for example, *Den kultiverade människan*, in which Jonas Frykman and Orvar Löfgren trace the trait in Swedish society.

2. Only about three percent of Norwegian land is arable. Mountains cover over sixty percent and forests over twenty percent of the land mass.
3. As Yi-Fu Tuan explains in *Topophilia*, "A symbol is a repository of meanings. Meanings arise out of the more profound experiences that have accumulated through time" (145).
4. Of course, Peter Rabinowitz is not the only scholar who discusses the entire "mock reader/author" relationship. It is a staple in Affective/Reader response criticism; but I prefer Rabinowitz' definitions because they are clear and because he pays particular attention to the conventions that readers bring to the text before opening the book. Expectations of readers are discussed further in a later chapter.
5. This frame narrator should not be confused with Asbjørnsen himself, since the somewhat condescending attitude of the frame narrator towards his informants does not reflect what is known about Asbjørnsen's attitude towards the storytellers. By all accounts, Asbjørnsen was a jovial and convivial fellow who thoroughly enjoyed hearing the tales he collected. The frame narrator is a literary construct who becomes a character in the story.
6. I have been unable to determine the identity of C. F. B. The review appears on pages 99–100 of issue 28 of *Frey*.
7. Vi fulgte stien under Grefsenåsen nedover høydene mot Grefsen. Hvitlige tåker svevde over elvedraget og myrene nede i dalen. Opp over byens røkslør hevet seg Akershus med sine tårn, der trådte klart frem mot fjordens speil, hvori Nesodden kastet seg langt ut som en mektig slagskygge. Himmelen var ikke ganske ren, og der var litt drag i skyer og luft; månens lys blandet seg med sommernattens demring og dempet omrissene i forgrunnen av det landskap, som utstrakte seg for våre føtter. Men over fjorden lå månelyset blankt og strålende, mens Asker- og Bærumsåsene, fortonende i sortblå skygninger, hevet seg over hverandre høyt opp i luften og dannet landskapets fjerne ramme.
8. Fra Tyristranden gikk vi en av de første dager i mai—det var lenge før jaktloven utklekkedes—opp igjennem lien for den følgende morgen å være på en tiurlek i Skjærsjøhaugen, som på disse kanter hadde ord for å være det sikreste.
9. It has been difficult to determine the exact literacy rate for Norway in 1845. Benedict Anderson writes that "as late as 1840, even in Britain and France, the most advanced states in Europe, almost half the population was still illiterate" (Anderson 1991, 75), but compulsory education had been instituted in Norway as early as 1739, primarily with the intent that the populace should be able to read the Bible in order to prepare for confirmation. In the countryside there were 166,000 students in 7,171 schools in 1837, 91.5 percent of these schools were ambulatory. See Fritz Hodne, *Norges Økonomiske Historie 1815–1970*. The public school was considered

inferior to private schools and many of the urban residents sent their children for private education. It seems safe to assume that by 1845, many Norwegians could read. However, a study by Kjell Ivar Vannebo, *En Nasjon av Skriveføre*, has shown that many of these readers had very minimal reading ability. That the initial audience for *Norske huldreeventyr og folkesagn* was probably mostly urban and more highly educated can also be assumed by the relatively small size of the editions in the 1840s. Vannebo suggests that 300 was a typical number of copies for works published between 1814 and 1847, although the 1848 collection of *huldreeventyr* was published in an edition of 1300. Collett's observation that "the book is in everyone's hands," really means "everyone who matters" in the small circle of the elite.

10. Of special interest is Julian Kramer's article, "Norsk identitet—et produkt av underutvikling og stammetilhørighet" [Norwegian Identity—A product of under-development and tribal attachment] in *Den Norske væremåten*, in which Kramer, who lives and works in Norway, sees resemblance between the Norwegian 17 May *bunad* display and the colorful costumes of the tribes of his native South Africa. This puzzled Kramer until he realized that Norway was for so many years a tribal society waging a long battle against colonialism. Nina Witoszek sees as well that elements of 17 May festivities compose a *rite de passage*. See *Norske naturmytologier* (148). Not everyone agrees that a colonial parallel is appropriate for Denmark/Norway, but there is little doubt that Norwegians felt themselves the inferior half of the "twin realms."

11. Moe actually writes, "for jakts skyld," which seems to be an expression he made up for the occasion.

12. Mot vest og nord utbredte seg for våre føtter den uendlige fjellslette, grågrønne, brunlige, sorgvekkende strekninger . . . gjennem denne halvt gjennemsiktige luft gjøt solen sitt strålevell utover Vestfjellenes sne- og isbreer; vinfarvede skyer med gyllen brem svevde over dem, og den rødlige funklende gullglans, fjellene lå i, gjenstrålte høyt opp i luften og gjennomtindret hele den nordvestlige himmel.

13. It is beyond the scope of this study to explore the enormous impact of the visual arts on the creation of the Norwegian imagined community. Particularly in the folk tale collections, generations of Norway's finest artists have reconceptualized the words of Asbjørnsen and Moe in pictures. See "Eventyrtegnerne" by Snorre Evensberget in the forward to the second volume of the Norwegian Bookclub's 1982 edition of *Norske folkeeventyr*. People the world over know what trolls are *supposed* to look like thanks to Erik Werenskiold and Theodor Kittelsen, but many other fine illustrators have helped to build the national narrative through their work.

14. [Vi] vandret opp gjennom Bjerkehagens løvrike lunder, hvor rødstjerten og bokfinken i oretoppene feiret dagen med raske velklingende slag;

fluesnapperne vimset om mellom grenene og gav sitt ord med i laget, mens havesangeren, beskjedent skjult bak løvet, lot sin muntre sang strømme ut fra de tette, dunkle kroner. Morgenen var så stille og lun; bjerkens blad rørte seg neppe, og da vi kom opp av stien gjennem engene, så vi, når der falt et solstreif i det grønne, ennu duggperlene funkle på kløveren og i maristakkens foldete blad. Svalene strøk lavt efter de fine libeller; buskskvetten satt gyngende på en tistel og kvitret i akeren. Her hadde vi lerkesang fra den blå himmel, der på alle kanter omgjerdedes av lyse sommerskyer, som skjermet oss mot den hete sol.

15. [D]et rike løvverk av moser og lavarter, som dekket de fuktige stokkevegger, spilte, forfrisket ved regnet, i det glimrende sollys. Utenfor, i skogen, var der en glede over alle planter og fugler. Pyroler og linnéer utsendte strømmer av vellukt, og granen drysset sin duft over oss.

16. oppover engene på østsiden av Akerselven forbi Torshaug og Sandaker gjennem Lillohagen til Oset ved Maridalsvannet.

17. Solen stod allerede i åskanten, og hvis jeg ville nå frem, mens folk var oppe, var det ikke å tenke på å gå den lange vei først om Dals Kirke opp til Midtskog, og derfra igjennem den største del av Gjerdrum den dårlige veien over Myrersletten, som nu måtte være dobbelt slem og kronglet efter den friske november kulde, vi hadde hatt. . . . Vi kom ut på Kulsrudsåsen, hvorfra man ser ut over Øvre-Romerikes store flate . . . like ned for meg hadde jeg Heni og Gjerdrums kirker.

18. It could be argued that these words indicate Asbjørnsen's fundamental place within the canon, but actually the characteristics praised here, nature description and description of the people, are the same characteristics that are *always* quoted in the literary histories, and are only part of the unified literary treatment I am claiming for this text. Asbjørnsen exists in the canon primarily as half of the "Asbjørnsen and Moe" entity.

19. Nina Witoszek writes of *Peer Gynt*: "Nowhere is the interplay of Nature and Culture so clearly defined. . . . Having indulged in the scandalous delights of Culture, Peer Gynt returns to Nature. There, in his seter, in the arms of Solveig, he discovers that love, truth and Nature are one" (102).

20. William Archer was one of the first Ibsen scholars to draw attention to the debt *Peer Gynt* owed to Asbjørnsen. In the introduction to his translation of *Peer Gynt*, Archer mentions the obvious source material of the Peer Gynt, Bøyg, and Gudbrand Glesne stories and then continues, "Many scattered traits and allusions, however, are borrowed from other legends in the same storehouse of grotesque and marvellous imaginings . . . the appearance of the Green-Clad One with her Ugly Brat, who offers Peer Gynt a goblet of beer (Act III, Sc. 3) is obviously suggested by an incident in 'Berthe Tuppenhaug's Stories' (p. 129). Old Berthe, too, supplies the idea of correcting Peer Gynt's eyesight according to the standard of the

hill-trolls (Act III, Sc. 6), as well as the germ of the fantastic yarn-ball episode in the last act (Sc. 6). The story of the theft of the bride by Bjørn Prestestulen, told in 'En Søndagskveld til Seters' has elements in common with Per's theft of the bride Ingrid at the end of Act I of *Peer Gynt*" (Archer, 182).

21. "Da han kom opp imot Høvringen, for der skulle han være i ei seter om natta, var det så mørkt, at han ikke kunne se en neve for seg, og hundene tok til å skoggjø, så det var reint spøkelig. Rett som det var, kom han inn på noe, og da han tok bort på det, var det både kaldt og sleipt og stort, og han syntes ikke han var kommet av vegen heller, så han ikke kunne vite hva det var for noe; men ohoglé var det. 'Hvem er det?' sa han Per, for han kjente det rørte på seg. 'Å, det er han Bøyg,' svarte det. Dermed var Per Gynt like klok; men han gikk utmed et stykke, for ensteds må jeg vel komme fram, tenkte han. Rett som det var, kom han innpå noe igjen, og da han tok bort på det, var det også både stort og kaldt og sleipt. 'Hvem er det?' sa Per Gynt. 'Å, det er Bøygen,' svarte det igjen. 'Ja, enten du er rett eller bogjé, så får du sleppe meg fram,' sa Per, for han skjønte, at han gikk i rund ring, og at Bøygen hadde ringt seg omkring selet. Dermed så lea den litt på seg, så Per kom fram til selet. Da han kom inn, var det ikke lysere der enn det var ute, og han fór og famla omkring veggene og skulle sette fra seg bøssa og legge av skreppa; men rett som han gikk og trevla seg fram, kjente han igjen dette kalde og store og sleipe. 'Hvem er det da?' ropte Per. 'Å, det er den store Bøygen,' svarte det, og hvor han tok og hvor han baud til å gå, så kjente han ringen av Bøygen. Det er nok ikke godt å være her, tenkte Per, sia denne Bøygen er både ute og inne, men jeg skal vel skjepe på denne tverrbleien. Så tok han bøssa og gikk ut igjen og famla seg fram, til han fann skallen på den. 'Hva er du for en?' sa Per. 'Å, jeg er den store Bøyg Etnedalen,' sa stortrollet. Så gjorde Per Gynt bråfang og skaut tre skudd midt i hue på den."

22. *Peer Gynt* has proven through the years notoriously difficult to translate, written as it is in rhymed verse. (Although this particular extract is an exception). The best available English translation is probably that of Rolf Fjelde, but I have chosen to render my own translation and relinquish rhyme for the more literal translation. Fjelde often takes considerable liberty in order to get his lines to rhyme.

23. It is worth noting that Peer Gynt has a lot in common with the younger son, the Ashlad, of the Norwegian fairy tales. He shares the recklessness and the sassy retorts of the fairy tale hero.

24. "En høst var han kommet i hold med en svær bukk. Han skaut på den og kunne ikke anna vite, enn at den var stokkdau, så falt den. Så gikk han, som en ofte pleier, og satte seg skrevs over ryggen på den, og skulle løyse på kniven og by til å skille nakkebeinet fra skallen. Men best han hadde

satt seg, spratt den opp, la horna tilbake og trykte han ned imellom dem, så han satt som i en armstol, og så gikk det av sted, for kula hadde bare strøket dyret på skallen, så det var svimeslått. Slik skyss har vel aldri noen menneske hatt, som den han Gudbrand fekk. Det gikk mot vær og vind, over de fæleste breer og styggurer. Så satte den over Gjenden-eggen, men da bad han til Vårherre, for da trudde han, at han aldri skulle få se sol eller måne mer. Men til sist la reinen på vatnet og svømte tvers over med skytteren på ryggen. Imens hadde han fått kniven laus, og i det samme bukken satte foten på landet, støtte han den i nakken, og dau var den, og Gudbrand Glesne hadde visst ikke gjort den reisa om igjen, om han kunne ha vunnet all den rikdom, som til var."

25. "Den Peer Gynt var en for seg sjøl . . . Han var riktig en eventyrmaker og en reglesmed, du skulle hatt moro av: han fortalte alltid, han sjøl hadde vært med i alle de historier, folk sa var hendt i gamle dager."
26. I am indebted to William Mishler for this apt comparison.
27. Cited in Kjell Ivar Vannebo's *En Nasjon av Skriveføre* after an 1849 study by H. Nissen.

CHAPTER 4

1. In his article, "The Field Study of Folklore in Context," Richard Baumann presents a series of contexts into which folklore is integrated, but rejects using his outline as any sort of checklist. Baumann states: "More important than any checklist is the basic contextual frame of reference, the conception of folklore as fundamentally rooted in the richness of human social and cultural life—not simply folklore and culture, or folklore in culture, but folklore *as* culture" (Baumann 1983, 367. Baumann's italics).
2. The language of *Norske huldreeventyr og folkesagn* will be discussed in chapter seven where Bakhtinian concepts as they apply to this text are further explicated.
3. A memorat is defined as a "personal story about a supranormal experience told by either the individual or a third person quoting him or her" (Kvideland and Sehmsdorf 1988, 19).
4. Liestøl's notes to the 1949 edition contain voluminous information about the people who actually told Asbjørnsen many of the stories.
5. See Hjalmar Christensen's *Det nittende aarhundredes kulturkamp i Norge* for a nice summary of these distinctions.
6. Liestøl is, of course, referring to the people of the mid-nineteenth century, although his verb tense does not make this apparent!
7. It is, of course, impossible to ascertain for certain what previous populations have really believed. See C. W. von Sydow's classic article from 1934, "The

Mannhardtian Theories about the Last Sheaf and the Fertility Demons from a Modern Critical Point of View," reprinted in *Selected Papers on Folklore*. Von Sydow writes: "An essential lack in former tradition research was that it understood everything the folk said in assertive form as belief. Nothing can be more absurd. All these bogy figures that the folk scare children with: the old man of the well who catches them if they go too near the well; and the wolf, witch, etc., who catches them if they trample down the corn, etc., are *purely fictitious* beings that the adults only *pretend* exist, but do not believe in themselves. They are *pedagogical* fictions, which the adults fancy for the children, and want them to believe in, until they understand better, and do not get into trouble or cause damage" (101. von Sydow's italics).

8. This study is not particularly concerned with the variants that Asbjørnsen had at his disposal. Since I am considering *Norske huldreeventyr og folkesagn* as a literary and cultural text with a folklore theme, rather than as a folklore text, the actual legends as re-told in the stories are of more interest to me than variants which Asbjørnsen chose *not* to use. A study of variants based upon Asbjørnsen's papers in the *folkeminnesamling* would undoubtedly be of great interest, but it is not the focus of this study.

9. Jeg ble grepet av en ubeskrivelig angst; det fór isnende gjennem meg ved disse lyd, og redselen forøkedes ved skummelheten mellem stammene, hvori alle gjenstander viste seg fortrukne, bevegelige, levende, utstrekkende tusener av hender og armer efter den villsomme vandrer. Alle mine barndoms eventyr fremmanedes for den oppskremte fantasi og gjorde seg gjeldende i de former, der omgav meg; jeg så hele skogen oppfylt av troll og alfer og gjekkende dverger.

10. Barre Toelken, in *The Dynamics of Folklore*, writes that a folklorist observing a folklore performance must always remember the Heisenberg principle, "the fact recognized by scientists that the very presence of an observer is bound to have some effect on the phenomenon under scrutiny. In folklore field work, this may produce negative results when the observer impedes the process under study, confusing results when the process takes place only because the observer is present, or positive results when the observer is able—as an outsider—to ask about things or observe matters that would be difficult or impossible for an insider to deal with" (51).

11. As Timothy Tangherlini defines the term, "The Other is constituted by all legend actants who belong to the 'outside' realm. This realm is in direct opposition to the 'inner realm,' which is bounded by the cultural borders of the tradition group. Sometimes these borders are physically discernible, such as the boundaries of the nineteenth century farm. Other times, the boundaries are more subtle and harder to recognize" (Tangherlini 1995, 32–33).

12. Som en fjorten års gutt kom jeg en lørdags eftermiddag kort efter sankthanstid til Øvre-Lyse, den siste gård i Sørkedalen. Jeg hadde så ofte kjørt og gått den slagne landevei mellem Kristiania og Ringerike; nu hadde jeg efter et kort besøk i mitt hjem til en avveksling tatt veien forbi Bogstad til Lyse, for derfra å gå kløvveien eller benveien over den nordlige del av Krogskogen til kjerraten i Åsa.
13. "Dem driver så med slåttonna, at dem mest inte får i seg maten . . . han finner nok fram."
14. Foran ilden satt en mørk skikkelse, som på grunn av sin stilling mellem meg og det flammende bål syntes å være av en aldeles overnaturlig størrelse. Krogskogens gamle røverhistorier fór meg plutselig igjennem hodet, og jeg var et øyeblikk i begrep med å løpe min vei; men da jeg fikk øye på barhytten ved ilden, de to karer, som satt foran den, og de mange økser, der var fasthugget i stubben ved siden av en felt furu, ble det meg klart, at det var tømmerhuggere.
15. "Han far var på hogst hos mannen på Ask uti Lier, og så hogg han oppe i Askmarka. Om kvelden gikk han til ei stue lengre nede mot bygda og holdt til hos Helge Myra."
16. As Liestøl points out in his notes to this story, the belief that the *underjordiske* should not be disturbed in the evening or at night is a common belief throughout Scandinavian folklore and one that is repeated in variations several times in the stories of *huldreeventyr*.
17. "Halvor, Halvor! Tidlig kom du, og seint går du". . . . "det har jeg hørt før . . . men det var ikke det jeg meinte, det var den gang han var til bryllups i vårfjøset på Kilebakken". . . . "Det var på vårsida, riktig straks før påsketider i 1815, da han far budde på Oppen-Eie, snøen var ikke borte enda." Liestøl informs us that Oppen-Eie was part of the farm Oppen in Ådal, about one and a half miles northwest of Hønefoss (A 2: 347).
18. Jeg måtte fortelle om Smørbukk og hunden Gulltann og enda gi til beste et par nissehistorier om Vagernissen og Burenissen, som drog høy fra hverandre, og møttes med hver sin høybør på nakken, og sloss så de ble borte i en høysky. Jeg måtte fortelle om nissen på Hesselberg, som tirret gårdshunden, til mannen kastet ham ut over låvebroen. Barna klappet i hendene og lo. "Det var til pass til ham det, stygge nissen," sa de og fordret mere. "Nei, nu plager I løytnanten for meget, barn," sa jomfru Cecilie; "nu forteller nok faster Mette en historie" . . . "Jeg blir redd, nei du skal fortelle løytnant; når du forteller, så blir jeg aldri redd." Liestøl notes that the stories about the Vager and Bure *nisser* were some that Asbjørnsen sent to Andreas Faye in 1835. He told Faye, "The tale about the *nisse* at Bure I heard from several people in the area during my two-year stay in Ringerike, but since I didn't care much about such things at that time, I had forgotten it again until

Jørgen Moe told me the story again about a year ago" (Liestøl, notes to A 1: 238).

19. Det var noe, jeg meget nødig innlot meg på, da der hørte sang til. Men de ville på ingen måte la meg slippe, og jeg begynte allerede å rømme meg for å forberede min overmåte uharmoniske stemme til å synge hallingdansen, som hørte til, da den omtalte smukke søsterdatter, til barnas glede og min frelse, trådte inn. "Ja nu barn, nu skal jeg fortelle, hvis I kan få kusine Lise til å synge hallingen for jer," sa jeg, idet hun tok plass, "og så danser I selv, ikke sant?"

20. This legend, ML 4015, is known in at least twenty-five variants in Norway, is widely spread throughout north and central Europe, and was known in the Middle Ages. "In folk legends the story is consistently focused on the fear of the dead and on the narrow escape of the unwitting observer" (Kvideland and Sehmsdorf 1988, 93).

21. See Niels Ingwersen's interpretation of this interplay in his article "The Folktale as Response to History" (SS 67). Ingwersen believes that the old woman's comforting words to the child actually are cold comfort to the alert adult members of the audience, because they falsify the situation. He states, "Asbjørnsen's sly use of the frame in 'En gammeldags juleaften' suggests that he did not intend to permit the question of what happens after death to be a general, vague concern; the opening and concluding details particularize the narrative and make his audience confront the issue of what happens next."

22. Most translators will translate the word used here, *brennevin*, as brandy or strong spirits, but in "Berthe Tuppenhaug's Stories," the old woman, in her home remedy to "fix" the frame narrator's sprained ankle, uses *brennevin* over which she mutters an incantation. The frame narrator writes, "Berthe got a squat blue flask and a shotglass with a wooden stem from the cupboard, poured in the aquavit, set the glass beside her on the hearth, unbuttoned my snow-sock and helped me get my shoe off" (A 1: 54–55). [Berthe hentet en undersetsig blå lerke og et brennevinsglass med trefot henne i det blommede skap, skjenket i akevitten, satte glasset ved siden av seg på skorstenen, knappet snesokken opp og hjalp av meg skoen.] If we were to translate *brennevin* as aquavit in the *huldreeventyr* as a whole, then we are dealing with strong spirits indeed! Aquavit is an 80–85 proof liquor made from potatoes.

23. "Det kan vel være så en ti, tolv år sia," begynte han, "jeg hadde ei kolmile inne på skogen ved Kampenhaug. Om vinteren låg jeg inne der, og hadde to hester og kjørte kol til Bærumsverket. En dag så kom jeg til å bli litt for lenge ved verket, for jeg traff noen kjenninger ovatil Ringerike; vi hadde nå litt snakk mellom oss, og litt drakk vi også—ja brennevin da—, og så kom jeg ikke tilbake til mila, før klokka var imot ti."

24. Eilert Sundt, Norway's famous first sociologist, studied the problem in *Om aedrueligheds tilstanden i Norge* [On the State of Sobriety in Norway], which was first published in 1859. According to Sundt's investigation, there were certain celebrations or situations in which *brennevin* was called for, among them Christmas celebrations, weddings, and to a lesser extent funerals. It was common for women in childbirth to be given alcohol, and it also belonged with hard work and traveling. It was especially common for the merchants in Kristiania to give the farmers a little *brennevin* for the long trip home from the city. There is evidence, however, that by the time *Norske huldreeventyr og folkesagn* was published, alcohol consumption was on the decline. See *Kampen om alkoholen i Norge 1816–1904* by Per Fuglum.
25. "Du må vel for brennande fanden tru vi er så dumme, at vi skjønner dette er løgn og kjerringrør? . . . Jeg kan nå for fanden ikke skjønne på det, at du kan sitte her og ljuge og si, at du har sett slikt sjøl."
26. "Er du nå ute med reglene dine og lyver igjen, smed?"
27. "Hå, hå, hå" lo Per i skjegget, kjennelig tilfreds med kapteinens spøkende ytring om hans fordelaktige ytre. "Jeg har ikke trudd på slikt, for jeg har aldri sett hverken troll eller hulder." "Men der bodde dog en bergkjerring borti Holleia her i gamle dager?" sa kapteinen. "Å, der er ikke anna enn et gammalt eventyr. Jeg har nok hørt slikt prat, men jeg tror det ikke," svarte Per. "Ja, men du vet da visst full beskjed derom, du som har ferdes her i marken så lenge? Du får fortelle hva du vet; ti denne bymann er en narr efter slike historier." "Kanskje det? Ja, kan det da, men jeg trur ikke det er sant," forsikret Per og begynte.
28. "Godaften, graver," sa jeg. Han målte meg fra øverst til nederst, spyttet i nevene, og tok igjen fatt på sitt arbeid. "Det er tungt arbeid du har i dette våte vær," forsatte jeg uforrtrødent. "Det er ikke lettere i solskinn," svarte han med et eddiksurt grin, og ble ved å grave. "For hvem graver du denne grav?" spurte jeg, i det håp at der måskje av dette spørsmål kunne utspinne seg en samtale. "For fanden og kjerka" svarte graveren. Over dette måtte jeg utbe meg en forklaring. "Fanden tar sjela og kjerka får pengene," svarte han. "Ikke således; jeg mente, hvem skal ligge i graven?" "Ei dau kjerring," svarte graveren. Der var broen avkastet. Dette innså jeg kunne ikke lede til noe ønskelig resultat. Utålmodig over regnet, som igjen begynte å ruske, og ergerlig over min efter all sannsynlighet mislykkede ekspedisjon fortalte jeg graveren, hvorledes jeg hadde søkt ham for å få høre eventyr og historier fra gamle tider; sa at han saktens ikke skulle fortelle meg dem for intet, at det endog måtte glede ham å ha en person å fortelle dem for som meg, der trodde på slikt, hva folk i alminnelighet ikke gjorde i våre dager, osv.
29. "Jeg har ikke fornummet noe, jeg kan ikke si det," sa den gamle. "Vatnet er nok blitt slått av og satt på for meg imellom, når jeg har dorma litt på saga om natta, or imellom har heg hørt det har tusla i bakhunen, men jeg

har aldri sett noe. Folk trur ikke på slikt mer heller nå," vedble han med et spørrende blikk til meg, "og derfor tør det ikke våge seg fram; folk er for kloke og beleste nå til dags." "Det kan du ha rett i," sa jeg, ti jeg merket godt, at der lå noe skjult bak det blikk han sendte meg, og ville heller ha ham til å fortelle gamle historier enn innlate meg på å drøfte hans tvil og den påstand at opplysningen skulle være en skremsel for nisser og underjordiske. "Det kan du ha rett i på en måte. I gamle dager var folk sterkere i troen på all slags trollskap; nu later de som de ikke tror på det, for å synes kloke og opplyste, som du sier. I fjellbygdene hører man dog ennu, at de underjordiske viser seg, tar folk inn til seg, og slikt. Nu skal du," føyde jeg til for rett å få ham på gli, "nu skal du bare høre en historie, som skal være hendt ensteds, men hvor og når det er hendt kan jeg ikke rett erindre."

30. "Jeg såg på henne, mens jeg gikk bortover vegen, men da jeg var kommet et stykke lengre fram, og der var kommet en bergrabbe imellom så jeg ikke kunne se henne lenger, så tenkte jeg; det er da galt, at mennesket skal gå der og vasse i myra, du skal gå opp på rabben og si til henne, at hun er gått av vegen. Jeg gikk opp, men der var ikke annet å se enn månen, som skinte på vasspyttene i myra, og så kunne jeg nok skjønne, at det hadde vært huldra". . . . Skjønt det forekom meg, at der skulle mere til å skjønne at det var huldren, beholdt jeg dog min tvil for meg selv, da jeg forutså, at mine innvendinger ikke ville rokke hans tro, men kun bringe ham til taushet; jeg spurte derfor kun, om han ikke oftere hadde sett sådant.

31. Here again Asbjørnsen's focus is clear. The frame narrator does not ask the Halling to tell just *any* legends, simply the ones dealing with the supernatural creatures. Asbjørnsen the selective editor chose not only variants but legend types as well.

32. " 'So va dæ ein dag trast etté, 'o Birgit gjætte kjydn burtundé Nysætknippé. Rett so dæ va, fekk 'o høyre gampa som kneggja, kjy som rauta, bjelleskrammel, å gjentu som svalla å leto på lu å prillahodn, plent som når dei buføre. Ho styrde kringum se på alle kanta, men såg korkji folk ell' krytyr, å so kunna 'o nokk veta, att dæ mått væra haugafolke, som kom med bølingen sin te stølé. No skunda 'o se drive krytyré heim att, å sa tå ve hine ko ho hadde fornåmé. So snugga dei se te buføre på heimsætern då, for dei tålde no 'kji drygjy lenger på langstølé; dei voro rædde, at haugafolkji skull bli ille, når dei soto over tié, sér du.' . . . Jeg voktet meg vel for å forstyrre den gamle i hans tro ved en meget naturlig forklaring av den historie, han sist hadde fortalt. Efter min kjennskap til egnens daler, dekker og steile høyder var det meg klart, at en hjemvendende buferd var dradd gjennem en av de fjernere smådaler, således at lydbølgene av hestenes kneggen, kyrnes brølen og bjeller, og pikenes tale, lokk og lur, formedelst de mellomliggende høyder og bakker ikke umiddelbart hadde nådd Birgits øre, men først efter å være kastet tilbake fra Nysætknippens steile sider, og at hun, da hun intet kunne

oppdage, hadde trodd, at det var huldren." Liestøl explains that much of the traditional material in "A Halling with Angelica Root," and particularly the masterly rendition of the idiomatic halling dialect, can be attributed to Asbjørnsen's friend, A. W. Grøtting.

33. Berthe fortalte ennu mange historier. Omsider knirket sneen under sleden, og hesten prustet for døren. Jeg stakk Berthe noen skillinger i hånden for kur og pleie, og innen et kvarters tid var jeg hjemme. Eddikomslag og koldt vann gjorde foten snart god; men da Berthe kom opp i kjøkkenet på gården, og pukkende på sine kunster ville tilegne seg æren for min hurtige helbredelse, kunne barna ikke holde seg; de skrålte henne i øret hennes signevers, som jeg hadde lært dem, og spurte om hun syntes en tår brennevin og slikt sludder kunne hjelpe for vred.

34. Således ble Matthias ved å fortelle fort vekk om puslinger, huldrer og nisser, til vi kom ut på Kulrudsåsen, hvorfra man ser ut over Øvre-Romerikes store flate, der nu lå for oss i det klare måneskinn; mot nord hevet Mistberget seg blånende, med enkelte snepletter; like ned for meg hadde jeg Heni og Gjerdrums kirker; etter disse kunne jeg bestemme min kos, og da jeg dessuten fra tidligere jakter var vel kjent i egnen, sa jeg min veiviser farvel, og var hellig nok til å nå mitt bestemmelsessted uten å bli drillet av nissen eller fristet av huldren.

35. For det første er nemlig opplysningen steget så høyt, at istedenfor å rishye byttinger tre torsdagskvelder på søppeldyngen eller knipe dem i nesen med en gloende ildtang, som skikk var i hine dager, så lar de nu mor Torgersen eller en annen signekjerring støpe over barnet for svekk, trollskap og fanteri, eller de sender en av barnets bleier til Stine Bredvolden, som er så klok, at hun på den leser barnets sykdom og skjebne, og derefter avgjør over liv og død.

36. "Ensteds i Solør var det, ja det var et bryllup. De spiste der og de drakk—de drikker alltid i bryllupene—, og mens de drakk og spiste, så hørte de en lyd fra en krok i stua. Naturligvis, ja, det var som en latter, en hes latter av flere mennesker—, men da de ikke så noen, og den kom fra en krok, hvor de kunne se, så var meningen den, at der var kommet ubudne gjester i laget. Naturligvis var det de underjordiske, for når der i gamle dager var noe på ferde, som de ikke kunne forstå, så var det alltid de underjordiske som var ute og hadde gjort det" . . . Derpå drakk han et glass øl og fortsatte: "Naturligvis bekreftet det seg også nå, at det hadde vært de underjordiske, som lo så hest i kroken; for det hendte siden, at en kone, som hadde forbindelse med disse underjordiske, kom til å tale med en huldrekulle, som naturligvis bodde i en haug tett ved, og som undertiden lånte smør og melk og annet sådant og alltid betalte ordentlig igjen—når kvinnfolka slipper slarven løs, så vet vi, hvorledes det går—naturligvis . . ."

37. "Det var i gamle dager naturligvis, men det var lenge etter de tider, da der

var bygd fjellstuer for de reisende som fór over Dovrefjell; for det var en, som skulle fare over fjellet ved juletider og reise sørover til Kristiania. Der skulle han naturligvis drikke jul, og det var dumt av ham, for naturligvis drikker de både mer og bedre alle årsens tider i Trondhjem enn i Kristiania . . . da han kom til en av fjellstuene—jeg tror det var Kongsvoll—, så skulle han hvile natten over der, og det var julenatten. Han kom inn, og naturligvis det brente på varmen og var lunt og godt og varmt."

38. Liestøl explains, "There is surely no doubt that the model is Hans Hansen Pillarviken (1798–1863), who then was the schoolteacher in Sel. . . . No doubt Asbjørnsen did not actually make a point of describing Pillarviken, but he borrowed so many characteristics from him that people recognized him right away. He himself was hurt by the caricature and broke off all correspondence with his friends" (Liestøl, notes to A 2: 301).

39. Det varte ikke lenge, før selskapet fra Tors seter innfant seg. Jenten var kjernesunn og rød og hvit; hun hadde et livlig ansikt og en trivelig figur. Ut av guttens åsyn lyste også frisk, ufordervet natur og åpen djervhet. Den tredje var skolemesteren; skjønt han ikke var meget over de tredve, var hans ansikt fullt av folder og rynker, som fornemmelig syntes å skrive seg fra en vedvarende bestrebelse for å gi seg en verdig mine. Hans klededrakt syntes også beregnet på å understøtte denne bestrebelse eller på å atskille ham fra de øvrige bønder: han gikk i en kjole av brunsort farve med uhyre lange, spisse skjøter; om halsen bar han hvitt halstørkle og store fadermordere, og på randen av disse var anbrakt egger, et slags utsydde spisser eller tagger. På den høyre side av hans vest stod der frem en uhyre bule, som jeg i begynnelsen antok hitrørte fra en gevekst; senere erfarte jeg, at det var et stort blekkhus, han alltid førte med seg. Denne manns hele fremtreden gjorde på den fremmede et meget ubehagelig inntrykk; ytterst ubehagelig var især den affekterte måte, hvorpå han snerpet sin munn sammen, når han talte. Fjellboens vitebegjærlighet og interesse for den fremmede han ser for seg, hans likefremme, naïve, undertiden såre ubeleilige spørsmål er bekjent. Men her opptrådte med skinnet av kultur en påtrengende nysgjerrighet og spørresyke, og hver gang han spurte, så han seg om med et blikk, som om han stod blant Vågås usepede ungdom, og på hans ansikt lå der en mine, om hans sammensnerpede munn et smil, der spurte de tilstedeværende: "Er det ikke godt sagt? Jo jeg kan føle sådanne karer på tennene!"

40. See *Bjørnstjerne Bjørnson og nasjonalismen* by Øystein Sørensen for a thorough discussion of Bjørnson's politics and his role in the cultural debates of his time.

41. It may be of some interest to note what Asbjørnsen thought of Bjørnson's early literary efforts. In October of 1858, Asbjørnsen sent a selection of Norwegian books and magazines to Jacob Grimm, with whom he corre-

sponded for many years. Among the books was Bjørnson's *Synnøve Solbakken*. Asbjørnsen writes that "there is perhaps more talent revealed [than in Ibsen] in *Synnøve Solbakken*; but although one can't deny the author a fine talent in the presentation of our people's idiosyncrasies, it still seems to me that he has studied the sagas more than life and nature, which also concerns his style, which is much too chronicle- and saga-like; but Bjørnson is young and let us hope that he will produce something better than this work; which is good, but which has been praised more than it really deserves in Denmark and Sweden" (pp. 263–64). This and four other letters from Asbjørnsen to Grimm appear in *Briefwechsel der Gebrüder Grimm mit Nordischen Gelehrten*.

CHAPTER 5

1. Of course the *huldreeventyr* contain plenty of women folk narrators, but they are all people whom an urbane story collector could be expected to meet more or less naturally. If Asbjørnsen cannot conceive of a plausible meeting between his frame narrator and the Gypsy wise woman, neither will he place him in the roadside tavern with the drunken card players of "The Lumber Haulers." Undoubtedly a wise decision! I will not use the usual translation of *signekjerring* as "witch" in this discussion, since it is not an accurate translation; but since the more accurate meaning of "a woman who heals with magic and incantations," is too cumbersome, I will use "wise woman." A witch in Norwegian is "heks."

2. There has been some discussion about whether the Norwegian term *tater* is an ethnic designation or simply a derogatory designation attached to a poor and itinerant segment of the population. See Bengt af Klintberg's review of Kvideland and Sehmsdorf's *Scandinavian Folk Belief and Legend* (*Journal of American Folklore* 103) in which Klintberg cautions against assuming that the term *tatere* in general refers to Gypsies. With some trepidation, I insist that in the stories "A Wise Woman" and "The Gypsies," Asbjørnsen was indeed discussing the ethnic Other, based on the physical descriptions of his characters. See also Eilert Sundt's *Beretning om fante-eller landstrygerfolket i Norge* [An Account of the Gypsy- or Tramp-populace in Norway] in which Sundt gives the conflicting meanings of the word *fant* and also distinguishes, based upon conversations with actual Gypsies, between *storvandringer*, who claimed a foreign origin and the *smaavandringer*, who simply were itinerant workers of one kind or another. Sundt seems to use *fant* and *tater* more or less interchangeably. The epigraph to this chapter is from this work.

3. Et stykke fra bygdeveien i en av de mellemste egner av Gudbrandsdalen lå det for noen år siden en hytte på en haug—Kanskje den ligger der ennu. Det var et mildt aprilvær utenfor; sneen smeltet; bekker bruste ned igjennem alle lier, marken begynte å bli bar; trostene skjentes i skogen; alle lunder var fulle av fuglekvitter, kort det tegnet til en tidlig vår . . . Inne i den røkfulle sperrestue var det uhyggelig og skummelt. En middelaldrende bondekone av et meget alminnelig og innskrenket utseende var i ferd med å puste ild i noen grener og rå trestykker, hun hadde lagt under kaffegryten på den lave skorsten.

4. Why early baptism should lead to death is not entirely clear from Grøn's text; but in the particularly harsh winter of 1755, all thirty infants born in Volda died, evidently because they were taken out in the cold conditions to be baptized in church.

5. "Folk sier det nytter ikke med denne støypinga, for barnet har ikke svekk, sier de, men er en bytting; der var en skinnfellmaker her om dagen og han sa det samme, for da han var liten, hadde han sett en bytting ute i Ringebu, og den var så blaut i kroppen og så lealaus som denne."

6. Den hun henvendte sin tale til, var et sværlemmet fruentimmer, der syntes å nærme seg de seksti. Hun var usedvanlig høy av vekst; ;men mens hun satt, syntes hun kun liten, og denne egenhet hadde hun å takke for, at man til hennes navn, Gubjør, hadde føyet økenavnet Langelår. I det taterfølge hun hadde flakket om med, førte hun andre navn. Grå hår stakk frem under skautet, der omgav et mørkt ansikt med buskede bryn og en lang ved roten bulket nese. Det opprinnelig innskrenkede, som antydedes ved en lav panne og ved ansiktets bredde over kinnbenene, stod i motsetning til det umiskjennelige uttrykk av list i hennes små, spillende øyne og til den inkarnerte bondefulhet, der utpreget seg i rynker og muskelspill. Hennes kledning betegnet henne som utvandrer fra et nordligere bygdelag; hennes ansikt og hele fremtreden antydet signekjerringen, eller i det minste den omstreifende, efter omstendighetene snart frekke og uforskammede, snart ydmyke og smiskende fantekjerring.

7. Liestøl notes that in nineteenth-century Norwegian literature, the word "Finn" can usually be considered synonymous with "Lapp" or "Sami" (Liestøl, notes to A 2: 352).

8. " . . . jeg skjønner meg på byttinger, for jeg har sett nok av dem."

9. "dette barnet er ikke mer en bytting, enn jeg er bytting."

10. "Til dokteren? Tvi!" sa signekjerringen og spyttet . . . "nei, gå til dokteren for slikt et barn, som har svekk, det skulle vel Fanden."

11. Casting involved dripping molten lead into cold water and then "reading" and interpreting the figures that were formed.

12. "Barnet har svekk, men der er ni slag svekk i verden. Ja, ja, det har jeg sagt deg, og du såg jo det, at han hadde vært ute både for trollsvekk og

vassvekk; for den første torsdagen så blei det en mann med to store horn og ei lang rumpe. Det var trollsvekk. Sist så blei det ei havfrue. Ja, du såg den jo så skjellig, som den var skildra. Det var vassvekken. Men nå er det torsdag igjen, og nå spørs det hva det blir, når vi støyper nå. Det er den tredje gangen det kommer an på, måvite. Der har du barnet," sa hun, og rakte det til konen, "La meg nå få i meg denne kaffedråpen, så skal jeg til."

13. "Sia sist torsdag," sa hun, "har jeg vært i sju kjerkesogn og skrapt vindusbly av kjerkevinduene ved natteleite; for det blei forbi med kjerkeblyet den gangen. Det kan leite på både sjel og kropp," mumlet hun hen for seg, mens hun av snushornet rystet ut i støpeskjeen noe av det efter sigende så møysomt innsamlede bly. "Du har vel henta nordenrennendes vatn høgstnattes?" spurte hun videre. "Ja, jeg var ved kvernbekken i gårnatt; det er det eneste vatn, som er nordrennendes på lang lei," svarte husmannskonen og tok frem et veltillukket spann, hvorav hun helte vannet i en ølbolle. Over denne ble lagt en byggbrødleiv, som der med en stoppenål var boret hull i. Da blyet var smeltet, gikk Gubjør hen i døren, så opp på solen, tok derpå støpeskjeen og helte det smeltede bly gjennem hullet langsomt ned i vannet, mens hun mumlet noen ord derover.

14. "Liksvekk, liksvekk!—først trollsvekk, så vassvekk, så liksvekk. En av dem kunne vært nok!" . . . "Ja, nå ser jeg, hvorledes det er gått til," vedble hun høyt og vendte seg til konen i huset: "Først har I reist gjennom en skog og forbi et berg, mens trolla var lause; der sa du Jesu navn. Så kom I over et vatn; der sa du også Jesu navn over barnet; men da du kom forbi kjerkegarden, var det før hanegal, så glømte du det, og her fanga barnet liksvekk."

15. "der spørs etter arvesølv. Har du arvesølv?" . . . "når det gjelder liv, så . . ."

16. "Skal barnet dø, før lauvet faller, så ser du bare svart, og ikke anna enn svart." Liestøl explains that from earliest times there was considered to be a special relationship between the eyes and life, and that impending death could be seen in the eyes (Liestøl, notes to A 2: 339).

17. Under denne fortelling viste der seg hos husmoren de umiskjenneligste tegn på engstelse. Mot slutningen ble de så påfallende, at selv fortellersken, der syntes å være grepet av sin egen fremstilling, ble oppmerksom derpå. "Hvad er på ferde?" spurte signekjerringen. "Å, det er mannen, som kommer" vedble hun med et blikk ut av døren og tilføyet høytidelig: "det er ikke blivendes for hun Gubjør ved pallen din; men vær ikke bange, mor; jeg skal gå nedenom kjerkegarden, så ser han meg ikke."

18. Kort efter kom Manden. Han tørrede Sveden af Panden med Trøieærmet, saa sig forskende om i Stuen, og fulgte med Øinene Konen, der forlegen gav sig noget at bestille ved Skorstenen; dernæst syntes Støbeskeen, som var bleven liggende under Bordet, at tiltrække sig hans Opmærksomhed. "Har du Noget Mad, Kjærring?" spurgte han. "Aa, Gud hjælpe mig," svarede

Konen, "jeg havde stegt lidt Flæsk; men det stjal denne Tyvekatten, mens jeg stelte Ungen." "Skulde En hørt saa galt," sagde Manden, "Flæsk til Fattigmandskost om Thorsdagen? Takke Gud, En kan faae det til Helgekost! Nei, det er vel gaaet med i Sørpen til Gubjør Langelaar; jeg syntes jeg saa det ene af de lange Benene hendes bag om Kirkemuren. Ja, jeg kunde tænke det, hun skulde komme igjen med Støbningen sin; men det siger jeg dig, at kommer hun igjen engang til, saa skal jeg see om jeg kan faae støbt hende ind i et Hul med Jernsprinkler for! Aa, dig Kjærring, dig skal jeg ogsaa tale lidt anderledes med!" The man threatens to report Gubjør for quackery, which was forbidden from an ordinance of 1794. See Olav Bø's article on wise women and country doctors in vol. 5 of *Norges kulturhistorie* for an enlightening overview of the medical situation in Norway of the nineteenth century. Considering the primitive state of knowledge and lack of doctors, it was perhaps not surprising that the people relied on age-old folk medicines.

19. Liestøl explains that Asbjørnsen was, of course, very interested in zoology and had heard the Swedish anthropologist Anders Adolph Retzius speak at a conference in Christiania in 1844. Retzius was the first to distinguish between "long" and "short" skull types. There was great interest in phrenology at this time.

20. I krokens halvskygge på den innerste seng eller bås av barakken lå en mann henstrakt på en skinnfell. Bak den lave panne, som han støttet mot en av muskelfylde svulmende håret arm, ferdedes tanker, hvis skygger svevet over et ansikt, like så mørkt som den sotete vegg, og hvis lyn glimtet frem i blikk så stikkende, stirrende og skumle, at selv den sløve vaktkar ble uhyggelig til mote, når de hendelsesvis falt på ham. Men intet ord røpet, hva der veltet seg i hans indre. Hans strie kullsorte hår, skarpe trekk, det lange ansikt, hvis underdel nu var bedekket med et kort sort skjegg, og dette egne blikk viste, at han hørte til de omvankende tatere eller langfantene, som vår almue i noen egner av landet kaller dem. Hans skumle utseende hadde skaffet ham navnet Svarte-Bertel. Av profesjon var han hesteskjærer, men fusket også med forskjellig hell på å kurere hester. Den annen lot til å være av en mere sorgløs natur, og hadde en lysere hudfarve; men taterstammens lave panne, skarpe ansikt, dyptliggende øyne og dette ubeskrivelige, på en gang utforskende, fikserende, stikkende blikk med dets uhyggelige fosforglans, utmerket også ham.

21. Of course Asbjørnsen and Sundt would later become the main antagonists in the famous "porridge war" which was waged in the newspapers. Asbjørnsen, who had written a cookbook under a pseudonym, insisted that the Norwegian peasant women made porridge in an inefficient manner while Sundt took the part of the housewives and insisted that they did not. Sundt was later proven to be correct.

22. The Gypsies evidently took advantage of the farmer's fear of this creature, which was supposed to be the familiar of witches. The troll-cat would steal milk from the farmer. See Bente Alver's *Heksetro og Trolddom* for a discussion of troll cats. Asbjørnsen includes a long footnote explaining how the Gypsies fool the unsuspecting farmer. First, the Gypsy poisons the cattle and buries the troll-cat, made of a bladder filled with red water surrounded by a cat-skin and including some kind of mechanism, in the barn. The next day, when the cattle are sick, the Gypsy appears and offers to cure the animals. This is done by digging up the troll-cat and chasing it from the barn. The Gypsy then gives the cows an antidote to the poison, unobserved by the farmer. The Norwegian novelist Johan Bojer writes of the troll-cat: "But the troll cat still lives. I remember that in 1914, when I was a lieutenant at Agdaness fortress, which is on the Tröndelagen seacoast, one day the housewives with whom my men were quartered resolved to raise the rent. Since the soldiers received only a few öre a day, and I could not see where the additional sums were coming from, I opposed the scheme. This naturally angered the women, and they warned me that I would regret it. And to be sure I was laid up in bed for the next three days with the very ailment that the troll cat is said to put upon one. The next time I marched by with my platoon, there stood a woman in each doorway, delightedly shouting, 'So you got what was coming to you!' There was not a doubt in their minds that one of them had got vengeance by setting a troll cat on me" (Bojer 1929, 724–725).

23. "Onde naboer har utsendt en trolldomsmaskan for å suge marg og blod av kuene dine," sa jeg, "det ser jeg; men får jeg råde, skal jeg vise den fram, og jeg skal hjelpe deg, så at den ikke får makt til å forderve fler." "Kan du det, min gode kone, skal jeg betale deg rundelig, og mat og klær skal du få attpå," sa bonden — "Følg med i fehuset, så skal jeg vise den, som suger blod og bryter bein," sa jeg til bonden; "men ta med hakke og spade." Han tok hakke og spade, og kona til bonden gikk etter han som en hund. "Jeg har aldri vært her," sa jeg, "men jeg værer godt og kjenner skjulte ting; gå til den svarte og kvite kua," sa jeg. — "Her er gravd før," sa bonden. — "Grav igjen!" sa jeg; "det som er skjult skal åpenbares." "Mannen grov, og best han grov, sprang der fram av båsen en katt og bort over golvet og skreik så fælt. I det samme gnistra det om øyene både på bonden og på kona hans som eld og luer." Her nikket hun betydningsfullt til tilhørerne og satte en hemmelighetsfull mine opp . . . "For det fikk jeg kaffe og tobakk, ullent og linnet, flesk og spekemat, seks sølvskeier og mange penger."

24. And how many enlightened citizens of the twenty-first century still may go out of their way to avoid walking under a ladder? It must also be mentioned that the short excerpts from Eilert Sundt's work cited here should not lead the reader to believe that Sundt found the Gypsies totally culpable for

their sometimes sorry treatment by the peasants. Sundt was just as likely to see the Gypsy as a victim of the society as he was to see him as a villain or a scapegoat. In all of his writings, Sundt does not allow his previous assumptions to interfere with later conclusions if changes are warranted.

25. "Der var en fut nord i dalen, han var så grovt ugudelig, at han ikke vørte hva han gjorde; men han fekk en urolig død. Når der ikke var folk i likstua, låg han stille; men når der kom folk inn, stod den døde mannen opp og tok dem i handa og takka for sist. Da han skulle begraves, satte de han i likkjelleren under kjerkegolvet. Nå var han rolig ei stund, men rett som det var, tok han til å spøke hver evige natt. En dag kom der en skomaker til en av gardene ved kjerka; han trudde ikke på spøkeriet, men vedda han skulle sitte på kjerkegolvet ved sida likkista ei heil natt og sy et par sko. De satte imot på det. Kista tok de opp av kjelleren, og skomakeren satte seg på golvet; men først kritta han en ring om seg. Da det leid ut på natta, kom sjølve Fanden flygende, reiv lokket av kista, slo hue av futen og flådde skinnet av han. Det dreiv han på med så hardt, at han ikke sanste skomakeren, som drog huden inn i ringen, ettersom Fanden fikk den av futen, og da det siste holdet slapp, drog han den til seg heil og holden. Da Fanden skulle ta den, kunne han ikke for ringen. Da blei han så arg og sint, som om han ville verpe både mord og brann, og han streik og bante, han ville ha igjen futeskinnet. 'Du får den ikke,' sa skomakeren. 'Men hva fanden vil du med skarvehuden?' spurte Fanden. 'Jeg vil barke den og gjøre sko av,' sa skomakeren."

26. Innen en time var forløpet, følte vaktkaren seg betatt av en uimotståelig tyngde og døsighet. Ilden ble svakere og svakere; til sist glødet den kun i levningene av den store tyrirot, hvis harpiksaktige deler undertiden utsendte en oppblussende flamme, som for et øyeblikk kastet et mørkerødt lys over taternes lurende ansikter. Endelig forkynte vaktkarens tunge åndedrag og dype snorken, at han ikke kunne legge noen hindring i veien for deres flukt.

27. Dog er der et spor av signekjerringen Gubjør Langelår. Forrige høst fant en renskytte, der forfulgte et skadeskutt dyr i en avsides bott oppe i Illmannshøen, hvorfra man ser nord over til Rondenes ville topper, levninger av et menneskelig skjelett som jerv og fjellrakk hadde søndergnaget. Mellem stenene lå et kobbersnushorn, fylt med småskåret bly. Dessuten fantes der et sammenrullet tanngjerde av en rokke, noen skaller av en venus og forskjellige andre sjødyr—rakerier, som ingen i dalen hadde sett eller kjente hensikten og bruken av, men som taterne anvender i sin ragusta—samt noen små flasker, hvorav en inneholdt en brunlig eller gullrød væske, der efter distriktslægens sigende var opium.

28. Anne Cohen Kiel has written a fascinating account of the way many Norwegians behave on public transportation and in crowds. See "Confessions of an Angry Commuter: Or Learning How to Communicate the Non-

Communicating Way" in *Continuity and Change: Aspects of Contemporary Norway*.

29. Nina Witoszek in *Norske naturmytologier* gives a convincing argument that the Norwegian worldview rests on a holistic cosmology and relationship to nature which still exists.

Chapter 6

1. The *nøkk* is a water spirit who tries to lure people into rivers and lakes. He can shift shape to that of a horse. Theodor Kittelsen has drawn *nøkken* in both forms in some very famous paintings. The *draug* is a similar spirit who inhabits the sea. See *Troll i Norge* by Eli Ketilsson for examples of Kittelsen's work.
2. The ban against Jews was repealed in 1851 and that against monastic orders in 1897. The ban against Jesuits was not repealed until 1956.
3. The Jante Law, a formulation of the novelist Aksel Sandemose, consists of a series of maxims for conformity, the most often cited is perhaps "You shall not believe that you *are* something." See *En flyktning krysser sitt spor: fortelling om en morders barndom*.
4. It must be remembered that what is known of pagan Nordic belief systems is suspect, since what is known was committed to writing after the conversion to Christianity by those who no longer believed and had an agenda of their own. A good overview of Scandinavian mythology, sources, and research is John Lindow's "Mythology and Mythography" in *Old Norse—Icelandic Literature*.
5. That legend does reflect worldview is a point on which there is not complete agreement. Niels Ingwersen, for example, writes that "legend tends to contradict legend and defies the notion that texts from a certain region present a uniform worldview," but at the same time he states that the function of counter-legends was to challenge an accepted worldview as reflected in conservative texts. If legends dealing with the inexplicable are contradictory, this does not necessarily mean that certain elements within those legends cannot still be consistent with majority thought. Variations may also simply mean that a particular worldview may be in transition. See *Scandinavian Studies* 67 for Ingwersen's article, "The Need for Narrative: The Folktale as Response to History."
6. Bascom's article, "Four Functions of Folklore" appeared in *Journal of American Folklore* 67 in 1954 and has been reprinted numerous times. Bascom asked, "What does folklore do for people who tell it and listen to it?" He identified the functions of amusement, education, validation of culture,

and the function of maintaining conformity to accepted patterns of behavior. All of these maintain the stability of culture.
7. As Ingwersen demonstrates in the article cited above.
8. Asbjørnsen himself counted only ninety, but this discrepancy can be accounted for by assuming that he may have considered all stories about one particular person to be one legend, while I have considered a narrative, as before indicated, to consist of a beginning, middle, and end, regardless of whether or not several stories in succession deal with the same character, with the exception of the Per Gynt episodes, which are connected by the oral narrator into what can only be considered one long story.
9. Four stories have both a male and female protagonist and one story is a fable with an animal protagonist.
10. Asbjørnsen spent large portions of his youth evading creditors and was never a wealthy man. It seems likely that the lack of a true feudal system, the land-owning farmer, and the virtual elimination of an aristocracy in the ravages of the fourteenth-century created in Norway a society that was and is in many ways more egalitarian than in many other countries. This does not negate the fact that the world of the cultured people, the *kondisjonerte*, was very different from that of the *bonde*.
11. That Asbjørnsen himself was very interested in this question is evident in the story "A Christmas Visit to the Parsonage," omitted from the 1870 edition, in which various characters discuss probable origins of the stories they relate. It seems likely that personification of natural phenomena could be the origin of at least some of the *underjordiske* characters, given human penchant for symbolization. Edvard Brandes writes of the *nisse*: "Who is not familiar with the various stories about the *nisse*, that little fellow in grey dress with the red pointed cap on his head, which has given the opportunity for so many symbolic stories; but who, on the other hand, knows the origin and original meaning of this little mischief-maker? Still, it has long been shown that the *nisse* is just a later form of fire, worshipped as a house god (*agni grihapati*), explaining his red cap. . . . Then his pranks and characteristics become clear. A man moves in order to get rid of him, but no sooner does he get to his new house before the fire god shows up there also: Fire always belongs to the hearth and the home. One still gives offerings to him as in the old days, and what he gets is porridge, but what the *nisse* cares about is that there is plenty of butter in it. For liquid butter (havis, ghrita) is the oldest offering that is thrown in the fire" (Brandes 1877, 335).
12. Or perhaps it is not so ironic after all. There is ample evidence that the Norwegian cosmology has integrated the pagan and the Christian to a remarkable extent. Speaking of the differences between the representation

of the dragon image in the Old Norse *Fåvnesmål*, as opposed to the representation in *Beowulf*, Nina Witoszek writes, "[T]he Norsemen offered a remarkable resistance to the Christian diabolisation of Nature. It is as if their affinity and kinship with the natural world was so strong that it never succumbed to theological cleansing. In the Nordic Middle Ages crosses and dragons are compatible, the ancient gods of nature co-exist with the transcendent Christian deity. Stave churches, adorned as they are with dragon heads, call to mind Vedic pagodas and perpetuate a dialogue of Christian and pagan memes. And the fact that King Olav Trygvasson, the apostle of Christianity, did not hesitate to call his ship "The Long Serpent" at a time when the serpent was the sworn enemy rather than the ally of saints seems to indicate not so much his secret adherence to paganism but the remarkable coexistence of two seemingly irreconcilable cosmologies" (72).

13. The eleven narratives that do not deal with the supernatural are for the most part hunting and fishing stories, or stories of search for treasure.

14. It is interesting that the opposite boundary shift, from Other to more nearly human, as is shown in the *hulder* marriage legends, does not carry these dire consequences.

15. The witch often appears in the shape of a black cat and may lose a hand when the human cuts off a paw. This bodily damage persists when the witch returns to human shape and is one way of identifying the witch. It would be intriguing to speculate on why cats are often seen as evil in legend, while in fairy tales they are usually helpful. See Jack Zipes' article, "Of Cats and Men: Framing the Civilizing Discourse of the Fairy Tale" in *Out of the Woods: The Origins of the Literary Fairy Tale in Italy and France*. Zipes writes, "It is said that a man's best friend is his dog, but those of us who read fairy tales know better. Time and again, cats have come to the aid of poor suffering young men" (176). But, of course, it is not only cats who are helpful to poor suffering young men. The animal helper is a widely spread motif which appears in a great many fairy tales.

16. See Kathleen Stokker's article "Between Sin and Salvation: The Human Condition in Legends of the Black Book Minister" in *Scandinavian Studies* 67.

17. Som hun satt i setra en ettermiddag, tykte hun, at kjæresten hennes kom og satte seg hos henne og begynte å tale om, at nå skulle de til å holde bryllup. Men hun satt ganske stille og svarte ingenting; for hun syntes hun blei så rar av seg. Litt om litt kom der flere og flere folk inn, og de begynte å dekke opp bord med sølvtøy og mat, og brurepiker bar inn krone og stas og en gild brurekjole, som de kledde på henne, og krona satte de på hue, som de brukte den gang, og ringer fikk hun på fingrene . . . "Hva betyr alt dette?" sa han, "du sitter jo pynta her som ei brur?" "Kan du spørre om det?"

sa jenta. "Du har jo sittet her og talt til meg om bryllup i heile ettermiddag." "Nei, nå kom *jeg*," sa han; "men det må vel hav vært noen, som har tatt på seg min liknelse."

18. Jenny Jochens writes in *Old Norse Images of Women* that "at some point in the nordic perceptual development, apparently, women and animals were grouped together" (Jochens 1996, 37).

19. It was possible for humans and the Other to marry, and the tail would normally fall off a *hulder* when she was baptized or blessed by a minister. In this sense, just as the human woman becomes the Other as a *trollkjerring*, the Other woman, the *hulder*, becomes nearly human through her acceptance of the sacraments of the church. No wonder that the line between the supernatural and the merely ethnic other was difficult to draw and difficult to keep. This tale type, called "Marriage to a Fairy Woman," 5090 in Christiansen's type index and Motif F 302 in Thompson's motif index, is known nearly all over the world and has been the subject of a considerable amount of study. In his massive study of the Norwegian mountain dairy folklore, *Norsk sætertradisjon*, Svale Solheim differentiates variants of this legend which end with a "happier ever after" scenario, right after the wedding, from those which he calls the full version of the legend, in which a show of strength from the hulder is required in order to bring the husband in line. It is of interest that Asbjørnsen selects only variants in which the show of strength is included, in order to integrate the tale with the frame story of the young girl dissuading a suitor in the case of "The Hulder Clan," and most probably for dramatic effect in the other versions.

20. stygg var hun og stygg blei hun, og kei var han av henne, og det var ikke fritt for, at han var litt slem iblant, så at han baud til å slå og denge henne.

21. Hun gikk til smia, og det første hun gjorde, var å ta skoen med begge never og rette den ut. "Se her," sa hun, "så skal du gjøre." Så bøyde hun den sammen, som om den hadde vært av bly. "Hold nå opp beinet," sa hun, og skoen passa så akkurat, at den beste smed ikke kunne gjort den bedre. "Du er nok stiv i finrene du," sa mannen og såg på henne. "Synes du det?" sa hun. "Hvordan meiner du det var gått med meg, dersom du hadde vært så stiv i fingrene? Men jeg holder for mye av deg, til at jeg skulle bruke kreftene mine på deg." sa hun. Fra den dag var han en aparte mann imot henne.

22. "Hva vil de meg? Min Gud! vet De hva De våger?" sa hun. "De kjenner jo min slekt! De vet vel, at jeg stammer fra huldrefolk, og at der rinner trollblod i mine årer?" . . . "Min oldemor eller tipoldemor var jo en virkelig hulder."

23. Da det led til høsten igjen og kålen ble stor, og kona skulle til å hakke og stelle til slaktingen, så hadde hun ikke noe hakkebrett og ikke heller noe

hakketrau. Hun bad da mannen ta øksa og gå opp i fjellet og hugge ned den store fura, som stod ved myra på seterveien; hun skulle ha den til et hakketrau. "Jeg mener du er styren, kjerring," sa mannen. "Skulle jeg hogge ned det beste tre i tømmerskogen til å gjøre hakketrau av? Og hvorledes skulle jeg få den hjem fra fjellet på denne tid, den er jo så diger, at ingen hest orker å dra den?" Hun bad mannen likevel; men da han slett ikke ville gå, så tok hun øksa, gikk opp i skogen, hogde furua ned og kom hjem med den på ryggen. Da mannen så det, ble han så forskrekket, at han aldri siden torde si henne imot, eller gjøre annet enn hun bad om, og fra den tid var der aldri uenighet mellom dem.

24. "De kan altså slutte Dem til hva De kan vente, hvis De for alvor gjør meg vred."
25. Marianne Gullestad writes that "a particular sign of Norwegian culture is that it is especially home-centered" (Gullestad 1989, 54). See also Nina Witoszek's discussion of the Norwegian home in *Norske naturmytologier*.
26. Han tok henne straks med ned til bygda, og for at der ikke skulle komme mere fanteri til henne, holdt de bryllup med det samme, og mens hun ennå hadde på brurestasen til de underjordiske. Krona og heile stasen blei hengt opp på Melbustad, og den skal være der den dag i dag er.
27. "Det var de underjordiske som tok henne, og de hadde vært etter henne lenge før også, for da der var festerøl for henne på Lier, tok de henne og satte henne på hue i et vasskar, men da var der så mange folk, som stod ute på tråkka, at hun ikke kom til skade; og så sa det borte i bakken ved stabburet, at det kom av hun ikke hadde festering. Men sia den tid går hver skarvejente, som har seg en fant, med festering."
28. It is interesting in this context that the concept of "going berserk," from the old norse word *beserkr*, includes the element of shape-shifting.
29. At this writing, it is now possible to speak of that Norwegian generation which has not experienced a colonized or occupied Norway.

Chapter 7

1. In this chapter I will include the original Scandinavian quotations within the text itself when language is the topic of the discussion.
2. To this hyphenated Norwegian-American, it seems bizarre in the extreme that Norwegian and Danish publishers routinely publish books *translated* from Danish to Norwegian and vice-versa. This can only be viewed as a political statement, since linguistically, it makes absolutely no sense at all. It is virtually effortless for Norwegians and Danes to read each other's languages.

3. At the time, this union was often referred to as *tvillingrikene*, the twin kingdoms.
4. As of 1 September 1999, 84.4% of Norwegian students selected *bokmål* as their primary language. ("Statistic Yearbook" available online at http://www.ssb.no/emner/04 [4 January 2002]). The original language controversy was between *riksmål* [the language of the realm, essentially Danish] and *landsmål* [the language of the countryside]. A series of spelling reforms and changes in vocabulary have created *bokmål* from *riksmål*, changes which incorporate elements from *landsmål*. *Landsmål* became *nynorsk* in 1929.
5. Jørgen Haugan writes about Norwegian as an academic discipline: "Language instruction acts as a linguistically political defense for the status quo. For example, you do not find many *riksmål* people at the University; evidently one has to be linguistically cleared in order to get a position in Norway. There is a predominance of language researchers at the Nordic Institutes whose primary language is *nynorsk* (Haugan 1991, 94).
6. The *nynorsk/bokmål* struggle is very complex, and it should be noted that I am not without bias. A favorite family story relates the only partly jocular reception a friend of my father's received from his father when he came home with the highest possible score on his *nynorsk* examination: "Du har brakt skam på hele familien!" [You have disgraced the whole family!]
7. It was so important to Asbjørnsen that the language of *Norske huldreeventyr og folkesagn* conform to the actual spoken language of the people that, before he died, he entrusted the continuing *fornorsking* of subsequent editions of *huldreeventyr* to Moltke Moe. The fourth edition of *Norske huldreeventyr og folkesagn* was published with revisions edited by Moltke Moe and Anders Krogvig in 1912 to 1914. This edition was somewhat controversial, since Moe insisted on using actual dialect forms of the folk narrators in all instances. He was criticized by Nils Kjær in several reviews in *Aftenposten*. Kjær doubted Moe's contention that Asbjørnsen had given him complete freedom to continue the *fornorsking* of the stories. Many critics saw the work as a way for Moe and Krogvig to advance the cause of *nynorsk*. See *En norsk elite. Nasjonsbyggerne på Lysaker 1890–1940* by Bodil Stenseth for more information. Even someone as sympathetic to Moltke Moe as Knut Liestøl could say that "for me personally it seems that several corrections were unnecessary" (Liestøl 1949, 107). Additional revisions appeared in the 1934 edition edited by Jan Jørgen Alnæs and Knut Liestøl. Liestøl's edition of 1949 is the text used in this study because it is based on Asbjørnsen's 1870 edition while incorporating modern spelling.
8. The development of *bokmål* included spelling reforms of 1907 and 1917, as well as a reform in 1938 to promote a convergence between *bokmål* and *nynorsk* (*samnorsk*) and another reform of 1959 which was unpopular and

led to a partial reversal of the trend to convergence with a spelling reform of 1981.

9. Of course when Camilla Collett started working on *Amtmandens Døtre* she originally was planning a novel of "everyday life" patterned on the work of Fredrika Bremer and Thomasine Gyllembourg. Certainly the rise of the modern Scandinavian novel was a pan-Scandinavian enterprise, with influences back and forth between Denmark, where Blicher was critical, Sweden, and finally Norway.

10. This term is used by Hans Robert Jauss in *Toward an Aesthetic of Reception*. Peter Rabinowitz has enumerated a series of "rules" of reading in his study of narrative conventions, *Before Reading*, which show how readers approach texts with preconceived ideas of what they will find, based on genre and other classifications.

11. In order to make the comparison more equitable, I have here used the *huldreeventyr* text from the first edition of 1845.

12. It is not surprising that the model for the schoolmaster, Hans Hansen Pillarviken, was offended by his depiction in this story. He was not alone. In his notes to *huldreeventyr* Liestøl includes the following sentences from a letter written to Asbjørnsen by Robert Meason Laing (the model for Sir John) in 1846: "If you have any desire to avoid hurting my feelings, you will not tug either me or any countryman of mine into your new book.—You may laugh as loud and as long as you like at my language; but I do most utterly detest having my *thoughts* travestied and my *meaning* misrepresented." There are no letters from Laing in Asbjørnsen's collection after the publication of "Mountain Images" (Liestøl, notes to A 2: 301).

Chapter 8

1. "But he doesn't have anything on!" This is the cry from the little boy in Andersen's fairy tale when he sees that the emperor's new clothes have been woven from imaginary threads. I expect those most likely to disagree with this reading of *Norske huldreeventyr og folkesagn* may be some Norwegian scholars, who can give the impression—perfectly understandable in a small country with a rich literature—of having a somewhat proprietary attitude towards their classics. The "Asbjørnsen and Moe" canon entity is so entrenched that any attempt to fiddle with it is likely to be met with scepticism.

2. And suggests that perhaps Norwegian academics should have part of their training in Denmark, where a variety of literary critical interpretive methods are used.

3. It is Julian Kramer's contention that the idea of a homogenous Norway is in many ways a myth. See his previously cited article "Norsk identitet—et produkt av underutvikling og stammetilhørighet" in *Den norske væremåten* for further discussion.
4. For example, no attempt has been made to trace the considerable residual effects of *Norske huldreeventyr og folkesagn* on nation building after 1905, when Norway finally became politically independent. That the work was appropriated for use by proponents of *landsmål* is evident from Bodil Stenseth's book *En norsk elite: Nasjonsbyggerne på Lysaker 1890–1940*.

Works Cited and Consulted

Aarnes, Sigurd Aa. 1991. *"Og nevner vi Henrik Wergelands navn": Wergelandkultusen som nasjonsbyggende faktor.* Oslo: Universitetsforlaget.
Aarseth, Asbjørn. 1976. *Episke strukturer.* Bergen: Universitetsforlaget.
———. 1981. *Realismen som myte.* Bergen: Universitetsforlaget.
Aasen, Ivar Andreas. 1848. *Det norske folkesprogs grammatik.* Kristiania: Werner.
———. 1850. *Ordbog over det norske folkesprog.* Kristiania.
Abrahams, Roger D. 1972. "Folklore and Literature as Performance." In *Journal of the Folklore Institute* 9: 75–94.
Abrams, M. H. 1988. *A Glossary of Literary Terms.* 5th revised and expanded ed. Fort Worth: Holt, Rinehart and Winston, Inc.
Alver, Bente Gullveig. 1971. *Heksetro og trolddom.* Oslo: Universitetsforlaget.
Alver, Brynjulf. [1962] 1989. "Historical Legends and Historical Truth." In *Nordic Folklore: Recent Studies.* Edited by Reimund Kvideland and Henning K. Sehmsdorf, in collaboration with Elizabeth Simpson. Bloomington: Indiana University Press. Originally published as "Historiske segner—historisk sanning" in *Norveg.*
Andenæs, Mads T., and Ingeborg Wilberg. 1987. *The Constitution of Norway: A Commentary.* Translated by Ronald Walford. N.p.: Universitetsforlaget.
Andenæs, Tønnes M., editor. [1949] 1989. *Grunnloven vår.* N.p.: Universitetsforlaget.
Anderson, Benedict. 1991. *Imagined Communities.* Revised and expanded edition, London and New York: Verso.
Archer, William. [1917] 1984. Introduction to *Peer Gynt.* Reprinted in *William Archer on Ibsen: The Major Essays, 1889–1919.* Edited by Thomas Postlewait. Westport, CT and London: Greenwood Press, 1984.
Arens, Ilmar, and Bengt af Klintberg. 1979. "Bortbytingssägner i en gotländsk dombok från 1690." In *Rig* 62: 89–97.
Arild, Lars, and Jørgen Haugan. 1986. "Novellen i teori og praksis." In *Edda* 4: 343–365.
Arneberg, Per. 1958. "Brekkesaga." In *Norsk skrivekunst.* Edited by Erling Nielsen. Copenhagen: Hans Reitzel.

Asbjørnsen, Peter Christen. 1845. *Norske huldreeventyr og folkesagn*. 1st collection. Christiania: W. T. Fabritius.

———. 1848. *Norske huldreeventyr og folkesagn*. 2nd collection. Christiania: C. A. Oybwad.

———. 1859. *Norske huldreeventyr og folkesagn*. 1st collection. 2nd expanded edition. Christiania: P. F. Steensballes Forlag.

———. 1866. *Norske huldreeventyr og folkesagn*. 2nd collection. 2nd expanded edition. Christiania: P. F. Steensballes Forlag.

———. 1870. *Norske huldreeventyr og folkesagn*. 1st and 2nd collection. 3rd edition. Christiania: P. F. Steensballes Forlag.

———. [1870] 1914. *Norske huldre-eventyr og folkesagn*. 4th edition. Revised by Moltke Moe and Anders Krogvig. Oslo: H. Aschehoug and Co.

———. [1870] 1949. *Norske huldreeventyr og folkesagn*. Edited and with an introduction and notes by Knut Liestøl. 2 vols. Oslo: Tanum.

———. 1871. *Norske folkeeventyr, fortalte af P. Chr. A.* New Collection, with contributions from Jørgen Moe. Christiania: Jac. Dybwad.

———. 1874. "Om Overtroens Væsen og Betydning." In *Morgenbladet*. 15 March.

———. 1876. *Norske folkeeventyr*. New collection. 2nd expanded and revised edition. Christiania.

———. 1879. *Norske folke- og huldreeventyr i Udvalg ved P. Chr. Asbjørnsen.* (With illustrations by P. A. Arboe, H. Gude, V. St. Lerche, E. Peterssen, A. Schneider, O. Sinding, A. Tedemann og E. Werenskiold). København: Gyldendal.

———. 1881. *Round the Yule Log: Norwegian Folk and Fairy Tales*. Translated by H. L. Brækstad. London: Sampson Low, Marston, Searle and Rivington.

———. [1879] 1896. *Norske Folke- og Huldre-Eventyr i Udvalg*. Copenhagen: Gyldendalske Boghandels Forlag (F. Hegel and Søn).

Asbjørnsen, P. Chr., and Jørgen Moe. 1841–44. *Norske folkeeventyr samlede ved Asbjørnsen og Jørgen Moe*. N.p.: Johan Dahl.

———. [1841–44] 1982. *Norske folkeeventyr. Samlede eventyr*. 2 vols. Oslo: Den Norske Bokklubben.

———. 1852. *Norske folkeeventyr, samlede og fortalte af P. C. A. og J. M.* 2nd expanded edition. N.p.: Johan Dahl.

———. 1866. *Norske folkeeventyr, fortalte af P. Chr. A. og J. M.* 3rd revised edition. Christiania.

———. 1868. *Norske folkeeventyr, fortalte af P. Chr. A. og J. M.* 4th revised edition. Christiania.

———. 1874. *Norske folkeeventyr, fortalte af P. Chr. A. og J. M.* 5th revised edition. Christiania.

Aubert, Elise Sofie Aars. 1921. *Fra Krinoline-tiden: Elise Auberts ungdomsbreve og dagbøker*. Edited by Sofie Aubert Lindbæk. Kristiania: H. Aschehoug.

Backer, Thomas. 1952. "Kongeveien." In *Den norske turistforening årbok:* 30–41. Oslo Cammermeyer.

Bakhtin, M. M. 1981. *The Dialogic Imagination.* Edited by Michael Holquist. Translated by Caryl Emerson and Michael Holquist. Austin: University of Texas Press.

———. 1984. *Rabelais and his World.* Translated by Hélène Iswolsky. Bloomington: Indiana University Press.

Bakken, Hallvard Sand. 1933. "P. Chr. Asbjørnsen og Universitetsbiblioteket." In *Overbibliotekar Wilhelm Munthe på 50-årsdagen 20. oktober 1933:* 299–324.

———. 1935. "Omkring Asbjørnsen: Hvorledes P. Chr. Asbjørnsen begynte som sagnforteller—for egen regning." In *Edda* 35: 463–497.

Bascom, William R. 1954. "Four Functions of Folklore." In *Journal of American Folklore* 67: 333–349.

Baumann, Richard. 1983. "The Field Study of Folklore in Context." In *Handbook of American Folklore.* Edited by Richard M. Dorson. Bloomington: Indiana University Press.

———. 1984. *Verbal Art as Performance.* Prospect Heights, Illinois: Waveland Press.

———. 1986. *Story, Performance and Event: Contextual Studies of Oral Narrative.* Cambridge and New York: Cambridge University Press.

Baumgartner, Walter. 1993. "Volksliterarische Erzählkultur und ihr Sympathisant Asbjørnsen." In *Literature as Resistance and Counter-culture: Papers of the 19th Conference of the International Association for Scandinavian Studies.* Edited by András Majórt. Budapest.

Berge, Rikard. 1919. "Norsk eventyrstil." In *Norske Folkekultur* 4: 156–172.

———. 1976. *Norsk sogukunst.* Oslo: Noregs Boklag.

Berggreen, Brit. 1989. *Da kulturen kom til Norge.* Oslo: H. Aschehoug and Co. (W. Nygaard).

Bettelheim, Bruno. 1989. *The Uses of Enchantment: The Meaning and Importance of Fairy Tales.* New York: Vintage Books. Originally published by Alfred A. Knopf, Inc., 1976.

Beyer, Edvard, and Harald Beyer. 1978. *Norsk litteratur historie.* 4th revised and expanded edition. Oslo: H. Aschehoug and Co. (W. Nygaard)

Beyer, Edvard, and Morten Moi. 1990. *Norsk litteratur-kritikks historie, 1770–1940.* Vol. 1. Edited by Edvard Beyer, Irene Iversen, Arild Linneberg, and Morten Moi. Oslo: Universitetsforlaget.

Boberg, Inger M. 1953. *Folkemindeforskningens historie i mellom og nord europa.* Copenhagen: Danmarks Folkeminder.

Bojer, Johan. 1929. "Landscape Myths in Norway." In *The American-Scandinavian Review* 17: 717–727.

Bottigheimer, Ruth. 1987. *Grimms' Bad Girls and Bold Boys*. New Haven: Yale University Press.

Brandes, Edvard. 1877. "Nye Samlinger af Folkepoesi." In *Det nittende Aarhundrede. Maanedsskrift for Literatur og Kritik*. (January-March): 319–336. Copenhagen: Gyldendalske Boghandels Forlag.

Bremner, Robert. 1840. *Excursions in Denmark, Norway, and Sweden*. London: Henry Colburn.

Brennan, Timothy. 1990. "The National Longing for Form." In *Nation and Narration*. Edited by Homi K. Bhabha. London and New York: Routledge.

Brooke, A. De Capell. 1823. *Travels through Sweden, Norway, and Finmark to the North Cape in the Summer of 1820*. London: Rodwell and Martin.

Bukdahl, Jørgen. 1926. *Det skjulte Norge*. Copenhagen: H. Aschehoug and Co.

Bull, Francis. 1923. "Dovre i Sagn og Digtning." In *Den Norske Turistforening Årbok*: 62–78.

———. 1952. "Dovre som Symbol." In *Den Norske Turistforening Årbok* : 8–17.

Bull, Olaf. [1913] 1999. *Nye Digte*. Kristiania: Gyldendal. Reprinted in *En himmel mot en annen. Utvalgte dikt*. N.p.: Gyldendal Norsk Forlag.

Burns, Thomas A. 1977. "Folkloristics: A Conception of Theory." In *Western Folklore* 36: 109–134.

Bø, Gudleiv. 1997. Lecture at the University of Minnesota. Minneapolis. October. In the memory of the author.

Bø, Olav. 1980. "Folkemedisinen: signekjerringar og bygdedokterar." In *Brytningsår-blomstringstid*. Vol. 5 of *Norges kulturhistorie*. Edited by Ingrid Semmingsen, Nina Karin Monsen, Stephan Tschudi-Madsen, and Yngvar Ustvedt. Oslo: H. Aschehoug and Co. (W. Nygaard).

Caspari, Theodor. 1917. *Norsk Naturfølelse i det Nittende Aarhundrede*. Kristiania: Aschehoug.

Christensen, Hjalmar. 1905. *Det nittende aarhundredes kulturkamp i Norge*. Kristiania: H. Aschehoug and Co. (W. Nygaard).

Christiansen, Reidar Th. 1938. *Norske sagn*. Oslo: H. Aschehoug and Co.

———. 1946. *Eventyr og sagn*. Oslo: Olaf Norlis Forlag.

———. 1958. *The Migratory Legends. A Proposed List of Types with a Systematic Catalogue of the Norwegian Variants*. Folklore Fellows' communications 175. Helsinki: Suomalainen Tiedeakatemia.

———. 1964. *Folktales of Norway*. Translated by Pat Shaw Iversen. Chicago and London: University of Chicago Press.

Clifford, James. 1986. *Writing Culture: The Poetics and Politics of Ethnography*. Berkeley and Los Angeles: University of California Press.

Collett, P. J. 1845. Review of *Norske huldreeventyr og folkesagn*, by Peter Christen Asbjørnsen. In *Den Constitutionelle* 215.

Connor, Walker. 1972. "Nation-Building or Nation-Destroying?" In *World Politics* 24: 319–355.

Dahl, Willy. 1981. *Norges litteratur 1: tid og tekst, 1814-1884*. Oslo: H. Aschehoug and Co. (W. Nygaard).
Darnton, Robert. 1984. *The Great Cat Massacre and Other Episodes in French Cultural History*. New York: Random House.
Dasent, George Webbe. 1859. *Popular Tales from the Norse*. Edinburgh: Edmonston and Douglas.
Deane, Seamus. 1990. Introduction to *Nationalism, Colonialism, and Literature*, by Terry Eagleton, Fredric Jameson, and Edward W. Said. Minneapolis: University of Minnesota Press.
Dégh, Linda, and Andrew Vázsonyi. [1971] 1976. "Legends and Belief." In *Folklore Genres*. Edited by Dan Ben-Amos. Austin and London: University of Texas Press. Originally published in *Genre* 4 (1971): 281–304.
Dentith, Simon. 1995. *Bakhtinian Thought*. London and New York: Routledge.
Dietrichson, Lorentz. 1866. *Omrids af den norske Poesis Historie*. Copenhagen: Gyldendalske Boghandel (F. Hegel).
Dorson, Richard M. 1966. "The Question of Folklore in a New Nation." In *Journal of the Folklore Institute* 3: 277–298.
Dundes, Alan. 1964. "Texture, Text, and Context." In *Southern Folklore Quarterly* 28: 251–265.
Eagleton, Terry. 1983. *Literary Theory: An Introduction*. Minneapolis: University of Minnesota Press.
———. 1990. "Nationalism: Irony and Commitment." In *Nationalism, Colonialism, and Literature*. Minneapolis: University of Minnesota Press.
Elster, Kristian d.y. 1924. *Illustreret Norsk Litteratur Historie*. Vol. 2. Kristiania: Gyldendalske Bokhandel.
Engelstad, Irene. 1976. *Fortellingens mønstre: En strukturell analyse av norske folkeeventyr*. Oslo: Universitetsforlaget.
Enzensberger, Hans Magnus. 1984. *Norsk utakt*. Oslo: Universitetsforlaget.
Erjavec, Aleš. 1994. "Mountain Photography and the Constitution of National Identity." In *Acta Philosophica* 2: 211–234.
Evensberget, Snorre. 1982. Introduction to *Norske folkeeventyr. Samlede eventyr*, by P. Chr. Asbjørnsen and Jørgen Moe. 2 vols. Oslo: Den Norske Bokklubben.
Faye, Andreas. [1833] 1948. *Norske folke-sagn*. Norsk folkeminnelags skrifter, no. 63. Oslo: Norsk folkeminnelags forlag.
Frykman, Jonas, and Orvar Löfgren. 1979. *Den kultiverade människan*. Lund: Liber Läromedel.
Fuglum, Per. 1972. *Kampen om alkoholen i Norge, 1816-1904*. Oslo: Universitetsforlaget.
Garborg, Arne. 1895. "Til deg, du hei og bleike myr." from *Haugtussa*. In *Lyrikkboken*, 1971. Oslo: Den norske bokklubben.
Gellner, Ernest. 1994. "Nations and Nationalism: General Perspectives." In

Nordic Paths to National Identity in the Nineteenth Century. Edited by Øystein Sørensen. Research Council of Norway, no. 1/94: 7–16. Oslo: University of Oslo.

Gilman, Sander L. 1985. *Difference and Pathology: Stereotypes of Sexuality, Race, and Madness.* Ithaca: Cornell University Press.

———. 1991. *Inscribing the Other.* Lincoln: University of Nebraska Press.

Gjefsen, Truls. 2001. *Peter Christen Asbjørnsen: diger og folkesæl.* Oslo: Andresen and Butenschøn A/S.

Gosse, Edmund W. 1881. Introduction to *Round the Yule Log: Norwegian Folk and Fairy Tales,* by Peter Christen Asbjørnsen. Translated by H. L. Brækstad. London: Sampson Low, Marston, Searle, and Rivington.

Grágás: Laws of Early Iceland. 1980. Translated by Andrew Dennis, Peter Foote, and Richard Perkins. Winnipeg: University of Manitoba Press.

Grimm, Jacob and William Grimm. [1885] 1974. *Briefwechsel der Brüder Grimm mit Nordischen Gelehrten.* Edited by Ernst Schmidt. Walluf: Dr. Martin Sändig Verlag.

———. 1916. "Jacob og Wilhelm Grimms brev til P. Chr. Asbjørnsen og Jørgen Moe." In *Festskrift til Gerhard Gran 9 desember, 1916.* Edited by Anders Krogvig. Kristiania.

———. 1987. *The Complete Fairy Tales of the Brothers Grimm.* Translated by Jack Zipes. Toronto, New York: Bantam.

Grunnloven vår. [1949] 1989. Edited by Tønnes M. Andenæs. N.p.: Universitetsforlaget.

Gullestad, Marianne. 1989. *Kultur og hverdagsliv.* Oslo: Universitetsforlaget.

Halvorsen, J[ens]. B[raage]. 1870. Review of *Norske huldreeventyr og folkesagn. Skilling-magazin* 45: 810.

———. 1885. "Asbjørnsen, Peter Christen." In *Norsk forfatter-lexikon.* Vol. 1. Kristiania: Den Norske forlagsforening.

Hansen, Børge. 1971. *Folkeeventyr: struktur og genre.* Copenhagen: Munksgaard.

Hansen, H. Olaf. 1862. *Den norske literatur fra 1814 indtil vore dage.* Copenhagen: Fr. Wøldikes Forlagsboghandel.

Hansen, Hans. 1932. *P. Chr. Asbjørnsen.* Oslo: H. Aschehoug and Co. (W. Nygaard).

Haugan, Jørgen. 1991. *400-årsnatten: Norsk selvforståelse ved en korsvei.* Oslo: Universitetsforlaget.

Haugen, Einar. 1976. *The Scandinavian Languages.* London: Faber and Faber.

———. 1987. "Danish, Norwegian, and Swedish." In *The World's Major Languages.* Edited by Bernard Comrie. New York: Oxford University Press.

Heber, Lilly. 1914. *Norsk realisme i 1830 og 40 aarene.* Kristiania: Olaf Norlis forlag.

Hertzberg, Nils Christian. 1910. *Minder fra min skolemestertid, 1844–1873.* Kristiania: Aschehoug and Co.

Herzfeld, Michael. 1987. *Anthropology through the looking-glass: Critical ethnography in the margins of Europe*. Cambridge and New York: Cambridge University Press.

Hodne, Fritz. 1981. *Norges økonomiske historie, 1815–1970*. N.p.: J. W. Cappelens Forlag.

Hodne, Ørnulf. 1979. *Jørgen Moe og folkeeventyrene: en studie i nasjonalromantisk folkloristikk*. Oslo: Universitetsforlaget.

———. 1982. *Jørgen Moe: Folkeminnesamler, dikter, prest*. Oslo: Universitetsforlaget.

———. 1994. *Det nasjonale hos norske folklorister på 1800-tallet*. KULT National Identity Series, no. 24. Oslo: Norges forskningsråd.

Hoel, Sigurd. 1948. "Eventyrene Våre." In *Tanker fra mange tider*. Oslo: Gyldendal Norsk Forlag. Originally published as a newspaper article, 1940.

Holbek, Bengt. 1987. *Interpretation of Fairy Tales: Danish Folklore in a European Perspective*. Folklore Fellows' communications 239. Helsinki: Suomalainen Tiedeakatemia.

Holter, Øystein Gullvåg. 1993. "Norwegian Families." In *Continuity and Change: Aspects of Contemporary Norway*. Edited by Anne Cohen Kiel. Oslo: Universitetsforlaget.

Honko, Lauri. [1964] 1989a. "Memorates and the Study of Folk Belief." In *Nordic Folklore: Recent Studies*. Edited by Reimund Kvideland and Henning K. Sehmsdorf, in collaboration with Elizabeth Simpson. Bloomington: Indiana University Press. Originally published in *Journal of the Folklore Institute*.

———. [1979–80] 1989b. "Methods in Folk Narrative Research." In *Nordic Folklore: Recent Studies*. Edited by Reimund Kvideland and Henning K. Sehmsdorf, in collaboration with Elizabeth Simpson. Bloomington: Indiana University Press. Originally published in *Ethnologia Europaea*.

Hougen, Frik. 1935. "Omkring Asbjørnsens reise til Gudbrandsdalen 1842." In *Edda* 35: 433–462.

———. 1940. "Omgangsskolehaldaren Hans Hansen Pillarviken." In *Edda* 40: 337–423.

Hultkrantz, Åke. 1960. "General Ethnological Concepts." In *International Dictionary of Regional European Ethnology and Folklore*. Edited by Åke Hultkrantz. Copenhagen: Rosenkilde and Bagger.

Ibsen, Henrik. [1867] 1980. *Peer Gynt*. Translated by Rolf Fjelde. Minneapolis: University of Minnesota Press.

———. 1991. *Peer Gynt*. In *Samlede Verker*. Vol. 1. Oslo: Den Norske Bokklubben.

———. 1904. *Breve*. Edited by Halvdan Koht and Julius Elias. Copenhagen: Gyldendalske boghandel.

Ingwersen, Niels. 1989. "Ethics Upheld/Ethics Defunct: The Magic Tale and the Fabliau in Scandinavian Tradition." In *Scandinavian Studies* 61: 304–317.
———. 1995. "The Need for Narrative: The Folktale as Response to History." In *Scandinavian Studies* 67: 77–90.
———. 1996. Afterword to *Tardy Awakening and Other Stories*, by Steen Steensen Blicher. Edited by Niels Ingwersen. Translated by Paula Brugge and Faith Ingwersen. Wisconsin Introductions to Scandinavia 2, no. 7. Madison: University of Wisconsin Department of Scandinavian Studies.
Iser, Wolfgang. 1980. "Interaction between Text and Reader." In *The Reader in the Text: Essays on Audience and Interpretation*. Edited by Susan R. Suleiman and Inge Crosman. Princeton: Princeton University Press.
Jauss, Hans Robert. 1982. *Toward an Aesthetic of Reception*. Translated by Timothy Bahti. Theory and History of Literature Series, no. 2. Minneapolis: University of Minnesota Press.
Jochens, Jenny. 1996. *Old Norse Images of Women*. Philadelphia: University of Pennsylvania Press.
Johannesen, Georg. 1994. "Den glemte Bjørnson." In *Moralske Tekster*. Otta, Norway: J. W. Cappelens Forlag.
Jusdanis, Gregory. 1991. *Belated Modernity and Aesthetic Culture: Inventing National Literature*. Theory and History of Literature Series, no. 81. Minneapolis: University of Minnesota Press.
Jæger, Henrik. 1878. *Litteraturhistoriske pennetegninger*. Copenhagen: Gyldendalske Boghandels Forlag (F. Hegel and Søn).
———. 1883. "Asbjørnsen og huldreeventyret." In *Norske forfattere*. Copenhagen: Gyldendalske Boghandels Forlag (F. Hegel and Søn).
Kedourie, Elie. [1960] 1994. *Nationalism*. Oxford: Blackwell.
Ketilsson, Eli. 1989. *Troll i Norge*. Oslo: J. M. Stenersens Forlag.
Kiel, Anne Cohen. 1993. "Confessions of an Angry Commuter: or Learning How to Communicate the Non-Communicating Way." In *Continuity and Change: Aspects of Contemporary Norway*. Edited by Anne Cohen Kiel. Oslo: Universitetsforlaget.
Kimball, Edwin. 1888. *Midnight Sunbeams, or Bits of Travel through the Land of the Norseman*. Boston: Cupples and Hurd.
King, James Roy. 1992. *Old Tales and New Truths*. Albany: State University of New York Press.
Klausen, Arne Martin. 1996. *Lillehammer-OL og olympismen*. Oslo: Gyldendal.
Klintberg, Bengt af. 1990. Review of *Scandinavian Folk Belief and Legend*, edited by Reimund Kvideland and Henning Sehmsdorf. In *Journal of American Folklore* 103: 232–233.
Koht, Halvdan. 1923. "Var 'Finnane' alltid Finnar?" In *Maal og Minne* 3: 161–175.

———. 1965. *Minnearv og historie: gamle og nye artiklar*. Oslo: H. Aschehoug and Co. (W. Nygaard).

Kramer, Julian. 1984. "Norsk identitet: et produkt av underutvikling og stammetilhørighet." In *Den norske væremåten*. Edited by Arne Martin Klausen. Oslo: J. W. Cappelens Forlag.

Krohn, Kaarle. [1926] 1971. *Folklore Methodology formulated by Julius Krohn and expanded by Nordic researchers*. Translated by Roger L. Welsch. Austin: University of Texas Press. Originally published in German as *Die folkloristische Arbeidmethode*.

Kvideland, Reimund, and Henning K. Sehmsdorf. 1989. "Nordic Folklore Studies Today." In *Nordic Folklore: Recent Studies*. Edited by Reimund Kvideland and Henning K. Sehmsdorf, in collaboration with Elizabeth Simpson. Bloomington: Indiana University Press.

———. eds. 1988. *Scandinavian Folk Belief and Legend*. Minneapolis: University of Minnesota Press.

Labov, William. 1982. "Speech Actions and Reactions in Personal Narrative." In *Georgetown University Roundtable on Languages and Linguistics 1981*. Edited by Deborah Tannen. Washington, D.C.: Georgetown University Press, 219–247.

Larsen, Karen. 1948. *A History of Norway*. The American Scandinavian Foundation: Princeton University Press.

Larsen, Tord. 1984. "Bønder i byen—på jakt etter den norske konfigurasjon." In *Den norske væremåten*. Edited by Arne Martin Klausen. Oslo: J. W. Cappelens Forlag.

Leitre, Arild, Einar Lundeby, and Ingvald Torvik. 1975. *Språket vårt før og nå: Språkhistorie, norrønt, dialekter, og nyislansk*. N.p.: Gyldendal Norsk Forlag.

Lid, Jon. 1931. "Ein folkeminnesamlar frå 1840-åri." In *Syn og segn* 37: 306–314.

Liestøl, Knut. 1947. *P. Chr. Asbjørnsen: Mannen og livsverket*. Oslo: Tanum-Norli.

———. 1949. *Moltke Moe*. Oslo: H. Aschehoug and Co. (W. Nygaard).

———. ed. 1949. *Norske huldreeventyr og folkesagn*, by Peter Christen Asbjørnsen. Oslo: Tanum.

Lindow, John. 1985. "Mythology and Mythography." In *Old Norse-Icelandic Literature*. Edited by Carol J. Clover and John Lindow. Ithaca and London: Cornell University Press.

———. 1995. "Supernatural Others and Ethnic Others: A Millenium of World View." In *Scandinavian Studies* 67: 8–31.

Linneberg, Arild. 1992. *Norsk litteratur-kritikks historie*. Vol 2. Edited by Edvard Beyer, Irene Iversen, Arild Linneberg, and Morten Moi. Oslo: Universitetsforlaget.

Lodge, David. 1990. *After Bakhtin*. London and New York: Routledge.

Long, Litt Woon. 1993. "Recent Immigration to Norway." In *Continuity and Change: Aspects of Contemporary Norway*. Edited by Anne Cohen Kiel. Oslo: Universitetsforlaget.

Lord, Albert. 1960. *The Singer of Tales*. Cambridge: Harvard University Press.

Lunden, Kåre. 1992. *Norsk grålysing*. Gjøvik, Norway: Det Norske Samlaget.

Lüthi, Max. 1970. *Once Upon A Time*. Translated by Lee Chadeayne and Paul Gottwald. New York: F. Ungar Publishing Co. Originally published in German as *Es war einmal*.

Løland, Ståle. 1997. "Rettskrivningsreformer i dette århundret." In *Språknytt*: 1/97: 12–13,36. Oslo: Norsk språkråd.

Malinowski, Bronislaw. 1926. *Myth in Primitive Psychology*. New York: Norton.

Miller, J. Hillis. 1995. *Topographies*. Stanford: Stanford University Press.

Moe, Jørgen Engelbretsen. 1845. "Om Fortællemaaden av Eventyr og Sagn." In *Den Constitutionelle* 231.

———. [1852] 1914. Introduction to *Norske folkeeventyr*. 2nd expanded edition. In *Jørgen Moe: Samlede Skrifter*. Edited by Anders Krogvig. Kristiania: H. Aschehoug and Co. (W. Nygaard).

———. 1915. *Fra det nationale gjennembruds tid. Breve fra Jørgen Moe til P. Chr. Asbjørnsen og andre*. Edited by Anders Krogvig. Kristiania: H. Aschehoug and Co. (W. Nygaard).

Moe, Jørgen, and Peter Christen Asbjørnsen. 1841–44. *Norske folkeeventyr samlede ved Asbjørnsen og Jørgen Moe*. N.p.: Johan Dahl.

———. [1841–44] 1982. *Norske folkeeventyr. Samlede eventyr*. 2 vols. Oslo: Den Norske Bokklubben.

———. 1852. *Norske folkeeventyr*. 2nd expanded edition. N.p.: Johan Dahl.

———. 1866. *Norske folkeeventyr, fortalte af P. Chr. A. og J. M*. 3rd revised edition. Christiania.

———. 1868. *Norske folkeeventyr, fortalte af P. Chr. A. og J. M*. 4th revised edition. Christiania.

———. 1874. *Norske folkeeventyr, fortalte af P. Chr. A. og J. M*. 5th revised edition. Christiania.

Moe, Moltke. 1927. "Det nationale gjennembrud og dets mænd." In *Moltke Moes Samlede Skrifter*. Vol. 3. Edited by Knut Liestøl. Oslo: H. Aschehoug and Co. (W. Nygaard).

Munch, Andreas. 1848. Review of *Norske huldreeventyr og folkesagn*, by Peter Christen Asbjørnsen. In *Norsk Tidsskrift for Videnskab og Litteratur*. Edited by Christian Dybwad Lange. Christiania.

Nicolson, Marjorie Hope. 1959. *Mountain Gloom and Mountain Glory*. Binghamton, New York: Cornell University Press.

Norske Turistforenings Årbok, Den. 1870. Kristiania: Albert Cammermeyer.

NOS Utdanningsstatistikk. 2001. http://www.ssb.no/emner/04/

Olrik, Axel. 1915. "Personal Impressions of Moltke Moe." Translated by Elisabeth Westergaard. In *Folklore Fellows' communications* 17: 3–76. Helsinki: Suomalainen Tiedeakatemia.

———. [1909] 1965. "Epic Laws of Folk Narrative." In *The Study of Folklore*. Edited by Alan Dundes. Translated by Jeanne P. Steager. Englewood Cliffs, N.J.: Prentice Hall. Originally published in German as "Epische Gesetze der Volksdichtung" in *Zeitschrift für Deutsches Altertum* 51: 1–12.

Ong, Walter. 1975. "The Writer's Audience is Always a Fiction." In *PMLA* 90: 9–21.

———. 1982. *Orality and Literacy*. London: Methuen.

Oring, Elliot. 1986. "Folk Narratives." In *Folk Groups and Folklore Genres*. Edited by Elliot Oring. Logan: Utah State University Press.

Paasche, Fredrik. 1932. "Fra 1814 til 1850-årene." In *Norges Litteratur*. Vol. 3. Edited by Francis Bull and Fredrik Paasche. Oslo: H. Aschehoug and Co. (W. Nygaard).

Pontoppidan, Erik [or, also, sometimes, Erich]. 1755. *The Natural History of Norway*. Translator unknown. London.

———. 1763. *Den danske Atlas eller Konge Riget Dannemark*. Copenhagen.

Popp, Daniel. 1977. *Asbjørnsen's linguistic reform*. Oslo: Universitetsforlaget.

Pratt, Mary Louise. 1992. *Imperial eyes: Travel Writing and Transculturation*. London and New York: Routledge.

Propp, Vladimir. [1928] 1968. *The Morphology of the Folktale*. Translated by Lawrence Scott. Austin: University of Texas Press.

Rabinowitz, Peter. 1977. "Truth in Fiction: A Reexamination of Audiences." In *Critical Inquiry* 4: 121–141.

———. 1987. *Before Reading: Narrative Conventions and the Politics of Interpretation*. Ithaca and London: Cornell University Press.

Reichborn-Kjennerud, I., Fr. Grøn, and I. Kobro. 1936. *Medisinens historie i Norge*. Oslo: Grøndahl and Søns Forlag.

Rosenberg, C. 1867. "Norsk folkedigtning." In *Steenstrups' Dansk maanedsskrift*. Copenhagen.

Sandemose, Aksel. [1933] 1996. *En flyktning krysser sitt spor: fortelling om en morders barndom*. Oslo, Gyldendal.

Scholes, Robert, and Robert Kellogg. 1966. *The Nature of Narrative*. New York: Oxford University Press.

Skirbekk, Gunnar. 1984. "Nasjon og natur: Eit essay om den norske veremåten." In *Ord: Essay i utval*. Oslo: Det Norske Samlaget.

Skjelbred, Ann Helene Bolstad. 1972. *Uren og Hedning: Barselkvinnen i norsk folketradisjon*. Oslo: Universitetsforlaget.

Smith, Anthony D. 1983. *Theories of Nationalism*. New York: Holmes and Meier.

Solheim, Svale. 1952. *Norsk sætertradisjon*. Oslo: Aschehoug; Cambridge: Harvard University Press.

Steen, Ellisiv. 1947. *Diktning og virkelighet: en studie i Camilla Colletts forfatterskap*. Oslo: Gyldendal Norsk Forlag.

———. 1954. *Den lange strid: Camilla Collett og hennes senere forfatterskap*. Oslo: Gyldendal Norsk Forlag.

Stenseth, Bodil. 1993. *En norsk elite. Nasjonbyggerne på Lysaker, 1890–1940*. Oslo: Aschehoug.

Stokker, Kathleen. 1995. "Between Sin and Salvation: The Human Condition in Legends of the Black Book Minister." In *Scandinavian Studies* 67: 91–108.

Store Norske Leksikon. 1978. Vol. 2, s.v. "Bjørnsjøen."

Sundland, Egil. 1995. *"Det var en gang . . . et menneske": Tolkninger av Asbjørnsen og Moes undereventyr som allegorier på menneskelig innsikt og erkjennelse*. N.p.: Cappelen Akademisk Forlag.

Sundt, Eilert. 1852. *Beretning om fante- eller landstrygerfolket i Norge*. Christiania: Abelsted.

———. [1859] 1976. *Om ædrueligheds-tilstanden i Norge*. Oslo: Gyldendal Norsk Forlag.

Sørensen, Øystein. 1994. "The Development of a Norwegian National Identity During the Nineteenth Century." In *Nordic Paths to National Identity in the Nineteenth Century*. Edited by Øystein Sørensen. Research Council of Norway, no. 1/94: 17–35. Oslo: University of Oslo.

———. 1997. *Bjørnstjerne Bjørnson og nasjonalismen*. N.p.: Cappelen.

Tangherlini, Timothy. 1995. "From Trolls to Turks: Continuity and Change in Danish Legend Tradition." In *Scandinavian Studies* 67: 32–62.

Tatar, Maria. 1987. *The Hard Facts of Grimms' Fairy Tales*. Princeton: Princeton University Press.

Thompson, Stith. [1946] 1977. *The Folktale*. Berkeley and Los Angeles: University of California Press.

———. 1961. "Folklore Trends in Scandinavia." In *Folklore Research around the World*. Edited by Richard M. Dorson. Bloomington: Indiana University Press.

Toelken, Barre. 1979. *The Dynamics of Folklore*. Boston: Houghton Mifflin Co.

Tompkins, Jane. 1985. *Sensational Designs: The Cultural Work of American Fiction*. New York: Oxford University Press.

Tuan, Yi-Fu. 1974. *Topophilia*. Englewood Cliffs, N.J.: Prentice Hall.

———. 1977. *Space and Place*. Minneapolis: University of Minnesota Press.

———. 1982. *Segmented Worlds and Self*. Minneapolis: University of Minnesota Press.

———. 1993. *Passing Strange and Wonderful: Aesthetics, Nature, and Culture*. Washington, D.C.: Island Press/Shearwater Books.

Vannebo, Kjell Ivar. 1984. *En Nasjon av Skriveføre*. Oslo: Novus Forlag.

Velure, Magne. [1983] 1989. "Nordic Folk Belief Research." In *Nordic Folklore: Recent Studies*. Edited by Reimund Kvideland and Henning K. Sehmsdorf,

in collaboration with Elizabeth Simpson. Bloomington: Indiana University Press. Originally published in *Studia Fennica*.
von Sydow, C. W. 1948. *Selected Papers on Folklore*. Edited by Laurits Bødker. Copenhagen: Rosenkilde and Bagger.
Wergeland, Henrik. [1845] 1973. *Hassel-Nøtter*. Oslo: H. Aschehoug and Co. (W. Nygaard).
———. 1867. *Breve*. Edited by H. Lassen. Christiania: P. T. Mallings Forlagsboghandel.
Westminster, Marchioness of. 1879. *Diary of a Tour in Sweden, Norway, and Russia, in 1827, with Letters*. London: Hurst and Blackett.
Wilson, William A. 1986. "Documenting Folklore." In *Folk Groups and Folklore Genres: An Introduction*. Edited by Elliot Oring. Logan: Utah State University Press.
———. 1989. "Herder, Folklore, and Romantic Nationalism." In *Folk Groups and Folklore Genres: An Introduction*. Edited by Elliot Oring. Logan: Utah State University Press.
Wimsatt, William K. 1954. *The Verbal Icon: Studies in the Meaning of Poetry*. Lexington: University of Kentucky Press.
Witoszek, Nina. 1991. "Der kultur møter natur: tilfellet Norge." In *Samtiden* 4: 11–19. Oslo.
———. 1998. *Norske naturmytologier: Fra Edda til økofilosofi*. Oslo: Pax Forlag A/S.
Wollstonecraft, Mary. [1796] 1889. *Letters written during a short residence in Sweden, Norway, and Denmark*. London: Cassell and Co.
X and Y. 1857. *A Long Vacation Ramble in Norway and Sweden*. Attributed to J. W. Clark and J. W. Dunning. Cambridge: Macmillan and Co.
Ziegler, Alexander. 1860. *Meine Reisen im Norden*. Leipzig: J. J. Weber.
Zipes, Jack. 1988. *The Brothers Grimm: From Enchanted Forest to the Modern World*. New York and London: Routledge.
———. 1991a. "Of Cats and Men: Framing the Civilizing Discourse of the Fairy Tale." In *Out of the Woods: The Origins of the Literary Fairy Tale in Italy and France*. Edited by Nancy L. Canepa. Detroit: Wayne State University Press.
———. 1991b. *Fairy Tales and the Art of Subversion*. New York and London: Routledge.
———. 1991c. *Spells of Enchantment: The Wondrous Fairy Tales of Western Culture*. New York: Viking.
Østerud, Øyvind. 1986. "Nasjonalstaten Norge: en karakteriserende skisse." In *Det Norske Samfunn*. Edited by Lars Alldén, Natalie Rogoff Ramsøy, and Mariken Vaa. Oslo: Gyldendal Norsk Forlag.
Øverland, Arnulf. 1967. *Sprog og usprog*. Oslo: Riksmålsforlaget A/S.

Index

Aarseth, Asbjørn, 45, 51–53
Aasen, Ivar, 18, 23, 94, 170, 171, 174, 188
Abrahamson, Werner: *Udvalgte danske Viser fra Middelalderen*, 26
Afzelius, Arvid August: *Svenska folk-visor från forntiden*, 26–27
Alcohol, 104, 113, 135, 213n. 22, 214n. 24
Andersen, Carl, 13
Andersen, H. C., 49
Anderson, Benedict, 12, 16
Animal, 97, 120, 153, 156–57, 226n. 15
Archer, William, 84, 208n. 20
Arneberg, Per, 71
Article, definite, 72
Asbjørnsen, Andreas, 12, 13
Asbjørnsen, Peter Christen: and Aasen, 188; and alcohol, 104, 113, 135, 213n. 22, 214n. 24; and ancestry, 93; and artists, 75; birth, 12; and Bjørnson, 116, 217n. 41; and Blicher, 31, 68; and *bokmål*, 172–73; and *bonde*, 46, 59, 72, 92–93, 104, 145; and characterization, 47, 95–96, 112–17; childhood, 12–13; and class, 147, 148, 150–51, 162, 163; and collaboration, 23, 33–38, 46, 78, 94, 150, 175–76, 188; and collection, 14, 34, 43, 44, 88, 89, 94, 97, 212n. 18; and Collett, 46, 78, 94, 150, 176; and combination, 48, 49, 91, 204n. 21; and common people, 90; and composition, 94; and Croker, 67; and culture, 76, 78, 115–16, 120, 140, 194; and Danish, 173, 174; and description, 51, 66–67, 68–70, 74–76, 77, 78, 86, 122–23, 125–26, 129–30, 208n. 18; and dialect, 14, 91, 174, 188–89, 215n. 32; and diction, 21, 36, 91; and editing, 43, 127–29, 143, 172–73, 215n. 31; education, 13, 33; and enlightenment, 32; family, 12; father, 12, 13; and Faye, 27, 43, 50, 90, 94, 149, 178–79, 180–81, 212n. 18; and folk belief, 44, 52, 90–91, 93, 94, 95, 107–8, 109, 110, 111–12, 113, 120, 121, 122, 123–24, 125, 127, 133, 144, 153, 194; and folk life, 66, 116; and folklore, 210n. 8; and forestry, 14–15; and gender, 147, 148, 149–51; and Grimm brothers, 21, 24, 29–30, 31, 32, 39, 42, 50, 201n. 6; and Gypsies, 130–32; and Hansen, 28, 31, 68; and horizon of expectation, 177–78, 181, 187; and *huldreeventyr* (term), 93–94; and Ibsen, 78–84, 116, 208n. 20; and identity, 142; independence of, 15, 23, 32, 41–42, 198n. 5; influence

Asbjørnsen, Peter Christen (*cont'd.*) of, 58–59, 69, 75, 77–86, 208n. 20; influences on, 21, 24, 29–32, 50, 67–68, 200n. 16; and informants, 14, 76, 88, 89, 94–95, 96, 119; and irony, 55, 110–11; *Kvernsagn*, 68; and landscape, 66, 68–69, 74, 75–76, 80, 82; and language, 14, 15, 16, 21, 27, 36, 38, 39, 43–44, 90, 91, 113, 114, 172–74, 176–77, 179–81, 186, 187–89, 191, 194, 215n. 32, 229n. 7; and legends, 41, 42, 43–55, 65, 91, 93, 94, 141–44, 145–46, 147–48, 149–50, 153–55, 156, 157, 158–60, 162, 163, 165, 204n. 21, 227n. 19; and literature, 15, 41, 44–48, 49, 52, 53, 89–90; and Moe, 13, 23, 33–38, 66, 68, 73–74, 173, 212n. 18; and nationalism, 23, 92, 143, 195; and national literature, 85–86; and nature, 34, 49, 50, 51, 59, 64, 66, 68–69, 73–74, 75–76, 78, 80, 82, 85, 194, 208n. 18; and *Norske folkeeventyr*, 34–35, 36, 37–38, 39, 40, 41, 42; and Norway, 27, 42, 76, 77, 85–86, 143, 144; and novel, 181; and Other, 119–20, 121, 122–30, 132–33, 134–37, 140, 141, 144, 165; and peasant, 53, 54, 143–44; and personality, 34, 38, 202n. 8; and philosophy, 31; and politics, 53, 205n. 25; and publication, 36, 37–40, 43; and purpose/motivation, 44, 50–51; and reader, 65–66, 70–73, 91–92, 106, 107, 108, 111, 119, 176–78, 181, 187, 206n. 9; and realism, 51, 52, 55, 70, 74–76, 173, 174; and romanticism, 12, 15, 43, 49, 50, 51, 52–53, 55, 74, 143, 173; and science, 14, 30, 31, 32, 75, 221n. 19; and simplification, 181; and style, 27, 34, 35, 36–37, 42, 45, 47–48, 50–55, 67–68, 70–71, 78, 103, 201nn. 3, 7; and subscribers, 37; and superstition, 90; and tradition, 65, 146; as tutor, 13, 14; and typicality, 46, 112, 116; and unreliable narrator, 68; and voice, 94; and "A Wise Woman" changes, 127–28; and writing, 13, 14. *See also Norske folkeeventyr* (Asbjørnsen and Moe); *Norske huldreeventyr og folkesagn* (Asbjørnsen); *specific stories*

Aubert, Elise Sofie Aars, 167–68

Audience, 66, 93, 97, 99–100, 101–2, 103, 104, 105, 106. *See also* Reader

Bakhtin, M. M., 53–54, 90, 176–77, 186

Bakken, Hallvard, 34, 201n. 4

Baptism, 122, 124, 161, 162, 219n. 4

Bascom, William, 146, 224n. 6

Baumann, Richard, 210n. 1

Baumgartner, Walter, 53–55

Belief, 94, 97, 142, 210n. 7. *See also* Folk belief

Bergtakning, 156

"Berthe Tuppenhaug's Stories" (Asbjørnsen), 43, 110, 156, 161

Bettelheim, Bruno, 203n. 13

Bjørnson, Bjørnstjerne, 145, 173, 177, 217n. 41; *Bondefortellinger*, 46, 116

Black Death, 15, 21, 142, 160

Blicher, Steen Steensen, 31, 70, 200n. 15; *Himmelbjerget*, 68; *Hosekræmmeren*, 68

Bokmål, 168, 170, 171, 172–73, 186, 190, 229nn. 4, 8. *See also* Language; Norwegian
Bonde: and alcohol, 104; and Asbjørnsen, 46, 59, 72, 92–93, 104, 145; and Bjørnson, 116; character of, 20; and folk material, 22, 28; idealization of, 46, 116, 145, 193, 194; kinds of, 92; and nationalism, 92–93; and nature, 57–58; and Other, 144–45; and peasant, 198n. 8
Border. *See* Boundary
Bottigheimer, Ruth, 145
Boundary, 144–45, 156–57, 160, 161–62, 163, 211n. 11. *See also* Other
Brandes, Edvard, 49, 225n. 11
Bremner, Robert, 63–64; *Excursions in Denmark, Norway and Sweden*, 62
Broch, Peter, 38
Brooke, A., 61–62
Bruun, Thurine Elisabeth, 12
Brække, Jakob Pladsen, 150
Bugge, Sophus, 39
Bukdahl, Jørgen, 55
Bull, Olaf, 73, 193; *Gobelin*, 11–12

Canon. *See* Literature
Caspari, Theodor, 68, 73, 74; *Norsk naturfølelse i det nittende aarhundrede*, 60
Changeling, 122, 123–24, 125, 156, 157. *See also* Folk belief; Supernatural/supranormal
Characterization, 42, 47, 71, 72, 92, 95–96, 112–17, 176. *See also Bonde*; Folk narrator; Frame narrator; Narrator; Style
Chaucer, Geoffrey, 65

Children, 111–12, 121, 124, 125, 126–27, 162, 210n. 7
Christiana, 13, 63, 64
Christianity, 120, 152, 155, 162, 225n. 12. *See also* Paganism; Religion
Christiansen, Reidar, 145, 146, 151–52, 153; *Folktales of Norway*, 142
"Christmas Visit to the Parsonage, A" (Asbjørnsen), 143
City. *See* Urban population
Class: and fairy tale, 41, 43, 203n. 14; and frame narrator, 151; and legends, 147, 148, 150–51, 162–63; and travelers, 62, 63. *See also Bonde*; Embets class; Rural population; Urban population
Collection: and Asbjørnsen, 14, 34, 43, 44, 88, 89, 94, 97, 212n. 18; and Herder, 21; and Hoel, 23; modern *vs.* nineteenth century, 87–88; and Moe, 34, 88–89; and Norway, 21; and observer, 96. *See also* Informant
Collett, Camilla, 46, 94, 150, 175–76; *Amtmandens Døtre*, 175, 230n. 9; "Badeliv og Fjeldliv," 78
Collett, Peter Jonas, 66, 175–76
Colonialism, 20, 22, 139, 164, 165, 207n. 10
Common people, 90. *See also Bonde*; Peasant
Connor, Walker, 16–17
Constitutionelle, Den, 43, 66, 100
Corpse, 153, 157
Croker, Crofton: *Fairy Legends and Traditions of the South of Ireland*, 50, 67–68
Culture: and Asbjørnsen, 53–55, 76, 78, 115–16, 120, 140, 194; and

Culture (*continued*)
　Bakhtin, 54; and nation-state, 17; and Norway, 22, 137–39; and Other, 137–39; and romanticism *vs.* realism, 55; and stereotype, 47; and Tompkins, 116. *See also* Society

Danish, 17, 21, 39, 168, 173, 174
Darnton, Robert, 196
Dass, Petter, 25
Dégh, Linda, 148
Denmark: aesthetics of, 29; and folk songs, 25, 26; and government, 55; and legends, 163–64; and Norway, 11, 18–19, 20, 73, 169–70, 228n. 2
Description: and nature, 51, 66–67, 68–70, 74–76, 77, 78, 86, 208n. 18; and Other, 122–23, 125–26, 129–30. *See also* Style
Devil, 52, 154
Dialect: and Asbjørnsen, 14, 91, 188–89; and informants, 14; and Moe, 14; and *Norske huldreeventyr og folkesagn*, 174, 215n. 32; and Norway, 17, 20, 168–69, 189–90. *See also* Language
Dialectic, 55
Dialogism, 54
Dickens, Charles, 175
Diction, 21, 36, 39, 43–44, 91. *See also* Language
Dietrichson, Lorentz, 115–16
Dorson, Richard, 20

Egalitarianism, 53, 144, 159, 160–61, 225n. 10. *See also* Pluralism; Polyphony
Embets class, 62, 155, 171, 195
Emblem, of contrast, 120, 123, 157, 160. *See also* Description

Enlightenment, 32, 54
Environment, 21, 149. *See also* Nature
Erjavec, Aleš, 58
Ethics, 88–89
Ethnicity: and homogeneity, 18; and Norway, 121, 164–65; and Other, 120, 121, 122–23, 132, 136, 137–38, 140, 141, 147, 163–64, 218n. 2; and stereotype, 120–21; and supernatural, 120
"Evening at the Neighbors, An" (Asbjørnsen), 95, 113–14
"Evening in the Squire's Kitchen, An" (Asbjørnsen), 53–55, 105, 158–59
Expectation, horizon of, 177–78, 181, 187. *See also* Review/reception

Fairy tale: and class, 203n. 14; definition of, 40–41, 42, 199n. 11; and legend, 42, 44; and nationalism, 43; and *Norske huldreeventyr og folkesagn*, 93; and oral wonder tale, 42; research on, 202n. 11; and style, 40, 42; and truth, 42, 203n. 13. *See also* Wonder tale
Family, 154, 161
Faye, Andreas, 43, 50, 90, 149, 212n. 18; *Norske folkesagn*, 27, 94, 177, 178–79, 180
Feudalism, 160–61, 225n. 10
Folk belief: and Asbjørnsen, 44, 52, 90–91, 93, 144, 194; and "Berthe Tuppenhaug's Stories," 110; and casting, 125, 126; and changeling, 122, 123–24; entities of, 97, 98, 152, 153; eradication of, 93; and "An Evening at the Neighbors," 95, 113; and frame narrator, 94–95; and "The Gypsies," 120, 133;

and "The Halling with Angelica
Root," 109; and illness, 125,
127; and "The King of Ekeberg,"
111–12; and "Legends of the Mill,"
107–8; and "Matthias the Hunter's
Stories," 109, 111; origin of, 152,
225n. 11; and Other, 120; and
paganism, 151; and Scandinavia,
26; and Sundt, 133–34; and
"A Wise Woman," 120, 121.
See also Belief; Changeling;
Haugfolk; *Hulder*; Legend;
Nisse; Supernatural/supranormal;
Underjordiske
Folk life, 66, 116
Folklore: and Asbjørnsen, 210n. 8;
and *bonde*, 22; and context, 87,
210n. 1; and *Norske huldreeventyr
og folkesagn*, 44–48; and Norwegian
character, 21; and romanticism, 24
Folk narrator: absence of, 119;
and audience, 106; and "Berthe
Tuppenhaug's Stories," 110;
characterization of, 112–17;
contradiction/subversion of,
94–95, 103–12; control of, 91–92;
creation of, 48; and frame narrator,
66, 93–95, 107, 108, 109, 159, 176–
77; and gender, 148–51; and "The
Halling with Angelica Root," 109;
idiosyncratic, 113; interruption of,
99–100; and "Legends of the Mill,"
107, 108; and names, 76; and
Norske huldreeventyr og folkesagn,
44, 93–95, 97, 99, 100–1, 102–16,
117; and "An Old-fashioned
Christmas Eve," 100–1, 102–3;
and partial retelling of legend, 147;
and performance context, 97; and
reader, 176–77; and "A Summer
Night in the Krok Forest," 99, 103,

104; and truth, 104, 105; typicality
of, 112; use of, 91; women, 218n. 1
Folk poetry, 21–22, 26, 28
Folk song, 25, 26
Folk tale: definition of, 199n. 11; and
fairy tale, 40; and Grimm brothers,
24; and nationalism, 23; oral, 40.
See also Collection
"Forest Valley in Western Norway, A"
(Asbjørnsen), 143
Fornorsking, 172, 229n. 7. *See also*
Language
Frame narrative: and Asbjørnsen,
47–48, 91; and Collett, 46; models
for, 67–68; and *Norske huldreeventyr
og folkesagn*, 44, 91, 98–99; and
"A Summer Night in the Krok
Forest," 98–99; and verisimilitude,
99, 100, 101. *See also* Narrative;
Performance context
Frame narrator: absence of, 119–20;
and Asbjørnsen, 45–46, 206n. 5,
215n. 31; and aside, 106, 107; as
authorial voice, 94; and "Berthe
Tuppenhaug's Stories," 110; and
class, 151; as control device, 91–92;
and conversation, 106; and "An
Evening at the Neighbors," 113,
114; and folk belief, 94, 95; and
folk narrator, 66, 93–95, 107, 108,
109, 159, 176–77; and gender,
149–51; and "The Grave Digger's
Stories," 91, 106–7; and "The
Gypsies," 129; and "The Halling
with Angelica Root," 109–10;
and "The Hulder Clan," 51; and
irony, 110–11; and language, 179,
181; and "Legends of the Mill,"
71, 107, 108, 179; and "Matthias
the Hunter's Stories," 108, 109,
111; and names, 76; and *Norske*

Frame narrator (*continued*)
  huldreeventyr og folkesagn, 44,
  45–46, 51, 71, 91, 92, 93, 94–103,
  106–12, 113, 114, 119–20, 129,
  179, 181; and "An Old-fashioned
  Christmas Eve," 100; and Other,
  119–20; and performance context,
  96–97; and reader, 71, 72, 91–92,
  106, 107, 108, 111, 119; and
  "A Summer Night in the Krok
  Forest," 92, 95, 98; and "A Sunday
  Evening at the Mountain Dairy,"
  181; and supernatural world, 160;
  and truth, 106; as typical, 46; and
  verisimilitude, 101–2. See also
  Narrator
"From the Mountains and the
  Dairies" (Asbjørnsen), 150, 175
"From the Sognefjord" (Asbjørnsen),
  174, 188
Frykman, Jonas, 62

Gedicke, Friedrich, 186
Geijer, Erik Gustaf, 31; "Den lilla
  Kolargossen," 97; "Om omqvädet,"
  26–27; *Svenska folk-visor från
  forntiden*, 26–27
Gender, 147, 148–51, 154, 159,
  162–63
Germany, 28–29, 46
"Giant and Johannes Blessom, The"
  (Asbjørnsen), 43
Gilman, Sander, 120–21, 132
Gjefsen, Truls, 201n. 4
"Goblins on Sandflesen, The"
  (Asbjørnsen), 143
Gosse, Edmund, 189
Government, 55, 169
"Grave Digger's Stories, The"
  (Asbjørnsen), 91, 106–7, 150,
  175

Grimm, Jacob: and Asbjørnsen, 21,
  24, 29–30, 31, 32, 39, 42, 50, 93,
  201n. 6; *Deutsche Grammatik*,
  31; *Deutsche Mythologie*, 29, 30;
  Deutsche Sagen, 31, 42; and fairy
  tale vs. legend, 42; and Germany,
  46; influence of, 25, 27, 29;
  Irische Elfenmärchen, 31; *Kinder-
  und Hausmärchen*, 29, 31, 32,
  36; and language, 21; on *Norske
  folkeeventyr*, 39; and Norway, 29;
  and wonder tale, 41
Grimm, Wilhelm: *Altdänische
  Heldenlieder*, 26; and Asbjørnsen,
  21, 24, 29–30, 31, 32, 39, 42, 50,
  93, 201n. 6; *Deutsche Grammatik*,
  31; *Deutsche Mythologie*, 29, 30;
  Deutsche Sagen, 31; and Germany,
  46; influence of, 25, 26, 29; *Irische
  Elfenmärchen*, 31; *Kinder- und
  Hausmärchen*, 29, 31, 32, 36; and
  language, 21; and Norway, 29; and
  wonder tale, 41
Grinder, Caroline Marianne, 14
"Grouse Hunt in Holleia, A"
  (Asbjørnsen), 72, 105
Grundtvig, Svend, 49
Grøn, Fredrik, 121–22
Guldberg, Carl August, 37, 38
"Gypsies, The" (Asbjørnsen), 120,
  129–30, 132–33, 134–37, 140, 188
Gypsy, 120, 122, 123, 130–32, 134,
  140, 218n. 2, 222nn. 22, 24

"Halling with Angelica Root, The"
  (Asbjørnsen), 109–10, 188
Hansen, Hans, 28–29, 34–35, 37,
  38–39, 93
Hansen, Hans Olaf, 51, 112, 204n.
  20; *Den Norske Literatur fra 1814
  indtil vore Dage*, 48–49

Index

Hansen, Maurits, 25, 27–28, 31, 68, 70, 173, 200n. 13
Haugan, Jørgen, 12, 18, 20, 170, 190, 194
Haugen, Einar, 168
Haugfolk, 152, 153. See also Folk belief; Supernatural/supranormal
Heber, Lilly, 173, 175–76
Heiberg, Johan Ludvig, 29, 46
Hemingway, Ernest: *A Farewell to Arms*, 71–72
Herder, Johann Gottfried, 21, 29, 31
Herzfeld, Michael, 16
History, 54, 55–56, 142
Hodne, Ørnulf: *Jørgen Moe og folkeeventyrene*, 88
Hoel, Sigurd, 23
Holbek, Bengt, 42, 147, 203n. 14
Holter, Øystein, 160–61
Home, 149, 161, 228n. 25
Homogeneity, 16–17, 18, 194, 231 n.3
Honko, Lauri, 87, 146, 148
Household, 161
Hulder: background on, 151, 152; and cow's tail, 157, 160; encounters with, 153; female, 154; marriage to, 156, 157, 158–59; and Other, 97, 145; and strength, 158, 159, 160, 227n. 19. See also Folk belief; Supernatural/supranormal
"Hulder Clan, The" (Asbjørnsen), 43, 51–52, 75–76, 159–60
Huldreeventyr, meaning of, 93–94
Human, and Other, 124, 141, 142, 145, 146, 149, 153–60, 165, 227n. 19

Ibsen, Henrik, 84–85, 116, 177; *Peer Gynt*, 23, 78–84, 208nn. 19, 20
Informant, 14, 76, 88, 89, 94–95, 96, 109, 119. See also Collection; Folk narrator
Irony, 55, 110–11

Jauss, Hans Robert, 79, 230n. 10
Johannesen, Georg, 46
Jusdanis, Gregory, 19, 46, 58, 195; *Belated Modernity and Aesthetic Culture: Inventing National Literature*, 17
Jæger, Henrik, 90, 193–94; *Norske Forfattere*, 49–52

Kielland, Alexander, 177
"King of Ekeberg, The" (Asbjørnsen), 43, 111–12
Klausen, Arne Martin, 195
Klaussøn, Peder, 25
Knudsen, Knud, 170
Kramer, Julian, 138–39, 164–65, 190, 207n. 10
Kristofersen, J. M., 97
Krogvig, Anders, 13, 34, 54–55, 197n. 3, 201n. 4
Kvernsagn (Asbjørnsen), 68
Kvideland, Reimund, 45, 142, 147–48

Landscape: and Asbjørnsen, 66, 68–69, 74, 80, 82; and "The Hulder Clan," 75–76; and literature, 19; and *Norske huldreeventyr og folkesagn*, 66. See also Nature
Landsmål, 170–71, 229n. 4. See also Language; Norwegian
Language, 167–91; and academe, 229n. 5; and Asbjørnsen, 14, 15, 16, 21, 27, 36, 38, 39, 43–44, 90, 91, 113, 114, 172–74, 176–77, 179–81, 186, 187–89, 191, 194, 215n. 32, 229n. 7; and character, 113, 114; choice of, 229nn. 4,

Language (continued)
5; and dialects, 14; dialogic, 91,
181; and "An Evening at the
Neighbors," 113, 114; and frame
narrator, 181; and Grimm brothers,
21; and informants, 14; and Moe,
14, 27, 181, 229n. 7; and nation-
state, 17; and *Norske folkeeventyr*,
14, 15, 38, 39, 181; and *Norske
huldreeventyr og folkesagn*, 15,
43–44, 91, 172–73, 174, 176–77,
179–81, 186, 187–89, 191, 194,
215n. 32; and Norway, 17–18, 20,
27, 168–84, 189–91; oral, 180; and
place, 174; and pluralism, 189; and
print, 14, 18; pronunciation of,
170; vernacular, 17; written, 15,
21, 168, 170, 180. See also Danish;
Dialect; Norwegian
Larsen, Tord, 139
Legend: and Asbjørnsen, 65, 141–43;
and belief, 142; and class, 150–51,
162–63; classification of, 151–52;
and Denmark, 163–64; and fairy
tale, 42, 44; functions of, 145–46,
224n. 6; and gender, 162–63;
historical, 142; migratory, 44;
mythical, 142, 146; and *Norske
huldreeventyr og folkesagn*, 41, 42,
43–55, 91, 93, 94, 141–44, 145–46,
147–48, 149–50, 153–55, 156,
157, 158–60, 162, 163, 165; of
Peer Gynt, 79, 177; provenance
of, 149; and tradition, 146; and
truth, 42–43; urban, 163–64; and
worldview, 141–46, 224n. 5. See
also Folk belief
"Legends of the Mill" (Asbjørnsen),
69, 71, 76–77, 94, 107–8, 149–50,
157, 178, 179–81
Lies. See Truth

Liestøl, Knut, 14, 186, 188; and
characterization, 95–96; and
Croker, 67; and *huldreeventyr*,
93, 94; and legends, 149, 150;
and Moe, 200n. 12, 201n. 4;
and place/locale, 69–70, 76; and
"A Summer Night in the Krok
Forest," 97; and "A Wise Woman,"
123–24
Lindow, John, 120, 137–38, 147, 157,
162
Literature: and Asbjørnsen, 89–90;
and canon, 23, 32, 46, 47, 116, 195,
196, 208n. 18; and expectation,
47; and fairy tale, 40, 41; and
folk songs, 25; and landscape, 19;
and Moe, 45; and nation, 22–23,
85–86; and nation-state, 17; and
Norske huldreeventyr og folkesagn,
15, 41, 44–48, 49, 52, 53; and
Norway, 22, 84, 88, 196; popular,
47; and Sweden, 25
Locale. See Place/locale
*Long Vacation Ramble in Norway and
Sweden, A*, 63
"Lumber Haulers, The" (Asbjørnsen),
51–52, 53
Lunden, Kåre, 20; *Norsk grålysing*, 19
"Lund Family, The" (Asbjørnsen),
162
Luther, Martin, 124
Lutheran church, 144, 155

Magic, 120, 122, 123, 134, 153, 199n.
11
Marriage, 156, 157–60, 161, 162,
227n. 19
"Matthias the Hunter's Stories"
(Asbjørnsen), 43, 77, 108–9, 111,
153
Medicine, 121–22, 125

Memorat, 93, 94, 123; defined, 210n. 3
Men, 149, 162
Modernity, 17, 194–95
Moe, Jørgen: and Asbjørnsen, 13, 23, 33–38, 66, 68, 73–74, 173, 212n. 18; and Blicher, 68; and Church, 14; and collection, 34, 88–89; contribution of, 34–35; and Danish, 174; and diction, 21; education, 33; and fairy tale, 44, 203n. 15; and Geijer, 27; and Grimm brothers, 21, 29–30, 36, 201n. 6; and Hansen, 28, 68; influences on, 24; and informants, 89; and language, 21, 27, 181, 229n. 7; and legend, 44; and literature, 45; and nationalism, 23; and nature, 34, 35, 66, 88; on *Norske folkeeventyr*, 38–39, 44; and Norwegian identity, 27; and novella, 203n. 17; personality of, 34; and politics, 53, 205n. 25; and prose, 173; and publication, 36; and publisher, 37–40; and Richter, 29; and romanticism, 29; and sagas, 39–40; and simplification, 181; and style, 27, 34, 35–37, 42, 45, 68, 201nn. 4, 7; and subscribers, 37. *See also Norske folkeeventyr* (Asbjørnsen and Moe)
Moe, Moltke, 24, 25, 27–28, 34, 36, 67, 93, 200n. 12
Montesquieu, 21
Multiculturalism, 138
Munch, Andreas, 50, 66
Munch, Johan Storm, 25
Munch, P. A., 23, 38, 39
Myth, 142

Name, 70, 76–77

Narrative, 78, 177, 180. *See also* Frame narrative
Narrator: and "An Evening in the Squire's Kitchen," 53; and "The Gypsies," 136; and "The Hulder Clan," 75; omniscient, 68, 95–96; and realism, 72; real *vs.* fictional, 101–2; reliable, 71, 72, 92, 176; unreliable, 68; urban, 55, 91, 93, 121, 129; and "A Wise Woman," 121, 128. *See also* Folk narrator; Frame narrator
Nation: defined, 16; and homogeneity, 16–17, 18; and literature, 22–23, 85–86; and *Norske folkeeventyr*, 43; and Norway, 11, 73, 140; and state, 16. *See also* State
Nationalism: and Asbjørnsen, 23, 92, 143; and Bjørnson, 116; and *bonde*, 92–93; definitions of, 16; and fairy tale, 43; and folktales, 23; and Moe, 23; and Norway, 17–18, 22, 30, 31, 143, 168–69, 195, 196, 198n. 6
Nationality, 21
Nation-state, 16–17, 19
Naturalism, 51, 52. *See also* Realism; Romanticism
Nature: and Asbjørnsen, 34, 49, 50, 51, 59, 64, 66, 68–69, 73–74, 75–76, 78, 80, 82, 85, 194, 208n. 18; attitudes toward, 59–60, 61–62, 63–64; and *bonde*, 57–58; descriptions of, 51, 66–67, 68–70, 74–76, 77, 78, 86, 208n. 18; and Moe, 34, 35, 66, 88; and *Norske folkeeventyr*, 39; and *Norske huldreeventyr og folkesagn*, 58, 66, 68–71, 72–73, 74–78, 82, 83, 85–86; and Norway, 57–62, 63–64,

Nature (*continued*)
204n. 22; and Other, 160; and state, 57–58. *See also* Landscape
"Night in Nordmarken, A" (Asbjørnsen), 69
Nisse, 97, 100–1, 151, 153, 154, 157, 225n. 11. *See also* Folk belief; Supernatural/supranormal
Nor, 36, 43
Norske folkeeventyr (Asbjørnsen and Moe): and canon, 32; criticism of, 38–39; editions of, 15, 39; and expectation, 181; and fairy tales, 41, 42; genesis of, 33–38; and humor, 39; and informants, 89; and language, 14, 15, 38, 39, 181; and nation-building, 43; and nature, 39; and *Norske huldreeventyr og folkesagn*, 36, 44; publication of, 38–39; and style, 34–35, 39–40
Norske huldreeventyr og folkesagn (Asbjørnsen): and audience, 66, 93, 97, 99–100, 101–2, 103, 104, 105, 106; and *bonde*, 145; and characterization, 47, 71, 72, 92, 95–96, 112–17, 176; and class, 147, 148, 150–51, 162, 163; and culture, 194; and dialect, 174, 215n. 32; and diction, 43–44; and ethnicity, 194; and fairy tales, 93; and folk belief, 93, 94–95, 107–8, 109, 110, 111–12, 113, 120, 121, 122, 123–24, 125, 126, 133; and folklore, 44–48; and folk narrator, 44, 93–95, 97, 99, 100–1, 102–16, 117; and frame narrative, 44, 91, 98–99; and frame narrator, 44, 45–46, 51, 71, 91, 92, 93, 94–103, 106–12, 113, 114, 119–20, 129, 179, 181; and gender, 147, 148, 149–51, 162, 163; and humor, 186; independence of, 15, 41–42; influence of, 58–59, 69, 75, 77–86, 85, 208n. 20; influences on, 30–32, 50, 67–68, 200n. 16; and informant, 45; and landscape, 66; and language, 15, 43–44, 91, 172–73, 174, 176–77, 179–81, 186, 187–89, 191, 194, 215n. 32; and legends, 41, 42, 43–55, 91, 93, 94, 141–44, 145–46, 147–48, 149–50, 153–55, 156, 157, 158–60, 162, 163, 165; and literature, 15, 41, 44–48, 49; and memorat, 93; and nationalism, 195; and nature, 58, 66, 68–71, 72–73, 74–78, 82, 83, 85–86; and *Norske folkeeventyr*, 36, 44; and Norway, 12, 43, 44, 46, 55, 58, 74–76, 77, 78, 79, 82, 85–86; and novel, 176; numbers of published, 206n. 9; and Other, 119–20, 121, 122–30, 132–33, 134–37, 140, 141, 165; and performance, 91; and performance context, 91–92; readers of, 206n. 9; and realism, 55, 70; and review/reception, 43–44, 48–49, 58–59, 66–67, 69–70, 76, 112, 187–88, 189, 193–94; and romanticism, 12, 43, 49, 50, 55; and short story, 45, 176; and style, 45, 47–48, 50–55, 67–68, 70–71, 78, 103, 201nn. 3, 7; title meaning, 93–94; and transcription, 45; and truth, 42. *See also individual stories*
Norske Selskapet, Det, 19
Norway: and Asbjørnsen, 27, 42, 76, 77, 85–86, 143, 144; and colonialism, 20, 22, 139, 164, 165, 207n. 10; constitution of 1814, 20; as construction, 22; and culture, 22, 137–39; and Danish aesthetics,

29; and Denmark, 11, 18–19, 20, 73, 169–70, 228n. 2; and dialects, 17, 20, 168–69, 189–90; and egalitarianism, 144, 159, 160–61, 225n. 10; and ethnicity, 121, 164–65; and fairy tale style, 35; and feudalism, 160–61; and folklore, 21; and folk tale style, 36–37; and gender, 159; and German aesthetics, 29; and government, 21, 22; and home, 161, 228n. 25; and homogeneity, 17, 194, 231 n.3; and Ibsen, 84–85; and identity, 11, 15, 18, 19, 20, 27, 46, 57–59, 73, 84–85, 140, 141, 144, 145, 164–65, 168–69, 171, 190, 194, 196, 199n. 10; imagined, 12, 77; and language, 17–18, 20, 27, 168–84, 189–91; and literacy, 206n. 9; and literature, 22, 84, 88, 196; and nation, 11, 73, 140; and national character, 18–19, 21, 22, 27; and nationalism, 17–18, 22, 30, 31, 143, 168–69, 195, 196, 198n. 6; and nation-building, 20; and nation-state, 19; natives of, 61, 62–63, 64; and nature, 57–62, 63–64, 204n. 22; and *Norske huldreeventyr og folkesagn*, 12, 43, 44, 46, 55, 58, 74–76, 77, 78, 79, 82, 85–86; and novel, 175, 177; and Other, 121, 137–40, 141, 155–56, 163–64; and realism, 175; and religion, 144; and romanticism, 11, 20, 28–29, 30, 31, 43, 49, 170, 175, 193; and style, 42, 88; and Sweden, 20, 73; and worldview, 160, 163

Norwegian, 14, 15, 17–18, 21, 23, 27, 38, 39, 168–74, 186, 188–91, 228n. 2, 229nn. 4, 5, 7, 8. *See also* Language; Norway

Novel, 16, 54, 174–86
Nyerup, Rasmus, 31; *Almindelig Morskabslæsning*, 27; *Udvalgte danske Viser fra Middelalderen*, 26
Nynorsk, 170, 172, 190, 229nn. 5, 7

"Old-fashioned Christmas Eve, An" (Asbjørnsen), 43, 100–3, 157
Ong, Walter, 65, 67, 71–72
Other: and Asbjørnsen, 132, 144; and *bonde*, 144–45; and boundary, 156–57, 160, 161–62, 163; and culture, 137–39; defined, 211n. 11; ethnic, 120, 121, 122–23, 132, 136, 137–38, 140, 141, 147, 163–64, 218n. 2; and frame narrator, 119–20; and gender, 154; and Gilman, 132; and *huldrefolk*, 145; and human, 124, 141, 142, 145, 146, 149, 153–60, 165, 227n. 19; integration of, 155; and nature, 160; and *Norske huldreeventyr og folkesagn*, 119–20, 121, 122–30, 132–33, 134–37, 140, 141, 165; and Norway, 121, 137–40, 141, 155–56, 163–64; and peasant, 145; recognition of, 154, 155; and self, 144, 155–56; supernatural, 97, 120, 136, 137–38, 140, 164

Paganism, 151, 225n. 12. *See also* Christianity; Religion
Parody, 176, 181
Paternity, 162
Peasant: and Asbjørnsen, 53, 54, 143–44; and *bonde*, 198n. 8; and Bremner, 62, 63; and "An Evening in the Squire's Kitchen," 53, 54; and Other, 145; and Pontoppidan, 18; and reader, 177; and romanticism, 20; and travelers,

Peasant (*continued*)
    62–63. *See also* Bonde; Common people
Performance: and folklore, 87; and interruption, 99, 100; and *Norske huldreeventyr og folkesagn*, 91; and observer, 96, 211n. 10
Performance context: absence of, 119; and characterization, 47; and class, 150; and gender, 150; and narrators, 96–99. *See also* Folk narrator; Frame narrator
Place/locale, 69–70, 76, 98, 100, 121, 174. *See also* Description
Pluralism, 46, 172, 177, 189, 195. *See also* Egalitarianism; Polyphony
Politics, 53
Polyphony, 55, 91. *See also* Egalitarianism; Pluralism
Pontoppidan, Erik, 18–19
Popp, Daniel: *Asbjørnsen's Linguistic Reform*, 172–73
Pratt, Mary Louise, 63; *Imperial Eyes*, 61
Print, 14, 18. *See also* Language; Writer/writing
Propp, Vladimir, 40

Rabinowitz, Peter, 66, 206n. 4, 230n. 10
Racism, 121
Rahbek, Knud-Lyne: *Udvalgte danske Viser fra Middelalderen*, 26
Reader: and Asbjørnsen, 65–66, 70–73, 177–78, 181, 187; effect on, 55; and folk narrator, 176–77; and frame narrator, 71, 72, 91–92, 106, 107, 108, 111, 119; history of, 196; and horizon of expectation, 177–78, 181, 187; and "Legends of the Mill," 107, 108; and *Norske huldreeventyr og folkesagn*, 206n. 9; and peasant, 177; and reliable narrator, 92, 176–77. *See also* Audience
Realism: and Aarseth, 53; and Asbjørnsen, 51, 52, 55, 70, 74–76, 173, 174; and Collett, 175; and culture, 55; and language, 174; and narrative discourse, 176; and narrator, 72; and Norway, 175. *See also* Naturalism; Romanticism; Verisimilitude
Recognition, 154, 155, 156–57
"Reindeer Hunt in the Rondane Mountains, A" (Asbjørnsen), 79, 80–81, 83
Religion, 174. *See also* Christianity; Paganism
Review/reception, 43–44, 48–49, 54, 58–59, 66–67, 69–70, 76, 112, 177–78, 181, 187–88, 189, 193–94. *See also* Expectation, horizon of
Richter, Jean Paul: *Vorschule der Esthetik*, 29
Rickets, 125
Riksmål, 171, 172, 186, 229n. 4. *See also* Language; Norwegian
Romanticism: and Asbjørnsen, 12, 15, 43, 49, 50, 51, 52–53, 55, 74, 143, 173; and Bremner, 63–64; and culture, 55; and Danish folk songs, 26; and folklore, 24; and Germany, 28–29; and Moe, 29; and Norway, 11, 20, 28–29, 30, 31, 43, 49, 170, 175, 193; and peasant, 20; and Scandinavia, 24–25; and urban population, 199n. 9. *See also* Naturalism; Realism
Rosenberg, C., 187–88

Rural population, 44, 139, 144, 154, 161. *See also* Bonde; Common people; Peasant

Saga, 39–40
Scandinavia, 24–25, 26, 147
Science, 14, 30, 31, 32, 75, 221n. 19
Scott, Walter, 13, 26, 31, 175
Sehmsdorf, Henning K., 45, 142, 147–48
Shape-changing, 120, 153, 156, 224n. 1. *See also* Folk belief; Supernatural/supranormal
Short story, 45, 176
Skillings magazine, 37
Skirbekk, Gunnar, 57–58
Smith, Adam: *Theories of Nationalism*, 19
Smith, Anthony D.: *Theories of Nationalism*, 17
Society, 15, 56. *See also* Culture
State, 16, 18, 57–58. *See also* Nation
Steen, Ellisiv, 78
Steffens, Henrich, 28, 29, 31, 200n.14
Stereotype, 47, 112, 120–21
Storyteller, 41, 44, 94. *See also* Narrator
Style: and Asbjørnsen, 27, 34, 35, 36–37, 42, 45, 47–48, 50–55, 67–68, 70–71, 78, 103, 201nn. 3, 7; and Croker, 67; expectations for, 177; and fairy tale, 40, 42; and legend, 42; and Moe, 27, 34, 35–37, 39–40, 42, 45, 68, 201nn. 4, 7; and Norway, 42, 88. *See also* Characterization; Description
"Summer Night in the Krok Forest, A" (Asbjørnsen), 92, 95, 97–100, 103–5
"Sunday Evening at the Mountain Dairy, A" (Asbjørnsen), 79, 181–86

Sundt, Eilert, 130–32, 133–34, 222n. 24
Supernatural/supranormal, 97, 120, 138, 141, 147, 151–63, 210n. 3, 225n. 11. *See also* Belief; Changeling; Folk belief; *Haugfolk*; *Hulder*; *Nisse*; Other; Shape-changing; *Underjordiske*
Superstition, 90, 133–34
Svendserud, Lars, 89
Sweden, 11, 20, 25, 26, 73
Syv, Peder, 26, 28; *200 Viser om Konger oc Kemper oc Andre*, 25. *See also* Vedel, Anders Sørenssøn
Sørensen, Øystein, 160–61

Tail, cow's, 157, 160
Tale-type, 145, 146
Tangherlini, Timothy, 141, 163, 211n. 11
Thiele, J. M., 31; *Danske Folkesagn*, 27; *Prøver af danske Folkesagn*, 27
Thompson, Aarni, 145
Thorpe, Benjamin, 89
Tidemand, Adolph: "Signekjærring," 75
Tieck, Ludwig, 28, 35, 36
Toelken, Barre, 211n. 10
Tompkins, Jane, 55–56, 116; *Sensational Designs*, 47
Tradition, 65, 146, 148, 194–95
Travel writing, 59–64
Treaty of Kiel, 11
Troll, 154
Troll cat, 132, 222n. 22
"Trolling for Mackerel" (Asbjørnsen), 143
Trollkjerring, 142, 154, 155, 156
Truth, 42–43, 97, 104, 105, 106, 107, 203n. 13. *See also* Verisimilitude
Tuan, Yi-Fu, 19–20, 76

Underjordiske, 97; and children, 111–12, 162; and church, 153; defined, 151, 152; and Gypsies, 136; and *haugfolk*, 153–54; and "The King of Ekeberg," 111–12; and "The Lund Family," 162; origin of, 225n. 11; and shape-shifting, 156. See also Folk belief; Supernatural/supranormal

Undset, Sigrid, 69

Urban population: and appropriation of nature, 59, 72–73, 195; and narrative dialectic, 44, 55, 93; and narrator, 55, 91, 93, 121, 129; and national identity, 73; and non-urban worlds, 63; and romanticism, 199n. 9; and rural worldview, 139, 194

Vedel, Anders Sørenssøn, 28; *It hundrede Vdvaalde Danske Viser*, 25, 26. See also Syv, Peder

Verisimilitude, 99, 100, 101. See also Realism; Style; Truth

Voice, 180, 181

Von Sydow, C. W., 210n. 7

Welhaven, Johan Sebastian, 29, 38, 54, 94, 202n. 9

Wergeland, Henrik, 23, 28, 29, 30

Westminster, Marchioness of, 62

"Wise Woman, A" (Asbjørnsen), 120, 121, 122–29, 132, 140, 162, 172

"Wise Woman's Stories, A" (Asbjørnsen), 43

Witch, 155, 218n. 1, 226n. 15

Witchcraft, 134, 138

Wollstonecraft, Mary, 61

Women, 149, 150, 161–62, 218n. 1, 227n. 18. See also Gender

Wonder tale, 40–41, 42, 199n. 11. See also Fairy tale

Working class, 150, 154. See also *Bonde*; Peasant

Worldview, 137–40, 141–46, 160, 163, 224n. 5

Writer/writing, 17, 19. See also Language; Print

Zipes, Jack, 40, 41, 203n. 14

Østerud, Øyvind, 22

Øverland, Arnulf, 173, 186–87